in association with

Decanter

THE WORLD'S WINE LEGENDS

First published in the UK 2022 by Sona Books an imprint of Danann Media Publishing Ltd

CAT NO: SON0525

Book design Darren Grice at Ctrl-d
Editor Martin Corteel
Proof reader Juliette O'Neill

With special thanks to Jim Greenhough who made this book possible

Made in Spain

ISBN: 978-1-912918-86-7

in association with

Decanter

THE WORLD'S WINE LEGENDS

Written by **Stephen Brook**

With a foreword by **Amy Wislocki**
Editor of *Decanter magazine*

CONTENTS

FOREWORD BY AMY WISLOCKI 6

INTRODUCTION BY STEPHEN BROOK 8

BORDEAUX 12

Château Angélus 1945 **14**
Château Ausone 2005 **16**
Château Figeac 1949 **18**
Château Haut-Brion 1945 **20**
Château Haut-Brion, Blanc 1989 **22**
Château Lafite-Rothschild 1959 **24**
Château Montrose 1990 **26**
Château Palmer 1961 **28**
Château Pichon Baron 2005 **30**
La Mission Haut-Brion 1929 **32**
Le Pin, Pomerol 1982 **34**
Pichon Comtesse de Lalande 1982 **36**

BURGUNDY 38

Bonneau du Martray 1990 **40**
JF Coche-Dury, Croton-Charlemagne 1986 **42**
Domaine Georges Roumier 1995 **44**
Domaine Leroy, Richebourg 1999 **46**
Domaine Rousseau, Chambertin 1993 **48**
Jayer, Cros-Parantoux, Vosne-Romanée 1990 **50**
Leflaive, Montrachet 1992 **52**
Ramonet, Montrachet 1986 **54**

CHAMPAGNE 56

Billecart-Salmon, Cuvée Nicolas François 1959 **58**
Bollinger, R.D. 1976 **60**
Dom Pérignon 1975 **62**
Louis Roederer, Cristal 1959 **64**
Philipponnat, Clos des Goisses 1964 **66**
Pol Roger, Cuvée Sir Winston Churchill 2000 **68**
Salon, Le Mesnil 1985 **70**

RHÔNE 72

M Chapoutier, Le Pavillon, Ermitage 1991 **74**
Château de Beaucastel 1981 **76**
Château Rayas, Réservé 1990 **78**
JL Chave, Cathelin, Ermitage 1990 **80**
Domaine J-P & J-L Jamet, Côte-Rôtie 1990 **82**
E Guigal, La Mouline 1969 **84**

OTHER WINES OF FRANCE 86

Clos Rougeard, Le Bourg 1990 **88**
Didier Dagueneau, Silex Pouilly-Fumé 2002 **90**
Hugel, Riesling SGN 1976 **92**
Mas de Daumas Gassac, 1982 **94**
Trimbach, Clos Ste-Hune 1990 **96**
Zind-Humbrecht, Clos St-Urbain 1989 **98**

GERMANY 100

Egon Müller-Schwarzhof TBA 1976 **102**
JJ Prüm, Wehlener Sonnenuhr 1971 **104**

ITALY 106

Biondi-Santi, Tenuta il Greppo 1975 **108**
Bruno Giacosa, Asili Barbaresco Riserva 2004 **110**
Conterno, Monfortino Barolo 1978 **112**
Isole e Olena, Cepparello 1982 **114**
Jermann, Vintage Tunina 1997 **116**
Mascarello, Monprivato Barolo 1970 **118**
Mastroberardino, Taurasi Riserva 1968 **120**
Nino Negri, 5 Stelle Sfursat 2001 **122**
Ornellaia 2001 **124**

SPAIN 126

Alvaro Palacios, L'Ermita 1993 **128**
Bodegas Roda, Roda i Reserva 1994 **130**
Dominio de Pingus, Pingus 1995 **132**
R López de Heredia 1964 **134**
Marqués de Griñón 1982 **136**
Marqués de Riscal 1964 **138**
Marqués de Murrieta 1925 **140**
Recaredo, Turó d'en Mota 1999 **142**
Torres, Gran Coronas Reserva 1970 **144**

OTHER OLD WORLD WINES 146

Casa Ferreirinha, Barca Velha 1966 **148**
Chateau Musar 1964 **150**
Royal Tukaji, Nyulászó Aszú Puttonyos 1993 **152**
Szepsy, Tokaji, Aszú 6 Puttonyos 1999 **154**

PORT AND MADEIRA 156

HM Borges, Terrantez 1862 **158**
Cockburn's Vintage Port 1947 **160**
Dow's Vintage Port 1955 **162**
Fonseca 1963 **164**
Quinta de Noval, Nacional 1931 **166**
Sandeman Vintage Port 1945 **168**
Taylor's Vintage Port 1927 **170**

AUSTRALIA AND NEW ZEALAND 172

Cape Mentelle, Cabernet Sauvignon 1983 **174**
Clonakilla, Shiraz-Voignier 2001 **176**
De Bortoli, Noble One 1982 **178**
Jim Barry, The Armagh 1999 **180**
Lindeman's, Bin 1590 Shiraz 1959 **182**
Moss Wood, Cabernet Sauvignon 1975 **184**
Te Mata, Coleraine 1998 **186**
Tyrrell's, Vat 1 Semillon 1994 **188**
Wendouree, Shiraz 1990 **190**
Wynns, John Riddoch Cabernet 1982 **192**

CHILE AND ARGENTINA 194

Montes, Alpha M 1999 **196**
Nicolás Catena Zapata 1997 **198**
Santa Rita, Casa Real 1989 **200**
Sena 1997 **202**
Viñedo Chadwick 2000 **204**
Weinert, Malbec Estrella 1977 **206**

SOUTH AFRICA 208

Kanonkop, Pinotage 1995 **210**
Klein Constantia, Vin de Constance 1986 **212**
Lanzerac, Pinotage 1959 **214**
Meerlust, Rubicon 1995 **216**
Nederburg, Cabernet Sauvignon 1974 **218**

UNITED STATES 220

Beaulieu Vineyard, BV, Private Reserve 1947 **222**
Chateau Montelena 1973 **224**
The Eyrie Vineyards, South Block Reserve 1975 **226**
Joseph Phelps, Insignia 1997 **228**
Martinelli, Jackass Hill Zinfandel 1994 **230**
Opus One 1991 **232**
Ridge, Monte Bello 1970 **234**
Screaming Eagle, Cabernet Sauvignon 1997 **236**
Williams Selyem, Summa Vineyard 1988 **238**

PICTURE CREDITS 240

FOREWORD

Sit down with your copy of *Decanter*, a glass of something at hand perhaps, and what do you turn to? Our pick of the best everyday wines on the shelves? Everyone loves a bargain, after all. Travel guides to the world's wine regions – holiday inspiration? Or the learning section, to boost your wine knowledge?

For almost a decade, between 2013 and 2021, it was the back page that many of our readers would turn to first. In the Wine Legends slot, we took readers on a tour of the wine world through its most famous names. These are wines that most of us will never be lucky enough to drink. But that doesn't matter. Here we can read about the world's most highly sought-after bottles. Wines that speak of incredible vineyard sites, whether the terra rossa soils of Coonawarra, the pudding stones of Châteauneuf-du-Pape or the gravel soils of the Médoc. Wines that over the years have acquired cult status and eye-watering price tags.

In choosing to highlight the most legendary vintage of these wines, we can tell the story not only of the soils, the grape varieties, and the winemaking genius behind the labels – but also of a particular year. What came together to make it such a remarkable vintage?

It's true that even if you could afford these wines, you'd often be unable to find them in the legendary vintages featured. Writer Stephen Brook refers in his introduction (*overleaf*) to the difficulty in tracking down tasting notes on occasion, so rare and historic are some of the wines chosen. But commercial availability is not the point, and was never a prerequisite for inclusion – the index of wines featured would look very different if it had been.

These are wines to covet, to drool over, to dream about. The labels have become reference points, touchstones, representations of what can be achieved given the right combination of what *Decanter*'s late, great consultant editor Steven Spurrier used to call the three Ps: place, people and product. Sit back, be transported to the wine world's most famous cellars, and just imagine uncorking some of these treasures.

Amy Wislocki

Editor, *Decanter* magazine

INTRODUCTION

When Amy Wislocki of *Decanter* first suggested a regular feature for the magazine entitled 'Wine Legends' I doubt either of us imagined that it would become hugely popular with readers, or that the column would run for the best part of a decade. Suggestions tumbled out for some 'legends': wines such as Le Pin, Guigal's 'La Mouline', Salon Le Mesnil and Jayer's Cros Parantoux were obvious candidates, even if some head-scratching and consultation were required before deciding on a vintage. And that was just French wine. Over the years every major wine region would be represented: Egon Müller's Scharzhofberg from Germany, L'Ermita from Priorat in Spain, Tyrrell's Vat 1 Semillon from Hunter Valley, Quinta da Noval Nacional from Portugal, Screaming Eagle from Napa Valley.

Although quality was an inevitable criterion, so was notoriety. I wasn't convinced that Screaming Eagle was distinctly superior to other top-of-the-range and pricy Napa Cabernets, but it was the label that had caught the attention of collectors, so it would have been perverse to ignore it. I had attended a horizontal tasting of the wine in 2003 and knew it was of high quality and that its reputation, if not exclusivity, was well deserved.

Another scarce and valuable wine came from the Loire: Clos Rougeard, known to a relatively small circle of winelovers. Its top wine, 'Le Bourg', from one hectare of old Cabernet Franc vines, was well on its way to being a cult wine. As only 2,500 bottles are produced each year, it's not a wine that appears on the tasting circuit of most contemporary wine critics, and it was impossible to find any tasting notes. This was awkward, since the column always included tasting notes. But in a few instances, they couldn't be included, as they never existed.

Just as scarce was Cuvée Cathelin from Chave. Gérard Chave's Hermitage was already a legendary wine, so it came as a surprise when in 1990 he released this special selection from the most prized sites on the Hermitage hill. I recall tasting the wine on release and thinking the £100 price tag per bottle was absurd. Maybe so, but the wine, all 2,000 bottles of it, took off and eclipsed the reputation of the magnificent regular Hermitage.

It was one thing to identify a 'wine legend'; it was quite another to find information about it in order to create the article. Sometimes it was easy. For example, the Chambertin from Rousseau or Opus One from Napa were widely appreciated and written about. There were often detailed websites that could be consulted, as well as articles and books by leading wine journalists. The same was true of the great champagnes, which were produced in considerable quantities and each cuvée was well documented.

Decades of travel related to researching wine articles

and books had put me in direct contact with hundreds of producers. This was a huge advantage in many instances. If I needed to know more about wines from Roumier, Zind-Humbrecht, Meerlust, or Mascarello, a quick email to the proprietor would soon get results.

But on other occasions, the research process was more laborious. Wendouree was a highly regarded Shiraz from Clare Valley in Australia, and tasting notes were not hard to find. But there was no website, and it was difficult to know whether some of the descriptions of the estate and the winemaking were accurate. An exchange of faxes eventually provided the necessary information.

The 1982 Cabernet Sauvignon from Marqués de Griñón was deservedly celebrated, but when the wine was released - and this was its debut vintage - there was scant interest in fine Spanish table wines, other than Rioja and Vega Sicilia. No contemporary reviews could be traced. By sheer good luck, I had tasted the wine at a London wine merchant's and had been so impressed that I bought a case. So I did end up with numerous tasting notes. The only problem was that I had written all of them. Even so, I had no choice but to use a couple of them in the tasting section of the article.

Other complications arose with very old vintages, such

as the 1929 La Mission Haut-Brion, 1925 Marqués de Murrieta, or 1931 Quinta da Noval Nacional port. Anyone who might have been involved with the property at that time would, if still alive, have been in his or her second century. So I was obliged to rely on published accounts of the estate and its wines. Fortunately they were copious and accurate, reflecting the fame of the properties.

I was dismayed at first when an 1862 Madeira – the Borges Terrantez – was selected. But despite the antiquity of the wine, there was, to my surprise, no shortage of information about it and there were plenty of critical reactions to quote. I should have realised that Madeira has always been a collector's wine, and that even very old vintages are often well documented.

Gradually the supply of legendary wines began to dry up. It would not do to scrape the barrel simply to justify the feature's existence. And so after many years of monthly appearances on the back page of *Decanter*, the feature was terminated. It had been fun to research and write, but even the best ideas will eventually run their course, so the plug was pulled. But looking back , it was gratifying to hear from many readers that when their copy of the magazine dropped onto the doormat, this was the article they turned to first.

BORDEAUX

With dozens of world-famous châteaux releasing wines over, in some cases, 200 vintages, there was clearly going to be little difficulty finding wines of legendary status. Wines from years such as 1929 and 1945, which were selected, might well be still drinkable, but more recent vintages such as 1989 and 2005 were demonstrably outstanding too.

Château Angélus 1985

St-Emilion, Bordeaux, France

A legend because...

This was the year in which Hubert de Boüard de Laforest took over the running of this St-Emilion estate from his father and uncle. At this time there were only a few barrels in the Angélus cellars, and they had been introduced by de Boüard from 1981 onwards. Overall quality was lacklustre. De Boüard, an oenologist, set about changing all this, and in 2012 would see the promotion of Angélus to the dizzy heights of Premier Grand Cru Classé A, alongside Ausone, Cheval Blanc and Pavie.

Looking back

In the 1950s Angélus had been highly regarded and took its place as a grand cru classé. But in the 1960s and '70s quality slumped, as it did almost everywhere in Bordeaux, due to high yields compounded by an absence of selection. Sorting the grapes, now routine at even the most humble property, was rare. De Boüard recalls the rows he had with his father Jacques when he introduced green-harvesting to reduce and concentrate the crop. He declared that either he was in charge or his father was. Hubert won. He also abandoned the use of fertilisers and returned to traditional barrel-ageing.

The vintage

Luck was on de Boüard's side in that his debut vintage was 1985. The summer was the driest since 1961 and hotter than 1982. It was a large crop but the Merlot ripened perfectly after a very warm September. Quality was very high except where growers allowed yields to increase.

The terroir

The Angélus vineyards lie mostly on the slopes, rather than on St-Emilion's famed limestone plateau. But in 1979 the estate bought 3ha from Château Beauséjour-Bécot, and this benefited the quality of the wine. There has always been a large proportion of Cabernet Franc – now about 47% – in the Angélus vineyards, which has contributed an aromatic lift and freshness, moderating the power of the very ripe Merlot. Merlot is planted on the higher parts of the property, near the limestone plateau, while the Cabernet Franc is on warm and well-drained slopes that suit the variety admirably.

The wine

While visiting Domaine des Comtes Lafon in Meursault in 1981, de Boüard noted how putting the new wine into barrels as soon as possible aided the integration of the wine with the oak. So in 1985 he increased the number of barrels at Angélus. The winemaking continues to evolve from year to year as de Boüard fine-tunes the process, a work of detailed attention validated by the estate's promotion.

The reaction

In 1993 Robert Parker assessed this wine: 'A seductively smooth, supple, broadly flavoured wine with aromas and flavours of berry fruit and herbs. Full-bodied, concentrated and delicious. Like many 1985s, it has reached full maturity more quickly than expected.' A year later James Suckling in *Wine Spectator* was impressed: 'Very concentrated, with plum and cassis and a hint of nuts. Full-bodied, with well integrated tannins, and loads of coffee and fruit on the finish.'

In 2005 Jancis Robinson was uneasy: 'Some leafy freshness on the nose but this wine is definitely on the way out, in the most gracious way. An old lady politely waving goodbye, to be Broadbentian about it. It was obviously very ripe at one stage but is just losing vigour and fruit. Just slightly sickly.' Tasting from magnum in 2011 she was more positive: 'Sweet and rather gorgeous and with some freshness. Kerpow! There is a bit of decay but also liquorice.' Sampling the same magnum, Stephen Brook noted: 'Slight evolution. The nose is faded, a bit mushroomy, with some red-fruits aromas. The palate shows sweet fruit, and it's quite elegant and fresh, still tannic but not to excess. Slightly dry but the fruit sweetness overrides it. Drink soon before the tannins become drier.'

THE FACTS

Bottles produced
100,000
Composition
55% Merlot, 45% Cabernet Franc
Yield
45 hl/ha
Alcohol
12.5%
Release price
89 Francs (€12)
Price today
€210

CHÂTEAU AUSONE 2005

St-Emilion 1GCCA, Bordeaux, France

A LEGEND BECAUSE...

Ausone was one of the appellation's top growths, until that exclusive band was expanded in 2012. Its history dates back many centuries; Bordeaux expert David Peppercorn MW recalls a tasting that included 17 vintages from the 19th century. The early 20th century also produced some remarkable wines, but a dull patch after 1945, followed by disputes among the owning families and winemakers, did not result in a golden period for Ausone. Since 1995 quality has soared and remained consistent. Ausone's superb location, outstanding soil and scrupulous viticulture all contribute to its fabulous quality.

LOOKING BACK

From 1985 Alain Vauthier was co-owner of the estate, but often found himself in conflict with the other co-owner, Heylette Dubois-Challon. By 1995 he was the sole director of the property, and two years later became sole owner, although Dubois-Challon had the right to inhabit the château until her death. Alain drily remarks: 'This short period was nothing compared to the three centuries during which my ancestors were here.' In 2005 his daughter, Pauline Vauthier, joined him.

THE VINTAGE

Climatic conditions were close to ideal in 2005. Flowering was unproblematic, and the summer proved hot and sunny, with a little rain in August and early September. This rainfall refreshed the vines and prevented hydric stress. The harvest took place under cloudless skies, yielding wines that were rich, tannic, and with a low pH that should ensure a very long life.

THE TERROIR

The tiny 7ha vineyard lies in a kind of amphitheatre beneath the château and cellars. Alain has maintained an average vine age of some 50 years, favouring very high-density planting, green-harvesting and deleafing. The small size of the vineyard allows him to harvest selectively. Cabernet Franc grows in just over half the vineyard, the remainder being Merlot. The higher part of the property is on the celebrated limestone plateau of St-Emilion, the remainder on steep slopes with more clay. In 2018 Pauline initiated conversion into organic viticulture, to result in certification in 2021.

THE WINE

Grapes are sorted in the vineyard; there is also a sorting machine at the winery, though it would have stood idly by in sunny 2005. The bunches are cold-soaked for a few days, then the temperature is gently raised until fermentation begins with indigenous yeasts in large wooden vats. The wine spends up to five weeks in those vats before being moved to new barrels for an ageing of around 21 months.

THE REACTION

Robert Parker Jr was enthusiastic in the *Wine Advocate* in 2008: 'Boasts powerful, super-layered, multi-dimensional flavours with tremendous extraction, yet they come across as incredibly sublime, even delicate for such a stunningly concentrated, full-bodied effort. A masterpiece of concentration and balance, it will no doubt be drinking well a century from now.'

In 2015 Neal Martin commented on *RobertParker.com*: 'A delicious, sensual Ausone, although it's just lost a little of the breeding I felt it had during its early years.'

Michael Schuster wrote in the same year: 'A very long-term Ausone, still youthfully marked by its new oak, but which will be a beauty given sufficient time.'

Jancis Robinson MW tasted the wine blind in 2017: 'More austere than some, but lovely freshness. Everything in its place. Long and prancing on the palate.'

Also tasting in 2017, Jeff Leve noted: 'Powerful, yet refined, this is quite tight at the moment... Give it at least another decade and a few hours of air, and the magic should happen.'

THE FACTS

Bottles produced
18,000
Composition
55% Cabernet Franc, 45% Merlot
Yield
30HL/HA
Alcohol
14%
Release price
N/A
Price today
£1,202-£2,093

CHÂTEAU FIGEAC 1949

St-Emilion 1GCC, Bordeaux, France

A LEGEND BECAUSE...

Long regarded as an archetypal Bordeaux, with a beguiling bouquet that has evolved over decades, plus remarkable distinction and length. 1945, 1947 and 1949 were all great vintages in Bordeaux – and in retrospect were great bargains at the time. It seems appropriate to focus on 1949, as this was the favourite wine of the late owner Thierry Manoncourt, and the first vintage under his sole control. He relished the wine's freshness and perfectly ripe Cabernet Sauvignon fruit.

LOOKING BACK

After time in a prisoner of war camp followed by studies in agronomy, Manoncourt returned to the family property in 1947. His studies gave him a level of technical expertise that was relatively uncommon in St-Emilion after the difficult war years. Careful study of Figeac's soils helped him to make the right choices about varietal balance in the vineyards, and he introduced a second wine in 1945 to improve quality of the grand vin further. Over many decades, until his death in 2010, Manoncourt, with his wife Marie-France always at his side, guided Figeac through a succession of great vintages.

THE VINTAGE

January and February were exceptionally dry. However, by the time of flowering in June, the weather had turned cold and rainy, which reduced the crop. In July the temperature topped 40°C, which in those days was highly unusual in Bordeaux. Storms gave some relief for the parched vines. Harvest began on 30 September, but yields were very low as hydric stress kept the berries small. These conditions gave the wine great intensity of flavour.

THE TERROIR

The 54ha estate is in a single parcel that has scarcely changed since 1892. The 40ha of vines spread over three gravel croupes that run from north to south. The soil has little clay and a good deal of sand, which probably accounts for the wine's elegance and also for the unusual grape mix in the vineyards: about a third each of Merlot, Cabernet Franc and Cabernet Sauvignon. The latter often doesn't ripen in St-Emilion, but usually does so here.

THE WINE

Thanks to his studies, Manoncourt understood the process of malolactic fermentation, as well as temperature control during alcoholic fermentation, and other winemaking techniques. The grapes were vinified in large wooden vats at about 28°C, using indigenous yeasts. Although today the wine is aged entirely in new oak barrels, this was only introduced in the 1970s.

THE REACTION

In 1991, James Suckling reviewed the wine for *Wine Spectator*: 'Perhaps the greatest Figeac ever made... Ripe fruit and black liquorice aromas, a hint of violets. Full-bodied, with masses of bitter chocolate and ripe fruit flavours and a very long finish. Superb.'

The late Michael Broadbent adored this wine: 'A particular feature is its extravagant fruitiness, glorious fragrance, and at [one] tasting, a taste I described as like raspberries and cream. [In 1998] it was sheer perfection: surprisingly deep in colour though a fully mature rim; a sweet, rich, totally delicious bouquet and flavour.'

Jeff Leve of *The Wine Cellar Insider* gave it a perfect score in 2018: 'This was majestic... From an imperial, opened at the château, heartstopping is the best word to describe it. Layer after layer of perfectly ripe, silky, textured, viscous, elegant cherries and plums topped with flowers, Cuban cigar wrappers, smoke, truffle and kirsch. The finish stuck with you for 60 seconds, or more. The memory lasts a lifetime.'

In 2020 Neal Martin wrote in *Vinous*: 'As with so many Figeacs of this era, you are beguiled by its sheer effortlessness... It is a brilliant, ageless St-Emilion that, with sound provenance, could give another two decades of drinking pleasure.'

THE FACTS

Bottles produced
N/A
Composition
50% Cabernet Franc, 34% Merlot, 12% Cabernet Sauvignon, 4% Malbec
Yield
25hl/ha
Alcohol
12%
Release price
N/A
Price today
A jeroboam of the wine was sold at Christie's in 2017 for £8,225

CHÂTEAU HAUT-BRION 1945

Pessac-Léognan, Bordeaux, France

A LEGEND BECAUSE...

It's astonishing to think that any wine was produced in Bordeaux following the devastation of the Second World War, and yet 1945 turned out to be a miraculous vintage. Its quality was due to remarkable climatic conditions that year, and the victorious outcome of the war makes it particularly memorable. A vintage that arguably eclipses even the celebrated 1961s, the 1945 Haut-Brion is a supreme expression of Graves at its seductive best.

LOOKING BACK

It was in 1935, during a period of economic crisis and political uncertainty, that American financier Clarence Dillon rescued Haut-Brion. He proved a dedicated guardian of the great estate, initiating extensive improvements in the vineyard and winery. His descendants still own the property.

THE VINTAGE

Snow and heavy frost on 2 May – an unusually late time for frost damage – reduced the crop by 80% in the Graves. Thereafter, the climate was superb, with a hot, dry summer and no more than 253mm of rainfall, which led to an early, uncomplicated harvest. The grapes were super-ripe, and some batches apparently reached an alcohol level of 15%, but would have been blended with less overwhelming lots. Quality was probably enhanced by the age of the vines, but quantities were considerably reduced; this was the smallest vintage since 1915, yet the wines had good acidity.

THE TERROIR

The great terroir of Bordeaux was formed by debris thrust northwards from the Pyrenees, depositing gravel over the Graves and the Médoc. Quartz pebbles are common among the gravels of Haut-Brion, a property composed of two croupes of stony soil that provide perfect drainage, while only rising to a height of 15m over the surrounding lands, which today form the suburbs of Bordeaux. The stony soil also retains daytime heat and gently releases it up onto the vines.

THE WINE

After harvest, the grapes would have been fermented in wooden vats, as Haut-Brion only introduced its stainless steel tanks (making it the first estate in Bordeaux to adopt the new technology) in 1961. Even Jean-Bernard Delmas, who began working at the estate in 1961, cannot recall further details of how the wine was made, but it is reasonable to suppose it was aged in older barriques, as new oak would have been hard to find at the end of the war.

THE REACTION

For Michael Broadbent, this is probably 'the best-ever Haut-Brion'. 'What this wine manages to do is to combine concentration with elegance and, despite being laden with 1945 tannin, it is relatively unobtrusive,' he said. 'Consistently deep in colour... with a rich, mahogany, mature rim; its bouquet fragrant, of course. Scanning my notes: vanilla chocolate, tobacco, earthy, harmonious, honeycomb, touch of liquorice, silky texture, crisp fruit, perfect weight, great length. A gentle giant.'

Robert Parker was blown away in 1994: 'Tasted five times with consistent notes... The colour remains a healthy, opaque garnet with only slight amber at the edge. A huge, penetrating bouquet of sweet black fruits, smoked nuts, tobacco and tar soars from the

'Probably the best-ever Haut-Brion. A gentle giant'

Michael Broadbent

glass. The wine possesses extraordinary density and extraction of fruit; massive, full-bodied, unctuously textured flavour that reveals little tannins, and copious quantities of glycerin and alcohol. It is a fabulously rich, monumental example of a fully mature Haut-Brion that exhibits no sign of decline. Awesome!'

Harvey Steiman, reporting in *The Wine Spectator* in 1995, noted: 'Powerful aromas centre around cedar, brick and leather, weaving a fine thread of strawberry and raspberry through toasty, earthy flavours.Finally, on the finish, black cherry asserts itself and everything comes together, becoming sweeter and silkier after time in the glass. Very distinctive, with a unique personality.'

In 2013, Jancis Robinson MW was impressed, with reservations: 'Served (blind) alongside the 1959, this was altogether nervier, chunkier, dense and, still, tougher. This wine seemed to have a very long life ahead, even now, and will probably never charm quite as much as the 1959. Quite marked acidity and some nuttiness on the nose. Impressive persistence and possibly not yet at its peak.'

THE FACTS

Bottles produced	Alcohol
N/A	**N/A**
Composition	Release price
N/A	**N/A**
Yield	Price today
18hl/ha	**£3,012**

CHÂTEAU HAUT-BRION, BLANC 1989

Graves, Bordeaux, France

A LEGEND BECAUSE...

Haut-Brion has long produced the most prestigious white Graves, although it faces strong competition from its neighbour La Mission Haut-Brion, which produced its own white wine under the label Laville Haut-Brion until 2009, when it was renamed La Mission Haut-Brion Blanc (both properties are under the same ownership). Produced in very small quantities since its first vintage in 1916, Haut-Brion Blanc has always been a wine of considerable power and longevity; its scarcity, and the fact that it is a white wine produced by the sole first growth in the Graves, make it much sought after by collectors. The château's first-growth status does not include the white wine, which remains unclassified.

LOOKING BACK

The Haut-Brion wines benefited from a surge of research by estate manager Jean-Bernard Delmas in the 1970s. He oversaw an intense study of the different clones and rootstocks present in the vineyards and, as a consequence, only the best were replanted (in 1977, two-thirds of the white vines were replanted). Delmas presided over production, and after his retirement in 2003 he was succeeded by his son, Jean-Philippe.

THE VINTAGE

Bordeaux has become accustomed to precocious vintages, but in 1989 it was highly unusual to be picking grapes in August. After the hottest summer since 1947, with 22 days above 30°C, the harvest was the earliest since 1893. Picking began in the Graves on 21 August, although Haut-Brion waited until 29 August. The challenge was to retain a degree of acidity in the fruit and thus avoid flabbiness.

THE TERROIR

Of the 52 hectares planted at the estate, only 2.9ha are white: 53% Sémillon, 47% Sauvignon Blanc. (Today there are also a few rows of Sauvignon Gris, but they were not planted in 1989.) They are planted on a 27m hillock across the road from the château. The soil is very deep gravel over a clay subsoil. There is less clay than at La Mission, and the varietal mix is also different, as there is considerably more Sauvignon Blanc at Haut-Brion. The whole estate lies within the city boundaries of Bordeaux, and thus benefits from a warmer microclimate. Yields vary from 25–40hl/ha.

THE WINE

The harvest is manual and takes place at maximum maturity, so the wine's alcohol varies from 13% to 14%. Sorting takes place in the vineyard and the grapes are whole-bunch pressed pneumatically; there is no skin contact. Fermentation takes place with indigenous yeasts in barrels, but the malolactic fermentation is blocked. The wine is racked every three or four months, and the ageing period ranges from 10 to 12 months, with little stirring of the lees. In the 1980s it was common for the wine to be aged entirely in new oak, but today that proportion is around 50%. Production ranges from 5,500 to 8,500 bottles.

THE REACTION

Robert Parker reported Jean-Bernard Delmas's view that 'the 1989 fully replicated the fleshy, chewy texture of a great grand

'Haut-Brion Blanc has always been a wine of considerable power and longevity'

cru white Burgundy'. Parker's own view of the wine (to which he gave 100 points) is that it was 'amazingly full and long... with a very distinctive mineral, honeyed character. The low acidity would seemingly suggest a shorter life than normal, but I am convinced this wine will last 25 or more years. A real show-stopper! Sweet, honeyed peach, caramel and buttery aromas tumble from the glass'. *Decanter's* Michael Broadbent preferred Laville Haut-Brion in 1989, and harboured some uncertainties about the wine, which he found 'surprisingly sweet for a dry Graves'. In 2000, UK critic Tom Cannavan was enthusiastic: 'Developed wax and wet-wool character on the nose, very buttery with a gorgeous weight of fruit and little floral notes among peach, vanilla and nuts. Fantastic ripeness of fruit gives a sweet impression on the palate with lots of orange and lush apricot... long, very focused and pure finish.' More recently, US critic Jeff Leve reported on a vertical tasting in 2010, noting that the 1989 'opens with aromas of fresh picked flowers, honey, caramel, grass, lemon, lime and orange. With textures of rich, polished fruit, the wine ends with a melange of citrus flavours'.

THE FACTS

Bottles produced
8,400

Composition
54% Sémillon, 46% Sauvignon Blanc

Yield
23 hl/ha

Alcohol
13.2%

Release price
N/A

Price today
£1,410

CHÂTEAU LAFITE-ROTHSCHILD 1959

Pauillac, Bordeaux, France

A LEGEND BECAUSE...

Despite stiff competition from the 1961, 1959 was widely regarded as one of the great Lafites. In the view of wine writer Edmund Penning-Rowsell, it was 'probably the best 1959' from Bordeaux.

LOOKING BACK

In 1959 Baron Guy was the major shareholder of Lafite, but since 1946 Baron Elie had been running the property. Andre Portet was the general manager while Georges Revelle was cellarmaster.

THE VINTAGE

1959, a very hot year, has long been recognised as a great vintage. According to Bordeaux négociant Frank Mähler-Besse, it wasn't appreciated for a decade or more. His firm re-released the wine in 1975, which happened to be the first year that *Decanter*'s Michael Broadbent tasted the 1959. The summer was fine, and rain in mid-September was welcome as it brought the grapes to full ripeness and the harvest began a week later. The wines were rich in tannin and quite high in alcohol, but low in acidity. The year is often cited by those who argue that high acidity is not an essential component in a fine red Bordeaux, and that low-acidity years such as 1959 can age splendidly. However, the wines can exhibit a dry, almost raisiny character, since the tannins remain prominent.

THE TERROIR

The vineyards lie on a plateau that rises to the majestic height of 27 metres, and two-thirds of the vines occupy a single parcel surrounding the château buildings. There are more parcels south of the main vineyard. The soil is welldrained gravel up to 4m deep. Further down is a layer of limestone to which some attribute the extraordinary finesse of Lafite. There was less Cabernet Sauvignon at Lafite than at its neighbour Mouton: about 65%, the remainder planted with Merlot and Cabernet Franc. The relatively high proportion of Merlot, which tends to be planted in lower- lying sectors, was retained to soften the wine and make it more supple. The 1959 contained 16% Merlot.

THE WINE

The harvest began on 23 September and André Portet notes in the château records that the year gave *'très grands vins'*. 158 tonneaux were made, equivalent to about 190,000 bottles. After destemming, the must was fermented in large oak vats. Temperature was adjusted by either heating some must separately and adding it to a vat, or by pumping cold water into coils piping around the vats. After fermentation the wine was decanted into new oak barrels, coopered at the estate, and aged for about 30 months with racking every three, before being egg white-fined and bottled at the château. Portet and Revelle would have discussed how much press wine to add to the blend, and it is likely that in 1959 very little would have been required.

THE REACTION

James Suckling, tasting the wine from magnum in 1991 for *The Wine Spectator*, said 'Its hallmark is a minty juniper aroma backed by luscious, rich, elegant flavours of black cherry so ripe and intense that they're almost pruney. Complete and delicious.'

In 1994, Robert Parker asserted that this wine 'is unquestionably the greatest Lafite that has approached full maturity'. He added: 'The bouquet of flowers, black truffles, cedar, lead pencil and red

'Probably the best 1959 from Bordeaux'

Edmund Penning-Rowsell

fruits is followed by one of the most powerful and concentrated Lafites I have tasted ...a testament to what this great estate can achieve when it hits the mark. Drink to 2024.'

In 2000 Michael Broadbent cited 'its extraordinary ability to exude not only an immediate cedary perfume but, very much a Lafite speciality, the way it opens up further avenues of fragrance and subtle by-paths, lingering in the mouth.' Five years later, tasting from magnum, he noted: 'Very deep, with dark cherry core. Nose at first holding back, unreleased fragrance, touch of iron. Sweet, glorious, mouthfilling flavour; great length, spicy, with teeth-gripping tannins. For Lafite, mammoth. And superb.'

Clive Coates MW in 1999 wrote: 'This has exceptionally classy fruit. Really lovely depth. Quite fantastic. Rich and voluptuous on the palate. Ripe and inviting on the follow-through.'

In 2013, Jeff Leve of *The Wine Cellar Insider*, recorded: 'Superb. The cedar, tobacco, cigar box, smoke, cassis and fresh herb nose was close to off the charts. A perfect blend of sweet and tart, black and red fruits, silky, elegant textures, ending with along cassis note.'

THE FACTS

Bottles produced	Alcohol
190,000	**N/A**
Composition	Release price
N/A	**N/A**
Yield	Price today
N/A	**£3,165**

CHÂTEAU MONTROSE 1990

St-Estèphe, Bordeaux, France

A LEGEND BECAUSE...

Montrose was long renowned for its impressive but austere and tannic wines that needed years of cellaring. Then in 1989 and 1990 it produced a pair of wines that established it as the finest property in St-Estèphe, with Cos d'Estournel its closest rival. Connoisseurs still discuss the relative merits of the two vintages, though the consensus is that the 1990 is, marginally, the finer of the two.

LOOKING BACK

Jean-Louis Charmolüe, whose ancestors had bought the estate in 1896, was the owner in 1990, and although he always maintained the very traditional style of Montrose, he was aware that wines of such severity were becoming less acceptable to a new generation of Bordeaux drinkers. He planted more Merlot, reducing the proportion of Cabernet Sauvignon. Charmolüe still produced massive wines in 1989 and 1990, though they were drinkable sooner than years such as 1959 and 1961 had been.

THE VINTAGE

The winter was mild and, after rain in April, May was very hot and dry. Flowering began well but was interrupted by poor weather that affected the set of the Cabernets. Extreme heat returned in July, leading to blocked ripening, August too was hot and dry, but there was some rain at the end of the month that relieved the parched vines and allowed the bunches to ripen fully. The harvest began in mid-September and continued until 3 October, giving ripe Merlots and concentrated Cabernets. Yields were generous across Bordeaux, despite energetic bunch-thinning; but in this regard Montrose seems to have been an exception.

THE TERROIR

With its deep gravel soils, Montrose differs little in its terroir from Château Latour, its riverside counterpart in Pauillac. The vineyards, about 68ha in 1990, are in a single block about 800m from the Gironde, and their average age was about 40 years. But the gravel is no more than 2m deep – ample for excellent drainage, but no match for the profundity of Latour's soils. Beneath the gravel is a layer of limestone and clay. Like other top châteaux in St-Estèphe, Montrose also has parcels with a high clay content, which may explain the hefty tannins of the wine, and also why more Merlot, always at home on clay, was planted in the 1980s. Charmolüe told me early in 1990 that he planned to bunch-thin the Merlot that year to ensure it would not weaken the wine's structure.

THE WINE

The grapes were fermented in wooden vats with frequent pumpovers, and the malolactic fermentation also took place in those vats. The wine was aged for 18 months in at least 50% new oak, racked regularly, and after a light egg-white fining, it was bottled unfiltered.

THE REACTION

Stephen Tanzer wrote in 2002: 'Distinctly exotic, even overripe. Then lush, sweet and opulent, with a typically velvety texture. But extremely young and structured, finishing with powerful tannins and great grip and length. Almost

California-like.' Jancis Robinson MW in 2009 said: 'At first the nose was not utterly pure and precise. But it seemed to clean itself up in the glass. Sweeter and richer than any Montrose I can think of... flattering and ready to drink, with some very fine tannins and just a little dustiness on the finish.' Robert Parker has always given this wine a perfect score, and was still enthusiastic in 2014: 'Majestic and opulent, with low acidity and fabulous fruit. It is close to full maturity.' Tasting the wine in November 2016, Jane Anson noted: 'Tertiary aromas and flavours are coming to the fore, but confidently so. There is still a sense of freshness to the black fruits, and this wine has a way to go – the pleasures of a ripe Bordeaux vintage are still very much intact.'

THE FACTS

Bottles produced
N/A

Composition
64% Cabernet Sauvignon, 32% Merlot, 4% Cabernet Franc

Yield
38hl/ha

Alcohol
13%

Release price
N/A

Price today
£638

CHÂTEAU PALMER 1961

Margaux 3CC, Bordeaux, France

A LEGEND BECAUSE...

Although it was not immediately apparent, this vintage would propel Palmer into the top ranks of the Médoc. Within two decades the price of this third growth rivalled, and in some cases exceeded, that of the first growths. To this day it is not entirely clear why Palmer should have performed so magnificently in this vintage. But it was no fluke: the 1962 was also a great wine. The fame of the Palmer may have been amplified by the fact that the other major player in the village, Château Margaux, was underperforming in the 1960s.

LOOKING BACK

In 1938 this celebrated property, owned for decades by the Periere banking family, was sold to a consortium of Bordeaux négociants, including the Mähler-Besse and Sichel families, who remain co-proprietors to this day. The Miaille family, once a significant force in the Médoc, were also part of the consortium in 1961, but are no longer involved. In the 1950s Jean Bouteiller was appointed manager of the property, and he would have had responsibility for the 1961 vintage, completed shortly before his death in 1962. Pierre Chardon, a greatly respected figure who was also mayor of Cantenac, was the vineyard manager, a role inherited by his children.

THE VINTAGE

A mild spring led to very early flowering, some three weeks in advance. But this only compounded the damage when two frosts hit the Médoc in April and May, particularly affecting the Merlot. Apart from a rainy July, the summer was very hot and dry, and drought stress delayed the harvest until the last week in September. The harvest took place in ideal conditions. The low yields led to highly concentrated wines, yet with supple tannins. The best wines, such as Palmer, were beautifully balanced and aged very well, though even the best bottles may be peaking. This was one of those vintages when there is no significant difference in quality between the Right and Left banks.

THE TERROIR

The 55-hectare Château Palmer is a neighbour of Château Margaux and also occupies some outstanding gravel soils. Whereas Margaux is overwhelmingly Cabernet Sauvignon, Palmer has long had a substantial proportion of Merlot, much of which was planted in the 1950s. Merlot is generally planted on clay soils, but at Palmer it is planted on some of the best gravelly parcels, which explains why Palmer retains such elegance despite so much Merlot in the blend. However, in 1961, Merlot would have played a negligible role after the devastating frost.

THE WINE

There was no mechanisation in the Palmer vineyards at this time, and horses rather than tractors conveyed the grapes to the vathouse. The grapes were fermented in large 15,000-litre wooden vats. The concentration of fruit was astonishing, since the yields in 1961 were just below 12 hectolitres per hectare. The wine was aged in barriques in the usual way, but it is almost certain that none of the barrels were new.

THE REACTION

In 1995 *Decanter*'s Michael Broadbent admired its 'silky and

'The 1961 Palmer manages to play on two contradictory notions: delicacy and force'

Jean-Paul Kauffmann

harmonious bouquet accelerating like Michael Schumacher from the starting grid. Full-bodied yet elegant, fleshy yet lissome'. By 2000 he found the wine 'less deep but an indescribably lovely bouquet and flavour. Perfection.' French writer Jean-Paul Kauffmann marvelled that the 1961 'manages to play on two contradictory notions: delicacy and force'. British wine writer and author Clive Coates MW in 2003 enthused: 'Medium-full body. Soft, smooth, silky and very ripe. Marvellous balance. Very, very long... Splendid grip. Beautiful fruit. Quite magnificent.'

In 2009, US wine author and journalist Benjamin Lewin MW noted: 'Fruit density is diminishing but that core of sweet fruits you get in Margaux is still there, now tinged by just a touch of acidity. A mature colour now, with soft fruits on the palate, an impression of mulberries, quite intense and ripe, with a supple, lovely finish. A touch of tertiary development shows as sous bois on the nose. Still top notch if now exceeded by Latour.'

THE FACTS

Bottles produced
36,000

Composition
52% Merlot, 30% Cabernet Sauvignon, 13% Petit Verdot, 5% Cabernet Franc

Yield
11.8 hl/ha

Alcohol
12.2%

Release price
7 Francs a bottle (release price to Bordeaux trade)

Price today
£1,980-£2,940 a bottle

CHÂTEAU PICHON BARON 2005

Pauillac 2CC, Bordeaux, France

A LEGEND BECAUSE...

Although this splendid second growth is now acknowledged as one of the top wines of the Médoc, this was not always the case. Until the 1980s Pichon Baron was in poor shape and its wines were inconsistent. The 19th-century château lay empty, and its owners, the Bouteiller family, lacked the resources to invest in the estate, including the vineyards, which had dwindled to around 30ha. In 1987, the Bouteillers sold to AXA Millésimes, whose estates were run by Jean-Michel Cazes, owner of Château Lynch-Bages. Suddenly there was immense investment: machine-harvesting and the use of herbicides and pesticides were halted, the château was renovated, a circular underground winery was constructed and new purchases brought the vineyards to 72ha. Quality improved swiftly, and the great Bordeaux vintage of 2005 was a huge success.

LOOKING BACK

By 2005, Cazes had retired and his place as managing director of AXA Millésimes was taken by Christian Seely. Production was supervised by Pichon's long-term winemaker Jean-René Matignon. From the outset Seely decided to limit the grand vin to the château's finest terroir and vines, even though this led to a reduction in volume. This decision came to fruition in this vintage.

THE VINTAGE

An early and speedy flowering, problem-free. The summer was very sunny and dry, but temperatures were not excessive, so there was no raisining. At Pichon, two phases of bunch-thinning increased the natural concentration of the fruit to a very high level. Light rain in September brought the grapes to perfect ripeness. Merlot was picked from 19-29 September, followed by Cabernet Sauvignon from 3-11 October. Thick skins ensured that tannins and sugars were high. Acidity was high too, suggesting the wines would be long-lived.

THE TERROIR

The historic vineyards that form the heart of the blend lie on 45ha across the road from Château Latour, and this sector is planted mostly with Cabernet Sauvignon. More vines are planted between St-Julien and the château on an undulating plateau. Merlot is planted on soils with a higher clay content.

THE WINE

In 2004, the château acquired a vibrating sorting table, though admittedly little sorting was required in such a perfectly healthy year. The grapes were fermented in steel tanks for more than three weeks, using selected yeasts. Malolactic fermentation took place in barrels and tanks, then the wine was aged for 18 months in 80% new oak. The blend was assembled in February after the vintage, and before bottling the wine was egg white-fined.

THE REACTION

James Suckling noted in *Wine Spectator* in 2008: 'Crushed currant and blackberry on the nose, turning to tar and liquorice. Full-bodied, with a solid core of ripe fruit and seamless tannins. Very, very beautiful.'

In 2015, Robert Parker wrote: 'Sweet crème de cassis fruit, lots of cedar wood and forest floor, medium to full body, ripe tannin, and a long finish... This is a beauty and one of the most successful Pauillacs of this vintage.'

Jancis Robinson was impressed in 2017: 'Dense, concentrated and briary. It does have relatively elevated acidity and still very marked tannins so I would not choose to drink it for quite a while, but it certainly has impressive persistence.'

In 2019, Stephen Brook was bowled over: 'Very rich and velvety, highly concentrated and broad-shouldered, showing lavish tannins and a chocolatey tone. The acidity seems moderate, so this is now beginning to open up. Imposing and monumental, textured and long.'

THE FACTS

Bottles produced
240,000
Composition
64% Cabernet Sauvignon, 33% Merlot, 3% Cabernet Franc
Yield
35HL/HA
Alcohol
13.6%
Release price
US$146
Price today
US$170-US$212 (£130-£162)

LA MISSION HAUT-BRION 1929

Pessac-Léognan, Bordeaux, France

A LEGEND BECAUSE...

Château La Mission Haut-Brion has always been known for producing wines that are more robust and masculine than those of its immediate neighbour Château Haut-Brion. In few vintages was this difference so marked as in 1929. Although the very firm tannins of the 1929 may have resulted in some individual bottles that now show some dryness, others are going strong.

LOOKING BACK

Frédéric Woltner acquired the Pessac-Léognan estate in 1919 but a few years later put his son Henri in charge of it; Henri ran it until his death in 1974. It remained in the Woltner family until 1983, when the estate was bought by the Dillon family of Haut-Brion, though its identity was to remain separate and distinct. Henri was an oenologist and a forward-looking one at that, installing glass-lined fermentation vats as long ago as 1926. Their squat shape maximised the ratio of skins to juice, ensuring the wines would be deep in colour and dense in structure. La Mission is recognised today as equal to a first growth in quality, which simply confirms the wine trade's view almost a century ago: the 1918 vintage was priced higher than Lafite, Latour, and Margaux, and only Haut-Brion itself was more expensive.

THE VINTAGE

The year was not only hot but exceedingly dry, with a mere 225mm of rainfall. The wines were incredibly concentrated and high in tannins, yet many of them had a youthful charm not always found in young Bordeaux from a great year. For legendary British wine critic Edmund Penning-Rowsell, 1929 was the finest vintage of the 20th century.

THE TERROIR

The soils are remarkably stony as well as gravelly, more so than those of its neighbour Haut-Brion. The gravel beds are many metres thick. Drainage is excellent and the proximity to the city of Bordeaux usually gives precocious harvests. Henri Woltner was always careful not to pick overripe fruit, and sought to retain exemplary acidity in his wines. But the wines have always shown more muscle and meatiness than those of the more elegant Haut-Brion, and this is probably explained by terroir more than winemaking.

THE WINE

This vintage would have been partially fermented in the glass-lined steel vats that Henri Woltner installed in 1926, though the bulk of the crop would have been vinified in wooden vats. Woltner's goal was to have a more even fermentation, without excessively high temperatures and the attendant risks of volatile acidity. However, the steel tanks at this time weren't temperature-controlled. The wine was then aged in barriques for up to 30 months before being bottled.

THE REACTION

Henri Woltner once remarked that the 1929 was superb in its youth but unlikely to age well. US critic Robert Parker proclaimed in 1994: 'How wrong [Woltner] was! Still deep garnet in colour, with only a trace of amber at the edge, this wine exhibits a fabulously exotic sensual bouquet filled with

'It is recognised today as equal to a first growth, confirming views held almost a century ago'

aromas of tobacco, blackcurrants, cedar and leather. On the palate it reveals high alcohol as well as the remarkably sweet, rich, expansive, staggering concentration of fruit necessary to stand up to the alcohol.' A few years earlier, in 1990, Michael Broadbent of *Decanter* and Christie's asserted that this was 'one of the best ever La Missions, certainly the richest'. In 2008, Jancis Robinson MW felt the wine was past its best: 'Still incredibly deep, almost a blackish tinge. A bit too old now? Very dry and lots of acidity, a bit too much volatile acidity. Old-fashioned and beginning to taste a bit hard and dank. I'm sure it was wonderful in its day.' At the same tasting Neal Martin of *The Wine Advocate*, noted: 'Deep broody nose, introspective but compelling. Notes of leather, mocha, roasted chestnut, sandalwood and roasted meats. The palate is full-bodied and sinewy... but the finish is a little disjointed and dry. Nevertheless this is an amazing 1929 that is in graceful decline.' My own note from the same tasting was a touch more positive: 'Almost opaque brickred. Sweet, stylish nose. Mushrooms and tobacco. Intense, highly concentrated and spicy, with mocha tones. Tremendous drive and no conspicuous tannins.'

THE FACTS

Bottles produced
N/A

Alcohol
N/A

Composition
N/A

Release price
N/A

Yield
N/A

Price today
£2,970

Le Pin, Pomerol 1982

Bordeaux, France

A legend because...

Le Pin seemed to burst into view overnight. The first vintage made by Jacques Thienpont had been in 1979, and was sold cheaply. Before then the wine had been sold extensively in Belgium, but was not widely known. Once the outstanding quality of the 1982 was recognised, notably thanks to Parker's perfect score, prices shot up on the secondary market.

Looking back

In 1982, Le Pin consisted of a single hectare, next to a pine tree. Jacques Thienpont, from a Belgian family with extensive interests in the wine trade in Bordeaux, had recognised the quality of the soil some years earlier. The original idea was to incorporate the parcel into Vieux Château Certan close by, but when that didn't work out, Jacques and his father and uncle contrived to buy the vineyard in 1979; it later fell into Jacques' ownership, with a small share being held by Alexandre Thienpont of Vieux Château Certan. In 1984 Jacques was able to buy a second hectare, but today the total area under vine still stands at a modest 2.7ha.

The vintage

Bordeaux enjoyed a superb growing season; there was some rain in September, probably beneficial, but much of the Merlot had already been picked by then. The lush, full-bodied wines were criticised by some as too Napa-like in style, and indeed some wines, picked at high yields, are now in decline. Many others, though mature, are still going strong.

The terroir

Le Pin's vines are located on one of the highest sectors of the Pomerol plateau. Its neighbours include Vieux Château Certan, Petit Village and Trotanoy. The soil is essentially gravelly, although there are patches of sand and clay on an iron-rich base. The gravel ensures excellent drainage. Despite the small size of Le Pin, variations in the soil result in varying bunch sizes and dates of maturation. In 1982, one third of the vines had been planted as recently as 1978 – a remarkably high proportion for a wine of this grandeur.

The wine

Jacques Thienpont was taught how to make wine by his uncle Léon, and he has seen no reason to veer from that tried-and-tested path. Fermentation takes place in stainless steel. If he requires more concentration, he may bleed some tanks, and in vintages when acidity is low, he will return some very ripe stalks to the tanks. Extraction is by traditional pumpovers. The malolactic fermentation has always been conducted in barriques, not out of conviction that it results in better wine, but because in the old cellars there was nowhere else to put the wine for this purpose. Le Pin spends between 14 and 16 months in new oak, with traditional rackings; it is bottled without filtration.

The reaction

Michael Broadbent tasted the wine in November 1983, finding it 'rich and fruity', and confessed he had no idea this was an infant cult wine. In 2001 he tasted it again: 'Glorious nose, very distinctive; sweet, soft, velvety, full of fruit. Fragrant.'

Neal Martin, who admits he prefers the 1983, has written: 'My solitary encounter with the 1982 [in 2008] suggested a pleasurable Pomerol, Burgundian and earthy on the nose, sumptuous on the palate, but fading a little in the glass.'

In 2008, James Suckling noted: 'A legendary wine. It's so exotic and very ripe, with chocolate, berry and light cream on the nose that follows through to the palate... Velvety and round... Super-exciting.'

In 2009, Robert Parker revisited it: 'Probably not a perfect wine for the classicist, this flamboyant, exotic, lavishly rich, concentrated, low-acid fruit-bomb exhibits remarkable aromatic complexity... This is another 1982 I thought would have one, possibly two feet in the grave at age 27, but lo and behold, it is still going strong.'

THE FACTS

Bottles produced
3,600

Composition
100% Merlot

Yield
30hl/ha

Alcohol
12.5%

Release price
US$400 per case

Price today
£9,512 per bottle

PICHON COMTESSE DE LALANDE 1982

Pauillac 2CC, Bordeaux, France

A LEGEND BECAUSE...

1982 was a splendid vintage, and many châteaux made terrific wines. Yet initial reactions were mixed. Some experts found a resemblance to opulent wines from Napa, and were suspicious of the style, since they were used to more austere and tannic clarets. Yet the 1982 Pichon Lalande has proved to be a near-perfect expression of this exuberant vintage, and it has confounded the sceptics by going the distance.

LOOKING BACK

Pichon's modern era began in 1925, when the estate was sold to the Miailhe family. One family member, May-Eliane de Lencquesaing, secured a majority holding in 1978. The previous decades had been lean ones for the property and the château itself was in a dilapidated state. The success of fine vintages, beginning with 1982, allowed her to invest heavily, with about £7 million spent on renovations. She lived at the property and ran it with an iron hand up to 2006, when she sold it to Roederer Champagne.

THE VINTAGE

Jean-Jacques Godin was estate manager since 1975, and would have overseen this vintage. A hot, dry summer allowed the grapes to reach perfect ripeness, with generous yields. Harvest began in mid-September in sunny weather, and subsequent rain did not diminish the quality of the Cabernets yet to be picked. The richness of the wines did lead to some problems during fermentation, such as high volatile acidity, but the best wines were well made, balanced and opulent.

THE TERROIR

Pichon Lalande is a large property with some 89ha under vine, although only 70ha were in production in 1982. There has always been a fairly high proportion of Merlot, around 30%, which contributes to the wine's sumptuous texture. The vineyards are dispersed, and most of those surrounding the château belong to Latour. The Pichon vines cross the border into St-Julien, where 11ha are planted, although just 1ha bears the appellation – the château has long been permitted to incorporate the St-Julien wine into its Pauillac wines. Soil is gravel over clay, with a deeper subsoil of sandstone, limestone and marl.

THE WINE

The hand-harvested grapes did not receive a cold soak, and selected yeasts were added to provoke fermentation. This was the first year in which temperature control was installed for fermentation. The wine was aged for about 18 months in 50%-60% new oak, with regular rackings, egg-white fining and filtration before bottling. In short, a conventional Médoc winemaking regime, allowing the superb terroir and ripe grapes to speak unhindered.

THE REACTION

In 2001, Michael Broadbent revelled in the wine: 'Prettily coloured, well upholstered, delectable, sweetness and fruit.' In 2009, Robert Parker tasted the wine in its prime: 'One of the monumental wines of the last century. It was a sprinter out of the gate, which gave rise to questions about how quickly it would begin its decline. However, at age 27, it retains all its glossy, flamboyant cassis fruit, chocolatey, berry jam-like notes, and earthy, foresty flavours.'

Jane Anson in 2016 noted: 'Just an incredible, stunning wine that hit me right from the very first moment and held its grip with the most confident of touches. Such intensity on the nose, with blueberry, blackcurrant and spicy mint, this is knock-your-socks-off great.'

A year later, Antonio Galloni was equally enthusiastic: 'Utterly profound from the very first taste. Powerful and explosive, with seemingly endless layers of flavour. Vivid, intensely aromatic and seamless, the 1982 has enough pedigree and depth to drink well for at least several decades. What a wine!'

THE FACTS

Bottles produced
275,000
Composition
N/A
Yield
40HL/HA
Alcohol
12.5%
Release price
Equivalent of €10.20
Price today
£511-£888

BURGUNDY

The region's hierarchy of crus meant that at the top level of the grands crus, quantities released would be small indeed. But they were also eagerly sought-after by tasters and connoisseurs as well as collectors, and there was no shortage of documentation on most of the wines selected.

HAMBERTIN

BONNEAU DU MARTRAY 1990

Corton-Charlemagne, Burgundy, France

A LEGEND BECAUSE...

Other than the Domaine de la Romanée-Conti, Bonneau du Martray is the only estate in Burgundy that produces nothing but grands crus. Only two wines are made: a red Corton and, in greater volumes, a Corton-Charlemagne that is widely recognised as the benchmark wine of the appellation. The 1990 is still going strong, confirming the longevity of the appellation in good vintages.

LOOKING BACK

The estate had been an ecclesiastical holding for 1,000 years, but was confiscated during the French Revolution and then sold to the Véry family. In 1835 Marie-Eugénie Véry married Charles Bonneau du Martray. It still remains in the hands of their descendants. In 1969 a family member bequeathed it to his niece Comtesse le Bault de la Morinière, and her husband Jean ran the estate. In 1994 the present co-owner and head of the domaine, Jean's son Jean-Charles le Bault de la Morinière, gave up a successful career as an architect in Paris to run the domaine. He reverted to ploughing the vineyards and replanted using massal selections from the the best vines.

THE VINTAGE

1990 was a glorious vintage in Burgundy, as in many other parts of Europe. The summer was hot and dry, although some welcome rain did fall during August and early September, helping to unlock any blocked maturation brought on by the heat. These vineyards are rarely exposed to excessive heat, so the grapes retained good acidity in this very warm year.

THE TERROIR

The hill of Corton, just north of Beaune, is divided among three communes: Aloxe-Corton, Pernand-Vergelesses and Ladoix-Serrigny. The 11 hectares owned by Bonneau de Martray lie in Pernand-Vergelesses and Aloxe-Corton, the most westerly part of the appellation. The average vine age is around 45 years. The vineyards all link up and are essentially in one block, facing west and southwest. Thus Bonneau du Martray is the largest proprietor in Corton-Charlemagne, where a total 72 hectares are authorised to produce the wine, and at present 50 hectares do so. The various elevations are a great advantage, allowing the domaine to harvest over a week-long period, selecting the ideal moment at which to pick each of the 16 parcels. Without any publicity, the estate has been converting its vineyards, which since the mid-1990s have not been subjected to herbicides or fertilisers, to organic farming.

THE WINE

Jean-Charles' father pioneered temperature control in the 1970s. He would begin the fermentation in small steel tanks, completing it in medium-toast barrels, one-third new. Today the lees may be stirred (if so, sparingly), but not in 1990, when the wine was simply aged on its fine lees. After a year in barrel, the wine spends six months in stainless steel tanks before being bottled, usually without fining but with a very light filtration, since the ageing in tank generally clarifies the wine very well.

THE REACTION

In 1995 Clive Coates wrote: 'At first it seemed a bit neutral, and I was more than a little disappointed. It is still a firm wine, reserved,

but underneath is a splendid opulence, marvellous concentration of fruit and great class.' By 2011 he was even more enthusiastic: 'Splendidly fresh still. Lovely fruit. Not quite the energy or power of the 1995, but very delicious. Marvellous vigour for a wine now 20 years old.'

Michael Broadbent in 1999 admired its 'delicious nose, like super-charged vanilla ice cream; distinctly sweet, a perfect blend of fruit and oak, smoky, elegant, good finish. Can't get much better than this.'

Jasper Morris MW in 2010 found the wine 'still marvellous'. In 2014 Jeff Leve of *Wine Cellar Inside* wrote: 'Spun gold in colour, this mineral-driven, citrus, floral and honey dominated wine ends with bright, firm lemon and grapefruit.'

THE FACTS

Bottles produced
54,000
Composition
100% Chardonnay
Yield
46-48 hl/ha approx
Alcohol
13%
Release price
£783 per case (in bond)
Price today
£262 per bottle

JF Coche-Dury, Corton-Charlemagne 1986

Burgundy, France

A legend because...

Jean-François Coche is recognised as one of Burgundy's greatest masters of white wine. He has achieved this status without leaping onto the circuit of winemaker dinners and tutored tastings. A retiring man, he has focused instead on meticulous work in the vineyards and cellar. About two thirds of the estate's production is Meursault Villages and plain Bourgogne Chardonnay, and Corton-Charlemagne is his sole grand cru. His holdings there are tiny, a mere 0.34 of a hectare. Thus the wine is scarce, which adds to its desirability as a collector's item. This, the first vintage, has stood the test of time.

Looking back

Jean-François, who has now retired in favour of his son Raphael, took over the domaine from his father in 1973. Georges Coche established a good reputation for the wines, but it was only after his son began making them that the estate was propelled into the top tier of white Burgundy producers, where it firmly remains. As for the difference between his Meursaults and this grand cru, Jean-François once told me: 'Corton-Charlemagne's character always lies in the aftertaste, that's its force.'

The vintage

Rainfall marred the red-grape harvest in 1986 but the whites were admired from the outset. The wet conditions did result in some botrytis infection in the Chardonnay grapes. Most white Burgundy producers quite like the additional richness and weight given to their wines by a little botrytis, and Jean-François admits that this wine contained about 15% of grapes with noble rot. Despite fears that the botrytis content in many of the whites could limit their ageability, many of them have gone the distance, showing good structure and firm acidity.

The terroir

The Coche-Dury parcel lies in a lieu-dit called Sous-la-Croix, a top sector of the vineyard above Aloxe-Corton. The vines face due south, and the soil has a high limestone content with little clay. They were planted in 1950, so by 1986, the first vintage under the Coche-Dury label, they were already mature.

The wine

Jean-François always made a great effort to reduce the yields of his vines - not by greenharvesting so much as by drastic pruning earlier in the growing season. Although in later years he would acquire a pneumatic press, in 1986 he was still using a Vaslin horizontal press. Vaslins would soon be scorned as too brutal, but ironically they came back into use after producers began to suspect that the ultra-clean juice produced by pneumatic presses might play a part in the premature oxidation that came to trouble winemakers and consumers alike from the late 1990s onwards. After pressing, the must is barrel-fermented in a high proportion of new oak, with regular stirring of the lees. The wine spends two winters in barrel before fining and bottling without filtration.

The reaction

An early assessment was given in 1992 by US critic Robert

> 'Great, lively white Burgundy. A terrific, indisputable thoroughbred'
>
> Jancis Robinson MW

Parker: 'The wine still boasts a spectacular, stony, mineral-scented nose intermingled with aromas of overripe oranges and apples. Full-bodied, with admirable concentration, crisp acidity... Large-scaled yet perfectly balanced.' The UK's Jancis Robinson MW reported in 1999 after a vertical tasting of various vintages of this wine: 'This has the deepest gold of all. Honey and flowers initially on the nose. This has a perfect full-on attack, which gets to every last little tastebud. Wonderfully fulfilling. Lifts of savoury and honey. The taste is big and long and this is a great lively white Burgundy. Very exciting indeed. A terrific, indisputable thoroughbred.' More recently, John Tolson wrote in *The Underground Newsletter* in 2014: 'The definition of complexity and perfection in white Burgundy. It is light golden in colour, with a perfume that soars from the glass offering hints of coconut, apricots, honey, and citrus with faint suggestions of spice. Deep, rich and supple, yet in perfect balance... Honeyed, with citrus, coconut, apricot and floral flavours. Opulent but with elegance and tremendous length. Perfection.'

THE FACTS

Bottles produced
About 1,800

Composition
100% Chardonnay

Yield
N/A

Alcohol
13%

Release price
N/A

Price today
In November 2014, two magnums were sold at auction for $18,375 (£11,722) the equivalent of £2,930 a bottle

DOMAINE GEORGES ROUMIER, BONNES-MARES GRAND CRU 1995

Chambolle-Musigny, Burgundy, France

A LEGEND BECAUSE...

The domaine is one of the three finest estates based in Chambolle-Musigny, the others being De Vogüé and Jacques-Frédéric Mugnier; like them, it includes one or more parcels of Bonnes-Mares in its portfolio. In recent years this grand cru has risen in esteem; it has always been highly regarded but for scarcity and, sometimes, quality it can be eclipsed by Musigny, Chambolle's other grand cru. Bonnes-Mares gives virile wines that can feel atypical of the supposedly more 'feminine' style for which Chambolle is known, but Roumier's is always renowned for its exceptional finesse.

LOOKING BACK

Christophe Roumier, born in 1958, became involved in the family domaine in 1982, and took over running it after his father Jean-Marie retired in 1992. The emphasis here has always been on maintaining healthy vineyards and aiming for reasonably small but not tiny yields. Roumier is flexible when it comes to such matters as destemming.

THE VINTAGE

The spring was mild, but May saw snow. The flowering was protracted and far from easy, and some hail diminished the crop further in Chambolle. But the summer was dry and hot, resulting in some water stress. September continued warm but conditions were also mixed, with some rain, which helped ripen the grapes, and the harvest began at the end of that month. The grapes needed some sorting, which further reduced yields. Initially tannic, they've turned out well.

THE TERROIR

The Roumier holdings are extensive, given this is a highly regarded grand cru. He owns 1.4 hectares of the total surface of 15ha, and these vines are divided among four parcels at elevations between 270m to 310m. The oldest vines date from 1928 and the 1940s, although there are younger plantings of clones from the 1980s and '90s. The soil has long been ploughed, and Roumier prefers severe pruning to green-harvesting to ensure low yields. Bonnes-Mares, which is on the mid-slope, is quite a large grand cru, and though most of it is in Chambolle-Musigny, part falls within the boundaries of Morey-St-Denis to the north. There are two distinct soil types, terres blanches and terres rouges, evenly distributed. The former is made up of marne soil with friable limestone, which results in perfumed, intense wines. The more fertile terres rouges give rounded but powerful wines. Since Roumier's parcels lie on both, he vinifies each separately, blending them later.

THE WINE

The grapes are mostly destemmed, in contrast to his Musigny, which is vinified from whole clusters. But in 1995 Roumier retained the stems of the Bonnes-Mares too, and fermented the must in large wooden vats, with a varying period of post-fermentation maceration. The different lots are aged in one-third to 50% new oak, as Roumier has never been keen on using a high proportion of new wood. It is bottled without fining or filtration.

THE REACTION

In the early 1990s Michael Broadbent gave the wine a four-star rating. In 1997 Pierre Rovani of *The Wine Advocate* tasted it in cask, noting its 'masculine but elegant nose [of] deep, sweet, spicy dark fruits ...Enthralling silky texture and finishes with a huge burst of powerful dark berries and a touch of earthiness'. In 2007 Jancis Robinson MW wrote: 'Heady perfumed nose ...Treacley and rich and concentrated. Really tingly. Long. Dense and sweet. Structure too.' Clive Coates MW tasted the wine twice in 2012 and both times referred to it as 'brilliant', 'splendid' and showing 'concentration' and 'dimension'.

THE FACTS

Bottles produced
N/A

Composition
100% Pinot Noir

Yield
N/A

Alcohol
12%

Release price
N/A

Price today
£1,995

DOMAINE LEROY, RICHEBOURG 1999

Côte de Nuits Grand Cru, Burgundy, France

A LEGEND BECAUSE...

Lalou Bize-Leroy created Domaine Leroy in 1988 by buying the richly endowed 12ha Charles Noëllat estate in Vosne, followed some years later by Domaine Philippe Rémy in Gevrey-Chambertin. Today she owns 22ha. She has always been utterly uncompromising, with a strong belief in biodynamic farming and very low yields that rarely exceed 25hl/ha. She converted the entire domaine to biodynamics in 1988. This refusal to cut corners is what justifies her very high prices, but few would question that the quality of her wines places the domaine among the very greatest properties in Burgundy.

LOOKING BACK

In 1993, severe mildew almost destroyed Madame Bize-Leroy's crop, allowing some to question whether the biodynamics was at fault – she insists this was not the case. When the decade ended with the 1999 vintage, she was thrilled with the quality, commenting on the wines' astonishing fruit and richness.

THE VINTAGE

Rain in June led to mildew, so treatments were essential, though at Leroy these were consistent with biodynamic principles. The summer was exceptionally warm, and by 20 September the grands crus were ready to be picked. Those who overcropped didn't achieve full maturation until October, by which time some rain had fallen. Overall, the problem in this vintage was not lack of ripeness but the very large crop – yields were very high, except, as usual, at Leroy. Here the excellent balance of fruit, acidity and tannin meant there was no dilution and ample structure.

THE TERROIR

This great site in Vosne-Romanée covers just over 8ha, and almost half is owned by Domaine de la Romanée-Conti. Leroy has the second largest holding, with 0.78ha. The soil is a mix of clay and sand, with limestone debris and pebbles. It lies mid-slope at 260m-280m. Vines are pruned severely to reduce yields.

THE WINE

Grapes are sorted twice at the winery. There is no destemming or crushing. Leroy favours a cold soak before a gradual fermentation in open-top vats of 18-20 days at a moderate temperature, with regular punchdowns. The grands crus are aged in new oak for 18 months, with just a single racking. The wines are bottled without filtration or fining.

THE REACTION

In 2008, Bruce Sanderson of *Wine Spectator* noted: 'Ripe and bordering on jammy, with black cherry and plum flavours. What texture... powerful and balanced, with a long finish.' Neal Martin admired the wine in *Wine Advocate* in 2009, finding it: '...full-bodied with very fine tannins; cranberry, wild strawberry, tart cherry but so tightly coiled and really not wanting to come out and play, rendering this a sulky Richebourg. But it purrs like a Rolls Royce.'

In 2010, Allen Meadows of Burghound wrote: 'Neither is it hard, dry or aggressive, merely quite firm, wrapped in a sappy and extract-suffused finish that goes on and on... This should be sensational in time.'

Clive Coates in 2012 tasted and wrote: 'Just about mature. Still quite closed on the nose. But lots and lots of depth and concentration. Very intense and very high-class. Full-bodied. Not yet ready. A very impressive, profound, multi-dimensional wine... Indisputably great.'

Jancis Robinson in 2018 found it: 'Intense, rich, broad and explosive and exuberant. Stuffed full of dramatic ingredients with a mass of fine tannins lurking underneath. Hint of something (deliciously) fungal and a floral note too. Extremely persistent.'

THE FACTS

Bottles produced
2,685
Composition
100% Pinot Noir
Yield
23hl/ha
Alcohol
13.5%
Release price
N/A
Price today
£5,570

DOMAINE ROUSSEAU, CHAMBERTIN 1993

Gevrey-Chambertin Grand Cru, Burgundy, France

A LEGEND BECAUSE...

Though there are other domaines with important holdings in Chambertin, Rousseau is widely regarded as the supreme exponent of this exceptional terroir. Chambertin is always powerful, demanding and ageworthy, but the Rousseau wines magically combine perfume, power and concentration with immense elegance. Although 1993 is not regarded as an outstanding vintage in Burgundy, Rousseau made exceptional wines, and his Chambertin is seen as superior to the much-acclaimed 1990.

LOOKING BACK

Charles Rousseau was at the peak of his powers in 1993, but also beginning to hand the reins to his son Eric. The transition brought no revolutionary changes, as Charles kept his expert eye on the domaine. But over the years Eric would make his own contributions, especially to work in the vineyard, consolidating his father's achievement.

THE PEOPLE

Armand Rousseau was one of the first growers in Burgundy to start bottling his own wines, in the 1930s - a period when cash-strapped merchants were unwilling to purchase more wine from growers. After his death in 1959, his place was taken by his son Charles (*see above*), a revered winemaker who has acted as mentor to many of the region's great names. Charles doubled the size of the domaine to 14 hectares through a series of shrewd acquisitions, primarily grands crus. Eric Rousseau reflects the interest of his generation in improving farming methods and controlling yields; in the cellar he works in much the same way as his father Charles, with some fine tuning.

THE VINTAGE

A wet, overcast July led to mildew and oidium, but August was warm and sunny. There was intermittent rain from mid- September to early October, but the Pinot skins were thick, days were cool, and there was neither rot nor dilution. Harvesting took place in the last week of September. The small berries resulted in concentrated reds that also had good colour and acidity. Rousseau's characteristic low yields paid off in terms of ripening and flavour, though the wines were notably tannic.

THE TERROIR

Rousseau is the largest owner of Chambertin, with 2.55ha of a total 12.9ha. The vines are in four parcels that lie on a gently sloping mid-slope at an elevation of 275m to 300m, protected from the colder upper slopes and avoiding richer soils lower down. The subsoil is Bajocian limestone, and the topsoil varies, with pebbles and clay distributed to varying degrees. The holdings are the result of purchases from 1921 onwards, the most recent in 2009. Average vine age is around 60 years, and the density an exceptionally high 12,000 vines/ha.

THE WINE

Yields rarely exceed 30hl/ha here, kept low by hard pruning and debudding rather than green-harvesting - and a ruthless selection is made in the vineyard. At the winery, grapes are mostly destemmed, chilled to 15°C, and left to macerate without temperature control for up to three weeks. Extraction is achieved initially by frequent pumpovers and subsequently by punching down the cap. After pressing, the juice is run off into 100% new barrels. The 1993 would have spent between 20 and 24 months in

barrel, though current practice at the domaine is to leave the wine in wood for only 18 months.

THE REACTION

In 2007 Jancis Robinson MW enthused: 'Sweet and scented nose. Very rich and sweet on the palate. Round and winning. Reverberates and dances. Lively. Racy.'

Benjamin Lewin MW in 2011 gave a detailed appraisal: 'Mineral nose with perfumed notes of violets. Beautiful, developed palate, just short of savoury, slightly tea-like and herbal finish, complex layers of flavour. Subtle palate, developed fruits integrating perfectly with acidity and tannins, a very long perfumed finish.'

In 2013 Neal Martin wrote: 'Scents of wild strawberry, raspberry, hints of wild mushroom and truffle. The palate is medium bodied but delivers a crescendo of flavours: raspberry preserve, ceps, hints of tobacco and dried herbs. It fans out gloriously, like a huge wave breaking upon a shoreline... Sublime.'

THE FACTS

Bottles produced	Alcohol
8,800	**13%**
Composition	Release price
100% Pinot Noir	**€50**
Yield	Price today
35hl/ha	**£1,340 (€1,115)**

JAYER, CROS-PARANTOUX, VOSNE-ROMANÉE 1990

Burgundy, France

A LEGEND BECAUSE...

Henri Jayer was not a major landowner in the Côte de Nuits, but of all red Burgundies, the wines he made from 1.5ha (hectares) of Cros-Parantoux, Richebourg and Echézeaux have become among the most sought after. Cros-Parantoux, a small premier cru, is often regarded as being of grand cru quality. The Jayer style may not seem that remarkable today - fully ripe fruit, low yields, complete destemming, a cold soak before fermentation and a generous use of new oak - but in the 1970s and 1980s he produced wines with a clarity and intensity that many found remarkable. Born in 1922, Jayer acquired many admirers and disciples among other Burgundian growers until he retired in 1995. Thereafter, his nephew Emmanuel Rouget sharecropped the vineyard, and Jayer himself retained a very small parcel until 2001, though sadly he died only five years later. Today, Rouget owns two-thirds of Cros-Parantoux.

LOOKING BACK

This exceptional premier cru had been abandoned after the devastation caused by phylloxera. Jayer sensed its great potential, even though for 20 years it had been used to grow Jerusalem artichokes. He used dynamite to clear the site and replanted it in 1953. Though Jayer had never intended to be a winemaker, he was asked by M Camuzet, the mayor of Vosne-Romanée at the time, to look after his vines on a sharecropping basis. One of the sites he tended was Cros-Parantoux, and part of the site belonged to Domaine Méo-Camuzet, which was inherited by Jean Méo, a well-known politician who lived in Paris and had little time to run his Burgundy estate. His son Jean-Nicolas took control of the family estate in 1989, and Jayer advised young Méo.

THE VINTAGE

The year 1990 did not begin auspiciously, as cool weather in June delayed flowering and led to problems with the fruit set. The summer was hot and dry, but rainfall in September was timely and brought the fruit to full ripeness. The harvest took place at the end of September. Sugar levels were high, and yields reasonably copious despite the problems at flowering. This vintage followed two other fine vintages, the more austere 1988 and the more opulent 1989, but had a finesse all its own. It takes its place among the most acclaimed postwar vintages, as a year when everything ripened, and the result was delicious wines from grand cru down to basic Bourgogne.

THE TERROIR

This exceptional premier cru, resuscitated by Jayer, lies on shallow, rocky soil and gives wine of remarkable longevity. Only 1ha in size, it lies just above Richebourg and to the south is Les Petits Monts, its neighbour. The slope is uneven, making it exceptionally hard to work. Tilted slightly to the north, it is also one of the cooler sites in Vosne.

THE WINE

Jayer treated Cros-Parantoux in the same manner as his grands crus, favouring a large proportion of new oak barrels, in this case 100%. Yields were low, and he aimed for full ripeness and entirely healthy fruit before harvesting. The grapes were destemmed and chilled for a week to stabilise colour before fermentation began in cement vats. Jayer was just as rigorous in the cellar, maintaining exemplary standards of cleanliness. The wines were aged for 18 months in medium-toast François Frères barrels. Jayer fined with

'Henri Jayer's methods led to robust wines, which hardly ever showed any traces of oxidation'

egg whites, but bottled by hand without filtration. It is universally agreed that Jayer's methods led to robust, full-flavoured wines, which hardly ever showed any traces of oxidation. Information about the wine in the fact box below is mostly absent because Jayer himself is dead, and very few other people would have had access to precise details on yield and alcohol.

THE REACTION

In 1996, wine critic and former *Decanter* columnist Michael Broadbent was impressed by the depth of colour, and said: 'Strangely sweet, then fragrant, spicy; marvellous fruit and flavour. I thought it was a bit over the top.' Broadbent noted that this was a blind tasting with other connoisseurs, and it 'received a large number of votes for the top wine of the range'. Such is the scarcity of the wine that I have been unable to locate other tasting notes.

THE FACTS

Bottles produced
3,500
Composition
100% Pinot Noir
Yield
N/A
Alcohol
N/A
Release price
N/A
Price today
£7,440 per bottle

Leflaive, Montrachet 1992

Côte de Beaune Grand Cru, Burgundy, France

A legend because…

For many decades, Domaine Leflaive was the benchmark estate in Puligny-Montrachet, with 22ha of fabulous vineyards (today almost 28ha) in many premiers crus and also in four grands crus. Its reputation had faded in the 1980s, possibly because generous yields had led to a loss of concentration. However, in 1990 Vincent Leflaive retired and his daughter Anne-Claude became a co-director alongside her cousin Olivier. By then she was formidably well trained as a soil expert and oenologist. In 1994 she was in charge, aided by Pierre Morey, the cellarmaster at the domaine for 20 years up to 2008, who shared her enthusiasm for biodynamic farming. The reputation of the domaine's 1992 Montrachet may have been enhanced by the fact that it was only their second vintage from this grand cru.

Looking back

Anne-Claude was a passionate convert to biodynamism, entirely convinced of its capacity to bring out the very best in a great site. Visitors to the domaine were often presented, blind, with two glasses from the same vineyard, one farmed organically, the other biodynamically, and asked to decide which was the better wine. Anne-Claude insisted the majority of her informed visitors chose the biodynamic wine. This was true in my case, and in that of neighbouring vigneron François Carillon, who wandered into the tasting room while I was there.

By 1992 she was just beginning her crusade. In 1990 she converted just one hectare of vines, and in 1992 added 3ha more. In 1997 the entire domaine had been converted to biodynamism. Given the domaine's eminence, it's surprising that Leflaive only managed to purchase its parcel in Montrachet in 1991. Thus 1992 was only the second vintage.

The vintage

The early summer was warm and humid, but July and August were fine, even resulting in some blocked maturation of the vines until welcome rain fell in late August. Early September was very hot, bringing speedy ripening and some loss of acidity. That made the precise moment of picking of great importance. The white wines were ample and relatively forward, with some lack of structure, although the finest wines aged well.

The terroir

Leflaive owns 0.08ha of Montrachet, which generally yields about 300 bottles. This single parcel, believed to have been planted in the 1950s, lies within the Chassagne-Montrachet sector, very close to the lane that separates Le Montrachet from Bâtard-Montrachet.

The wine

After careful sorting in the vineyard, the wine was pressed in pneumatic presses, then fermented in a single new barrel, with regular stirring of the lees until the end of the year. The wine was then aged for a total of one year in the same barrel, before being decanted into a stainless steel vat for the second winter.

The reaction

Robert Parker tasted the wine in 1993: 'The quintessential Chardonnay, it is an awesomely rich, highly extracted wine oozing with flavour, yet it is marvellously precise and focused…

The [Leflaive Montrachet] wines are renowned for their purity and elegance, but the 1992s also display a special level of richness and intensity.'

More recently, Allen Meadows of *www.burghound.com* tasted the wine in 2018: 'Even at almost 30 years of age, the 1992 Montrachet is still cruising along like it was only 10, as the freshness of the aromas is uncanny... exotic fruit aromas with fantastically complex secondary nuances as well as those of wet stone, honeysuckle and anise. The thick, concentrated and opulent, broad-shouldered flavours possess an incredible level of mouth-coating dry extract that... confers a distinct texture onto the mineral-driven and gorgeously long finish. This is one powerful effort, in fact so much so that this can only be drunk slowly. A stunner of a wine by any definition.'

THE FACTS

Bottles produced
300
Composition
100% Chardonnay
Yield
Approx. 30hl/ha
Alcohol
13.5%
Release price
US$300
Price today
£12,400

Ramonet, Montrachet 1986

Grand Cru, Burgundy, France

A legend because…

It is hard to think of another Burgundian white wine estate with a pedigree and reputation as substantial as that of Ramonet. As long ago as the 1930s its bottled wines were being imported into the US. The 1986 vintage was superb for white wines in the region and Montrachet, then as now, reigns supreme as its most prestigious and lauded vineyard.

Looking back

In 1986 the patriarch Pierre Ramonet was still alive, but by then he was into his 80s. The estate had been operated since 1983 by his grandsons Noël (born 1962) and Jean-Claude (1967). Pierre died in 1994, at the age of 88. His grandsons were always very respectful of the traditions and styles laid down by Pierre, and the rich and fleshy style of the wines has been perpetuated.

The vintage

The spring was damp, but flowering took place in warm, dry conditions. Summer was warm and mostly dry until mid-August, and there were downpours in September too. Rot was widespread, but affected the red grapes more than the white. By late September the Chardonnay was fully ripe – in some cases too ripe – but Montrachet is a site that preserves freshness. Almost all wines are fully ready to drink.

The terroir

The domaine's main focus is on the vineyards of Chassagne-Montrachet, where the cellars are located. It has superb premiers crus, but the wines that drinkers and collectors yearn for are the grands crus Bienvenues-Bâtard-Montrachet, Bâtard-Montrachet, Chevalier-Montrachet and Le Montrachet. Sandwiched between Bâtard below and Chevalier above, the 8ha Montrachet is a gently sloping and perfectly situated site that often combines the power and richness of Bâtard with the finesse of Chevalier. Its clay subsoil retains moisture so it rarely suffers from drought stress. Ramonet's 0.5ha is more or less equally divided between Chassagne and Puligny, as Montrachet straddles both communes. The old vines were taken out in the late 1980s and replaced in 1990.

The wine

Ramonet's wines are only produced from vines that are at least 18 years old. After vinification in stainless steel tanks, the wine is transferred to oak barrels. The Ramonets favour the Allier and Vosges forests and buy their barrels from up to 10 coopers. The wines are aged in one-third new oak for 12-15 months, with the exception of the Montrachet, which spends its ageing period in entirely new oak. Lees-stirring is minimal, but the brothers favour long lees contact (including a proportion of gross lees), which helps to fashion the rich and voluminous style of the Ramonet wines. Neither fining nor filtration is systematic.

The reaction

Robert Parker found it 'stunning' in August 1992: 'With a bold, even dramatic nose of buttered popcorn, honeyed apples, oranges... its velvety, viscous, chewy texture is crammed with sweet, expansive Chardonnay fruit. There is barely enough acidity to hold everything together, and the finish is explosively long, rich, and buttery.' Harvey Steiman in *The Wine Spectator* wrote in 1995: 'Lithe, even sinuous, and supple, showing off toasty, spicy hazelnut and pear flavours with a flourish of mushroom at the edges. The texture is especially wonderful...with a lacy core of acidity. Delicious now, but should go on until 2000 at least.' In 1997, Michael Broadbent tasted the wine from salmanazar and found it: 'Very pale; rich, toasty bouquet that spread its wings magnificently; distinct sweetness, full-bodied, nutty flavour – what a pathetic, inadequate description! Rich of course, and with very good acidity. Will keep for ages.'

THE FACTS

Composition
100% Chardonnay
Release price
US$725
Price today
£3,000 ex-tax

CHAMPAGNE
BOLLINGER
MAISON FONDÉE EN 1829

CHAMPAGNE

The producers, or marques, were not difficult to select. How could one not include Cristal or Salon or Bollinger R.D.? The vintages, though, would prove less clear-cut, as not all champagne enthusiasts relish *le gout anglais*, the aromas and flavours of well-matured sparkling wines.

BILLECART-SALMON, CUVÉE NICOLAS FRANÇOIS 1959

Champagne, France

A LEGEND BECAUSE...

This was the wine that triumphed in a blind tasting of 150 vintage Champagnes organised in 1999 by an expert team led by Richard Juhlin from Sweden. It won first place as 'Champagne of the Millennium', and second place was, remarkably, taken by the 1961 vintage. François Roland-Billecart was reluctant to submit any of the house's cuvées, but his brother Antoine went behind his back and entered both the triumphant wines.

This cuvée is dominated by Pinot Noir, but in more recent years a scarcer wine has taken its place alongside it – Le Clos St-Hilaire, produced solely from 1ha of Pinot Noir grapes planted in the former park of the mansion at Mareuil-sur-Aÿ. Vinified in casks, it is aged on the yeasts for 14 years before being bottled with low dosage. Rare and costly, it shows that the Billecart family doesn't rest on its laurels.

LOOKING BACK

The family history dates back at least to the 17th century, but it was the marriage in 1818 of Nicolas François Billecart to Elisabeth Salmon that marks the creation of the house in its present form. It is run today by seventh-generation Mathieu Roland-Billecart, who succeeded François in 2018. Jean-Jacques Frey became a minority shareholder in 2004, bringing his Champagne vineyards to the estate. In 1959, this cuvée, which had been produced since 1955, was not marketed under the family label, but in 1964 it was named Cuvée NF Billecart.

THE VINTAGE

1959 was a superb year in Champagne. From May onwards the summer was hot and there was little rain. Flowering took place in ideal conditions. The growing season delivered substantial volumes as well as exceptional quality. These were wines of weight and power that in many cases have aged exceptionally well.

THE TERROIR

Although the house now owns a good range of its own vineyards, in the 1950s it relied on contracts with a body of excellent growers with good sites and the same commitment to quality as the Billecart family. Only grapes from Mareuil-sur-Aÿ and grand cru sites are selected for this cuvée.

THE WINE

Each parcel is vinified separately. The Roland-Billecart family uses a distinctive technique when it comes to fermenting the wine, derived from experience centuries ago as brewers. The must is settled and clarified twice, chilled to a temperature of about 5°C. The gross lees are then removed before the temperature is slowly raised to allow the yeasts to get to work on juice that is free of any oxidation. The fermentation, at relatively cool temperatures, generally takes about three weeks, and for this cuvée would have taken place in oak barrels. Barrel-fermentation was later abandoned, but revived again in the mid-1990s.

THE REACTION

In his 2001 book, *Champagne: The Great Tasting*, Richard

Juhlin wrote that the Cuvée Nicolas François 1959 '...had everything one would expect of a luxury Champagne, but in a seldom-seen concentration, and simultaneously with harmonious balance.

A totally perfect Champagne in its category, with a smoky, honey-smooth, extremely long taste of walnut, orange blossom and chocolate.' Serena Sutcliffe MW, who also participated in the 1999 tasting, noted: 'Very pale with a greenish tinge. The ultimate "divine hedgerows" bouquet – like coming home. This is it! Creamy delicacy and yet huge flavour (this must be the Holy Grail for which all Champagne blenders search). Mega dimension. Great depth and yet finesse. Perfect composition. Remains fabulous in the glass.'

THE FACTS

Bottles produced
N/A

Composition
60% Pinot Noir, 40% Chardonnay

Yield
36hl/ha

Alcohol
12.5%

Release price
N/A

Price today
N/A

BOLLINGER, R.D. 1976

Champagne, France

A LEGEND BECAUSE...

R.D. stands for 'Récemment Dégorgé' and although Bollinger is not the only Champagne house that sometimes ages its vintage wines on the lees for longer than the usual three years, this has become a legendary wine.

The style was created by Madame Bollinger in 1961 with the 1952 vintage. Although it is usually assumed that this prolonged ageing is beneficial, the precise date of disgorgement is important, and it is not Bollinger's practice to disgorge every R.D. cuvée at the same time. Enthusiasts argue that the extended period of lees-ageing preserves freshness and magnifies richness; however, others believe a vintage wine is fully mature when originally disgorged, and will not benefit from further bottle-ageing. The outcome will vary depending on the vintage, as well as other factors such as storage. The 1976 is particularly esteemed as it came from a torrid year yet has lasted well.

LOOKING BACK

Bollinger had been criticised in the early 1980s for releasing some of its non-vintage wines too young, giving them a rawness that British drinkers especially found disagreeable. Giving their wines long lees ageing was a response to this complaint, and proved very successful. The firm registered 'R.D.' as a trademark, which meant other houses following the same method could not use the initials. At this time the usual ageing period was around eight years, but that soon became a minimum, and some releases have been kept on lees for far longer.

THE VINTAGE

1976 was a notoriously hot year, with high temperatures and no rain during the summer. As a consequence the harvest started early, from 1 September. The wines were very rich, powerful and high in extract, but the scorching temperatures meant acidity was low. One might assume the wines would have peaked early and be in serious decline by now, but quite a few 1976s from top producers have aged very well.

THE TERROIR

The Champagne would have been produced from the Bollingers' 140 hectares of vineyards from 30 different crus, all classified as premier cru or grand cru. Pinot Noir dominates the vintage wines and generally composes 70% of the blend.

THE WINE

Like other Bollinger vintage cuvées, this would have been vinified from the first pressing. The must would have been fermented in oak barrels of varying sizes (up to 400 litres), with minimal malolactic fermentation, giving a more oxidative style, though the Bollinger team ensures there is no actual oxidation, which would tire the wine from the outset. At this stage in its life, the R.D. is the same wine as Bollinger Grande Année; it is the decision to give some of the production additional ageing that transforms it into an R.D. The R.D. will be aged under cork for a minimum of eight years, compared to five for the regular vintage wines. The riddling and disgorgement are performed by hand, and the dosage is low at 3g/l to 4g/l.

THE REACTION

It is important to note that an R.D. released after eight to 10 years on the lees will not be the same wine as the same vintage disgorged after 35 years. In 2010, Jancis Robinson MW tasted a bottle disgorged that same year and noted: 'Pale bronze. Extremely rich and candied on the nose. Toasty, this just washes over you. Really hedonistic. In view of the relatively low acidity, it's amazing how well this has lasted. Presumably the very late disgorgement helps.' In 2013 Stephen Brook tasted a magnum disgorged four months earlier: 'Rich toasty nose, with power and weight but no heaviness. Perhaps a touch soft but still has acidic bite. Ready to drink.' In 2014 Michael Edwards noted of a bottle disgorged in 2010: 'Very solid, sturdy character but miraculously with little loss of freshness and vitality.'

THE FACTS

Bottles produced
N/A

Composition
65% Pinot Noir, 35% Chardonnay

Yield
66hl/ha

Alcohol
12.2%

Release price
N/A

Price today
£940

DOM PÉRIGNON 1975

Champagne, France

A LEGEND BECAUSE...

Roederer's Cristal was the first prestige cuvée, made for the Russian court. Moët & Chandon was next, with the 1921 vintage of a wine that, when it was released in 1936, was named Dom Pérignon after the 17th-century cellarmaster of the Hautvillers abbey. Although Dom Pérignon is only released in vintages that are considered outstanding, the 1975 has always been recognised as one of the very finest.

LOOKING BACK

Champagne styles can evolve, but even 40 years ago, the taut, lean style of Dom Pérignon was established. It has always been a roughly equal blend of Chardonnay and Pinot Noir. The principles of vinification were the same as for the regular Moët bottlings, the difference being stricter selection of grapes, and longer ageing on the lees. The bottle is based on one created in 1735, but its current prestige is linked to the marketing power of owner LVMH, the luxury goods group created in 1987. The 1975, made under chef de cave Dominique Foulon, proves that great quality was also attained in preceding decades.

THE VINTAGE

On paper, 1975 was not an ideal vintage. Spring was cold and budbreak late, though flowering took place in fine conditions. The summer was warmer than usual, with a few August storms. Harvest began on 29 September and had to be completed fairly rapidly, as the weather soon worsened. A small crop produced wines high in acidity, which gave many 1975 Champagnes the structure for long ageing.

THE TERROIR

Today Dom Pérignon is sourced from 17 grands crus and a single premier cru, Hautvillers, but in 1975 it only drew on Hautvillers and eight grands crus. The Chardonnay comes from the villages of Avize, Chouilly, Cramant and Mesnil, while the Pinot Noir is from Aÿ, Bouzy, Mailly and Verzenay.

THE WINE

Almost all Champagne is a blend, and Dom Pérignon is no exception, the chef de cave choosing from the very best lots, dictated both by the quality of the wines available and by the cuvée style. Unlike other prestige Champagne producers, Moët's chef de cave does not want a super-rich style, but seeks aromatic finesse, a silky texture and a honed elegance. Until 1969, the must would have been fermented in wood, but by 1975 it was all fermented in steel tanks. The style has always placed an emphasis on reduction; that is, protection from oxygen and thus from oxygenation, as the cellarmasters want wines that age well. The final blend spends at least six years on the lees before being disgorged.

THE REACTION

Michael Broadbent found the 1975 acidic in 1983, but 12 years later when he tasted it from a six-litre bottle, wrote: 'Very fine bubbles; creamy, first reaction glorious, refined, then "a bit tame", which is rather ungrateful.'

Bruce Sanderson of *The Wine Spectator* reported in 2009 that the Vinothèque release, which was disgorged in 2007: 'Offers a bouquet of toffee, coffee, truffle and toast. A graphite note emerges with air. In the mouth, citrus and ginger notes chime in with the vibrant acidity, keeping this fresh and driving the long finish. Firm and taut, with a mineral finish.' In the same issue, Michael Edwards, tasting the regular release, was concerned that the 1975, 'a once superb but fine-drawn year, may be in decline'.

In 2012, Tom Stevenson enthused: 'How can Moët cram so much delicious fruit in one bottle and yet produce a Champagne of incomparable finesse and charm? Absolutely complete, with a creamy vanilla richness backed up by toasty acidity, this vintage is still in fruit-driven mode and will take a long time to build up an extraordinary complexity. Lots of life ahead, with caramel, cedar wood and candy floss notes.'

THE FACTS

Bottles produced
N/A
Composition
50% Chardonnay, 50% Pinot Noir (subject to vintage variation)
Yield
N/A
Alcohol
12.7%
Release price
N/A
Price today
£536

LOUIS ROEDERER, CRISTAL 1959

Champagne, France

A LEGEND BECAUSE…

Created in 1876 for Tsar Alexander II, a great admirer of and customer for Roederer wines, this Champagne remains universally recognised due to its presentation in a clear bottle, cellophane-wrapped to protect it further. The wine created for the tsar is remote from the modern incarnation, as it was extremely sweet. The unique packaging was patented in 1928, when the brand, which ceased production after the Russian Revolution, was revived as a prestige cuvée. It is rare for any vintage of Cristal to disappoint, given the scrupulous attention paid to quality and balance before the Champagne is declared and released. The 1959 is clearly exceptional, and so too were past vintages such as 1949, 1955, 1962 and 1964.

LOOKING BACK

Then as now, the wine was produced solely from grapes grown in the Roederer vineyards. Although the original Cristal was very sweet, once the Russian connection had been severed due to the Revolution, the blend gradually evolved to its present dry style. Its iconic character – above all its packaging, which established its status as a brand – remained unchanged. The wine was made to the most exacting standards, as is still the case today. The even more revered Cristal Rosé did not exist at this time, and was first produced in 1974.

THE VINTAGE

As in other parts of France, the summer in the Champagne region was hot and dry, generating a large crop of very ripe grapes. The grapes were picked between 12-25 September. Pinot Noir attained natural alcoholic ripeness – that is, without chaptalisation – of 12°-12.5°, and Chardonnay was even riper at 13°. Acidity was low, but as with the top wines of Bordeaux, the best 1959 Champagnes have stood the test of time.

THE TERROIR

The vines were given a severe pruning and the bunches thinned during the growing season to give optimal ripeness and concentration. In this vintage the Pinot Noir was sourced from top vineyards in Verzenay, Verzy, Beaumont-sur-Vesle and Aÿ; the Chardonnay came from Avize, Mesnil, Cramant and Chouilly.

THE WINE

For Cristal, only the first pressing is used, and even those pressings are tasted and graded to ensure the base wines are of the highest quality. All the wine is fermented in oak, using barrels of 205 litres and casks of 6,000 litres. There is no fixed rule about malolactic fermentation, but in this vintage there was no malolactic, presumably because the acidity was low. After bottling, it is aged six years on lees, and then for a further eight months after disgorgement. The dosage is relatively high, at up to 11 grams per litre, but this is required to balance a wine that typically has high acidity and is intended to be capable of prolonged cellaring. Indeed, immediately after release Cristal can seem closed and inexpressive, but that is because it is styled as a Champagne for the long haul.

THE REACTION

In 1996, Swedish Champagne expert Richard Juhlin found it

'majestic and irresistible', saying: 'As usual Cristal manages to charm both the expert and the novice with its beautiful, exotic sweetness and creamy toffee flavour. This wine doesn't show us anything new or unexpected, but quite simply offers more of all the good things one finds in these wines.'

In 2013 the current cellarmaster at Roederer, Jean-Baptiste Lécaillon, who has been responsible for recent vintages of Cristal since 1999, tasted the wine and noted: 'Delicious sweetness, charming and irresistible. Almost exotic in character with caramelly creaminess but also rich in extract. Yet there is a strong acidity, giving a powerful, concentrated wine.'

THE FACTS

Bottles produced
N/A
Composition
60% Pinot Noir, 40% Chardonnay
Yield
N/A
Alcohol
12%
Release price
N/A
Price today
£2,400

PHILIPPONNAT, CLOS DES GOISSES 1964

Champagne, France

A LEGEND BECAUSE...

Many Champagnes aim to achieve a consistent house style through blending, using different grape varieties, vineyards or vintages. There are exceptions, such as Krug's Clos du Mesnil and Philipponnat's Clos des Goisses, which are always vintage wines, so if conditions have been poor, the producer is under no obligation to make and release them in any given year. However, when they are produced, they are Champagnes with a distinctive terroir, reflecting the soil and exposition of the place where the grapes are grown. Unlike most other single-vineyard Champagnes, Clos des Goisses is produced in most vintages. From 1935 to 2007, only 12 vintages were skipped – since 1988 it has been produced every year.

LOOKING BACK

The house, based in Mareuil-sur-Aÿ, was formally incorporated in 1912 by Pierre and Auguste Philipponnat, although the family traces its activity as wine-growers in Aÿ back to 1522. The chef de caves in 1964 was Achille Souply, the unsung hero of a great wine.

THE VINTAGE

This was a superb year for Champagne, with excellent flowering and a hot, dry summer. Rain in early August was a relief to the parched vines – grapes continued to ripen and were ready for harvesting by the second week in September.

THE TERROIR

The Clos des Goisses is a true clos, in the sense that it is a walled vineyard under single ownership. Quite a large site, with 5.83ha planted (Philipponnat today owns 22ha in total), its main distinction is that it is a steep hill overlooking the Marne canal, facing south towards the Côte des Blancs, so that it receives constant sunshine – it is probably the warmest single vineyard in Champagne. Pinot Noir is the dominant grape; however, until 1964 the Clos had been planted mostly to Chardonnay. The soil is pure chalk. Part of the Clos is planted on a small plateau on top of the hill, giving a slightly different microclimate. Overall the Clos is on average 1.5°C warmer than neighbouring vineyards, and in some vintages such as 1959 and 1976, grapes have reached a natural ripeness of 13° potential alcohol.

THE WINE

The must was fermented in older barrels of various dimensions. Because of the size of the Clos, 15 lots are each fermented separately. The wine is never chaptalised, and the malolactic fermentation is always blocked. The dosage of the 1964 was 4.5g/litre.

THE REACTION

Tom Stevenson organised a vertical tasting in 2008; this magnum had been disgorged in 2007. 'This was the star of the entire tasting... such amazing youth, vitality, and freshness that I wondered how it would have performed against the 1966, which has always been the fresher, more lively of these two great Clos des Goisses vintages. It is hard to imagine that the 1966 could have had more vigour and vivacity than this 1964. The balance of the 1964 is impeccable; it seems so light in the mouth for such a fabulously rich wine, with great depth, length and finesse of fruit. This is possibly the most evenly balanced vintage of them between minerality and spicy complexity. A great, great Clos des Goisses.'

In 2015, Antonio Galloni tasted the wine from magnum (disgorged March 2008): 'A profound Champagne, the 1964 is timeless. The flavours are mature, as one would expect from a wine of this era, yet there is a fabulous sense of freshness throughout. Apricot, spice, brioche and almond are some of the nuances that open up in the glass, but the 1964 can't be described in terms of its flavours, rather it is a wine of sublime textural finesse and magnificent complexity.'

THE FACTS

Bottles produced
37,358 bottles, 538 magnums
Composition
Mostly Chardonnay
Yield
50hl/ha-55hl/ha
Alcohol
13%
Release price
Approx. 100 French francs
Price today
£1,000-£1,300

POL ROGER, CUVÉE SIR WINSTON CHURCHILL 2000

Champagne, France

A LEGEND BECAUSE...

First made in 1975, this cuvée has become one of Champagne's best and most admired wines. As a vintage, it is only made in top years and aged for about nine years before release. The warm conditions in 2000 particularly suited the rich, weighty style of the cuvée.

LOOKING BACK

Pol Roger was founded in 1849, in Epernay.

For decades it was Winston Churchill's favourite Champagne (his first order was in 1908), but the personal connection can be traced back to the liberation of Paris in 1944, when a lunch organised by Lady Diana Cooper brought Odette Pol-Roger and Churchill together. The two got along famously, establishing a long-lived friendship. When Churchill died in 1965, Pol-Roger ordered all Pol Roger labels destined for the UK to be bordered in black in tribute to him, and 10 years later the house released a more lasting tribute: Cuvée Sir Winston Churchill. It was intended to reflect his personality – robust, muscular and full-bodied – and thus dominated by Pinot Noir.

THE VINTAGE

As in other parts of France, 2000 was a warm and humid year, but complicated here by outbreaks of mildew and botrytis. The weather was fine during harvest, though some sorting was required. The year produced Champagnes of great opulence, yet many have evolved quite rapidly. It was a vintage that favoured Chardonnay over the Pinots, but this hasn't impacted on the quality of this wine.

THE TERROIR

Sir Winston Churchill is sourced from various vineyards, in this case solely from grand cru sites. Pinot Noir is always the dominant variety, but Pol Roger doesn't disclose the blend. The house owns 92 hectares of vineyards, mostly around Epernay. About half of its grapes are purchased from growers.

THE WINE

This was the second Churchill cuvée made by cellarmaster Dominique Petit. Although one would be forgiven for thinking the wine was barrel-fermented to develop its rich style, this is not in fact the case. The young wine goes through malolactic fermentation. The cuvée spends at least eight years in the cellars, which are particularly cold, retarding the maturation process and ensuring tiny bubbles after the cork is pulled. Riddling is manual, now a rarity in Champagne.

THE REACTION

In 2012 Alison Napjus in *The Wine Spectator* noted: 'Smoky, with firm structure and a minerally base note, this offers a fine, creamy texture and hints of dried apricot, lemon curd, cassis, biscuit and blanched almond. The lingering finish echoes the minerality...'

In the same year, Antonio Galloni in *The Wine Advocate* commented: 'I don't see the 2000 being an especially long-term ager, but it is wonderfully radiant and open today. Hints of pastry, spice, apricots and succulent ripe pears blossom on the expansive, broad-shouldered finish.'

In 2015 Stephen Brook reported: 'The apple-compote nose is reserved, but has purity of fruit and finesse. The attack is lean, tight and racy, very youthful, with a wonderful tension and dynamism. It is in its prime but should keep well thanks to its racy acidity.'

A year later, Jancis Robinson MW, tasting the cuvée blind, wrote: 'With time this really tightens up on the palate and seems younger, quite powerful and great length. Power and precision.'

THE FACTS

Bottles produced
N/A
Composition
Predominantly Pinot Noir
Yield
N/A
Alcohol
12.5%
Release price
N/A
Price today
£190

SALON, LE MESNIL 1985

Champagne, France

A LEGEND BECAUSE...

Salon is a unique Champagne house. It is the smallest of the grandes marques but, more importantly, it is defined by three criteria that were unique until Krug started producing its Clos du Mesnil in 1979: it is made from a single variety, Chardonnay; from a single but outstanding village, Mesnil; and is only made as a vintage wine. That means that in many years no Salon is produced. This approach is, of course, the direct opposite of the widespread Champagne philosophy of blending varieties from a range of sources. Like other vintage Champagnes, it is only produced in exceptional years. Thus only 37 vintages have been produced since 1905.

LOOKING BACK

Salon was named after its founder, Eugène-Aimé Salon, a furrier from Paris who set up the house to furnish wines for the enthusiastic consumption of his friends. He produced wines from 1905 onwards, but it was only with the 1921 vintage that Salon was released commercially. After his death in 1943, his niece inherited the property, and later sold it to Dubonnet. By 1985 Dubonnet had been absorbed by drinks giant Pernod Ricard. This would be their last vintage as, in 1988, Salon was sold to Laurent- Perrier, who still owns and manages the property. Winemaker Didier Depond observes that because the wine is made in very small quantities (60,000 bottles maximum), he is encouraged to focus solely on quality, since Laurent-Perrier does not need to rely on Salon for its profits. Nonetheless the wine has always been very expensive.

THE VINTAGE

The winter was exceedingly cold, but as the vines were dormant in January, no damage was done. However, fierce frosts continued into the spring, and some vines were destroyed. 'There is certainly something to be said for the "survivor" grapes of the terrible 1985 winter – they gave this wine an energy that can still be felt today,' recalls Vianney Gravereaux, export director of Salon. Then the weather improved and flowering took place normally. The summer was warm, with high temperatures in August, and the harvest began in late September, resulting in healthy grapes of very high quality, though volumes were reduced by one-third.

THE TERROIR

Salon owns just over a hectare of vines, called the Jardin de Salon and located behind the house, but they were virused and had to be replanted in 2002. Most of the grapes are purchased from 19 growers in Mesnil, from 13ha (hectares) of vines. Many of those are more than 40 years old and planted on mid-slopes, the best location for hillside vines. Some of the growers are from the same families from which Salon himself bought grapes. The crumbly chalk soils allow the roots to descend deeply in search of nutrients. The chalk also promotes high acidity in the grapes, which is one reason why the Salon wines need ageing before disgorgement and consumption.

THE WINE

Selection during harvest ensures only top-quality grapes reach the winery. Only the first pressing is used. Fermentation takes place in stainless steel tanks, and once the alcoholic

'Its weight and vinosity make it one of the few blancs de blancs that can be drunk with food'

fermentation is completed the decision is made whether the wine will be worthy of Salon. There is no malolactic fermentation. The wine is aged in bottles for eight to 12 years before disgorgement, and the dosage is low at 4–8g per litre. Since the wine is always from a single vintage, there is no use of reserve wines. The style of Salon is very distinctive: austere in its youth but with tremendous weight and vinosity that make it one of the few blancs de blancs that can be drunk with food. It is perhaps for this reason that it has always found more favour with export markets than with French consumers.

THE REACTION

The tiny production (for a Champagne) means recorded tasting notes are rare. In 1998 Tom Stevenson wrote: 'Very fine, elegant and pure. Delightful now, but will mature gracefully for another 30 years.' Leading sommelier Enrico Bernardo commented: 'Magnificent effervescence, rich in elegant and persistent bubbles... In the mouth, the structure is very subtle and of extreme elegance. I cannot resist tasting it a second time to savour the frankness and precision of a Champagne that will surely have a long life.'

THE FACTS

Bottles produced	Alcohol
20,000	**12%**
Composition	Release price
100% Chardonnay	**(in 1999) €150**
Yield	Price today
Varied from grower to grower	**£780**

RHÔNE

With the Syrah variety throughout, the northern Rhône was always going to be the more obvious source for ageworthy and admired wines. But a handful of estates from the southern Rhône, notably Rayas and Beaucastel from Châteauneuf-du-Pape, would clearly be contenders too, magnificent wines of complexity and grandeur.

M CHAPOUTIER, LE PAVILLON, ERMITAGE 1991

Rhône, France

A LEGEND BECAUSE...

In 1988 Michel Chapoutier took control of this distinguished Rhône producer in a kind of family coup. He soon made radical changes, such as throwing out ancient chestnut barrels and moving rapidly towards biodynamic farming. Another innovation was the release of very limited luxury cuvées from top appellations, such as white and red Hermitage, Côte-Rôtie and Châteauneuf-du-Pape, all from very old vines. Some of these wines were aged entirely in new oak. They made an immediate impression and were hailed as among the greatest wines of the Rhône Valley.

LOOKING BACK

This was a period of flux at Chapoutier, with Michel making his mark with great energy, not to say ruthlessness. By the late 1980s its big, burly, somewhat rustic wines were no longer selling and bankruptcy was looming. A cash injection from its American importer saved the day, but in return Michel was encouraged to take control and implement his innovative ideas. New bottlings showed more precision and freshness, while the special cuvées attracted attention - not only because of their high prices. The revolution was set to continue, with the acquisition of vineyards in Provence and Australia.

THE VINTAGE

There was a tendency to underestimate 1991, as 1988, 1989 and 1990 were all sunny and hot. After a cold spring, the summer was pleasant but not especially hot, and there was some rain at harvest, so growers were on alert for rot. Picking for this wine took place on 10 October, and low yields gave fine concentration. Initially perceived as a lightweight vintage, it later became clear that wines from the best sites, such as Le Pavillon, had considerable staying power.

THE TERROIR

The grapes, from vines around 70 years old, were sourced from the oldest plants in the Les Bessards lieu-dit near the top of the Hermitage hill. They are planted on poor sedimentary soils over a granitic subsoil. This sector gives what are probably the most structured wines from the Hermitage hill.

THE WINE

The grapes were destemmed before being treated to a cuvaison of four weeks in an old and unsealed oak vat. Extraction was achieved by punching down the cap once or twice a day. Fermentation took place at a temperature that did not exceed 32°C. After the wine had fermented to dryness it was aged for 12 months in older barrels acquired from Drouhin in Burgundy. No press wine was used, and it was bottled without filtration.

THE REACTION

In 1996, Robert Parker hailed this as a 'perfect wine... Enormously concentrated yet with brilliant focus and delineation to its awesomely endowed personality, this should age effortlessly for three-plus decades... A seamless beauty!'

In 2011 Jamie Goode noted: 'Very fine, fresh and bloody with lovely cherry fruit and some meatiness. Firm tannins… A fresh, vital and beautifully complex wine with some earthy, spicy maturity but also lovely freshness.'

In 2017 Matt Walls wrote: 'Still seriously concentrated and remains remarkably youthful – this will last from now until 2040 with ease.'

In the same year Jeff Leve commented: 'Powerful, big, full-bodied, rich and deep. Believe it or not, I think it needs more time to develop to its full potential. This is really such a super wine.'

THE FACTS

Bottles produced
9,000
Composition
100% Syrah
Yield
15hl/ha
Alcohol
13.5%
Release price
160 French francs
Price today
£467

CHÂTEAU DE BEAUCASTEL 1981

Châteauneuf-du-Pape, France

A LEGEND BECAUSE...

Beaucastel is not the only great estate in Châteauneuf-du-Pape, but it has been admired for its consistency and elegance over many decades. What makes its wine distinctive is the 25% to 30% of Mourvèdre in the blend. This is one of the 13 permitted varieties for the appellation, but it is rare to find such a high proportion in a wine usually dominated by Grenache. The Mourvèdre gives the wine a finesse that is rare in the region. It also gives it backbone, doesn't oxidise easily, and the wine is rarely high in alcohol. Beaucastel ages remarkably well, and the high proportion of Mourvèdre is part of the explanation.

LOOKING BACK

The Perrin family acquired this estate in 1909 and it remains firmly in family hands. It has tenaciously applied the principles laid down by the late Jacques Perrin, who died in 1978: organic (and then biodynamic) farming, massal selections in the vineyards, low yields and manual harvesting.

THE VINTAGE

1981 was not an obviously outstanding vintage. The spring was cold and there was some frost. June was cool too, resulting in uneven fruit set and a fairly small crop. The summer was extremely dry, and harvesting began in mid-September. Quality was uneven, and at many estates strict selection was required to determine the best wine for bottling. The tannins proved gutsy and robust, and the wine benefitted from bottle age.

THE TERROIR

The 70 (today 100) hectares of vineyards, on flat reddish soil strewn with the potato-sized stones known as galets, encircle the winery. Beneath the 1.5m of galets is a complex subsoil of clay, sandstone, and limestone. Since 1974 the domaine has been farmed biodynamically, but the Perrins have never made a song and dance about it, and the word doesn't appear on the label. Yields are very low, and the bush vines are picked manually, with the Mourvèdre, which represents about a third of the blend, usually the last variety to be harvested.

THE WINE

Each variety – and Beaucastel uses all 13 that are permitted – is fermented separately, with punchdowns, either in open wooden vats or cement vats, depending on the variety. Only indigenous yeasts are used. Blending is done in the spring following the malolactic fermentation. The wine is then aged for a year or so in large casks, which are kept for up to 25 years, racked a few times, egg white-fined, and bottled by gravity without filtration.

THE REACTION

In 1992, *Decanter*'s John Livingstone-Learmonth quoted François Perrin's view that the wine combined austerity and roundness, adding: 'It has since 1988 an extraordinarily pungent bouquet – very gamey and musky and typical of ageing Mourvèdre... The palate's early richness is supported by a firm structure and the depth of extract is memorable.'

In 2000 Jamie Goode, on his *Wine Anorak* site, wrote: 'Drinking beautifully. Nose of spice and herbs with a touch of caramel and some gaminess. Firm tannins and spicy complexity (tea, leather, and herbs). Excellent.'

Robert Parker has written positively about the wine on many occasions, and in 2003 added: 'One of the all-time classics, the 1981 is fully mature and should be consumed. It's a big, sweet, candied fruit bomb offering notes of smoke, pepper, dried herbs, truffles, leather, cedar, as well as black and red currants. Full-bodied and opulent, it is one of the most delicious, complex and stunning Beaucastels ever made.'

Though most experts believe the 1981 has peaked, Jeff Leve of *Wine Cellar Insider* wrote in 2014: 'This wine must be immortal, it never fades... It tastes at least a decade younger.'

THE FACTS

Bottles produced
120,000
Composition
40% Grenache, 25% Mourvèdre, 10% Syrah, 5% Counoise, 20% others
Yield
23hl/ha
Alcohol
12.5%
Release price
50 French francs (about £4.75 in today's money)
Price today
£134

CHÂTEAU RAYAS, RÉSERVÉ 1990

Châteauneuf-du-Pape, Rhône, France

A LEGEND BECAUSE...

This wine's legendary status is down to a happy coincidence of factors. The first was the remarkable quality in general of vintages from this domaine. Another was the highly eccentric personality of then owner Jacques Reynaud, which often seemed at odds with the stature of the wine. The 1990 vintage played its part too, delivering wines of power, density and succulence. Today the property is run by Jacques's nephew Emmanuel, who has altered little and has maintained the style of the wines.

LOOKING BACK

Jacques Reynaud, who died in 1997, inherited the property from his father Louis in 1980. He was an intensely shy man, and there were stories of visitors seeing him dart into the bushes when a merchant or journalist (even one with an appointment) was heard approaching the winery. Reynaud was not very forthcoming if one did get to meet him, and there was nothing within the winery to suggest that it was capable of producing drinkable, let alone great wines. The casks were jumbled, the floor cluttered and the tasting glasses, usually with broken stems, looked no cleaner than the rest of the winery. Yet there was no doubting the extraordinary quality and personality of the wines – both Rayas itself, white as well as red, the second wine known as Pignan, and even the Côtes du Rhône sold as Fonsalette.

THE VINTAGE

The summer was very hot and dry, blocking the maturation of the grapes, which ripened slowly, with high sugar. By mid-September the Grenache, of which Rayas is mostly composed, had potential alcohols of well over 14%, but Reynaud, who always preferred optimal ripeness, delayed picking until late September. Consequently some tanks showed alcohol closer to 16%. The final wines exhibited density and chewiness, in contrast to the elegant 1989 vintage.

THE TERROIR

Rayas is a secluded estate northeast of the village, not far from Courthézon. The vines are almost exclusively Grenache, many aged between 20 and 35 years. Rayas is renowned for its minuscule yields, which many attribute to the numerous missing vines in the 13 hectares of vineyards rather than to any severe reduction of the crop, even though Reynaud claimed to thin bunches in July to assure a yield of no more than 20hl/ha. The vineyards were divided into 15 small plots, and soils are varied, though they do not resemble the stoniest sectors of the appellation. At Rayas there are vines planted on sandy soils, others on clay-limestone. Many face north, which also slows ripening. (Whites account for about one fifth of plantings and production.)

THE WINE

The winemaking at this time was simplicity itself. The juice was fermented in concrete vats without temperature control, and transferred to casks of various sizes in the spring. Bizarrely, given the ramshackle conditions at the winery, it was equipped with a pneumatic press. The press wine was blended in and the wine left undisturbed for about a year, although Louis Reynaud had aged the wine for much longer. It was then bottled without fining or filtration. Because of the very low yields, there were usually no more than 20,000 bottles of Rayas from any vintage.

'Rayas is renowned for its minuscule yields... usually no more than 20,000 bottles'

THE REACTION

British wine author and merchant Remington Norman found the 1990 'more obviously forward and elegant than the 1989, but with greater weight underneath; very long, complex, opulent. Ultimately, the greater of this remarkable pair'. Tasting it between release and 1996, Robert Parker observed: 'The 1990 Rayas may be the most prized wine in my personal collection.' *Decanter*'s Michael Broadbent blind-tasted it in 1996: 'I noted a piquant, high-toned, bilberry-like fruitiness; very sweet, immensely rich, full of fruit.' In 2001 he wrote: 'Rich spicy, soft, full, fleshy, with a fairly swingeing tannic finish.' In 2011, Jeff Leve of website *Wine Cellar Insider* found the wine fully mature: 'Spicy cherries, earth, kirsch, jammy raspberry and spice scents.... The palate enjoys layers of soft, ripe, polished, sweet red fruits. This is the epitome of finesse in Châteauneuf-du-Pape.'

THE FACTS

Bottles produced
About 16,000
Composition
100% Grenache
Yield
18 hl/ha
Alcohol
14.5%
Release price
250 French francs per bottle (€53/£44.50 today)
Price today
£3,392-£4,499

JL CHAVE, CATHELIN, ERMITAGE 1990

Rhône, France

A LEGEND BECAUSE...

For decades Gérard Chave has been regarded as the supreme exponent of the wines of Hermitage, white as well as red, with in some vintages Jaboulet's La Chapelle level-pegging. After all, the Chave family has been farming in these parts since 1481, and bought its first parcels in Hermitage in 1865. So it came as a surprise when in the 1990 vintage he decided to release a special bottling. Chave owns parcels in different sectors of the Hermitage hill, and his skill has always been in composing the best balanced and most ageworthy blend from those blocks. Cathelin is also a blend, but the proportions differ from those in the regular Hermitage. It is named after the late Bernard Cathelin, a painter who was a friend of the family. It is not made every year. The debut vintage was 1990, followed by 1991, 1995, 1998, 2000, 2003, 2009 and 2010.

LOOKING BACK

In 1990 Gérard Chave, who was born in 1935, was in his prime. Two decades had gone by since he took over from his father. A modest man, he seems happier in his cellar than replying to the enquiries of the privileged few. Yet he responds warmly to genuine and informed enthusiasm. Gradually he passed the baton to his son Jean-Louis, who returned to the domaine in 1992 after his studies at the University of California (Davis), but in 1990 Gérard still had full control.

THE VINTAGE

The spring in the northern Rhône was mild, leading to early flowering. The summer was not as torrid as in 1989, but it was very dry, which in some areas, such as Côte-Rôtie, forced growers to wait well into the autumn before harvesting. However, some rain fell in early September in Hermitage, which speeded the maturation and did not cause much delay in harvesting. Indeed, Chave is always among the last Hermitage growers to pick. Jean-Louise Chave has explained that, despite the renown of the vintage, it was at first difficult to discern the red's tannic structure, which prompted his father to create a different and more structured blend.

THE TERROIR

It is difficult to speak of the terroir behind the Chave Hermitage, since the family owns 14 hectares, of which 10ha are Syrah, in seven parcels. They are located in many of the most highly regarded sectors of the hill (such as Le Méal, Les Bessards and L'Hermite) and the wines are always a blend. The 1990 Cathelin came mostly from Les Bessards and was aged in new barrels.

THE WINE

After harvest the grapes are partially destemmed, then fermented either in open wood vats or in concrete tanks. The wines, with each parcel kept separately, are aged in casks of different sizes, with a modest proportion of new wood, never exceeding 20%, for up to 18 months. After blending, the wines are fined with egg white and bottled without filtration. The limited-production Cathelin, however, is aged entirely in new barrels.

THE REACTION

In 1996 Robert Parker described the wine as 'prodigious... Remarkably, the new oak takes a backseat in the wine's superb raw materials. The wine exhibits fabulous concentration, richness, intensity and length, as well as a mind-boggling finish. It is not superior to the classic cuvée, just different... It has the potential to

'Chave's skill has always been in composing the best balanced and most ageworthy blend'

last 30-50 years.' Not all tasters prefer the 1990 Cathelin to the regular Hemitage. Jeff Leve, of *The Wine Cellar Insider*, wrote in 2009: 'Coffee, chocolate, liquorice, black cherry and blackberry aromas. This full-bodied, concentrated wine did not seem as rich or complex as the normal Chave, which seems to express more minerality.' But in 2002 *Decanter*'s John Livingstone- Learmonth was impressed: 'Dense, warm, sappy bouquet, live fruit here... Very pretty attack, bounces out - very tasty impact. Sustained and wide through the palate - very elegant fruit and fat. Suave, but tight on finish. The regular 1990 is mild and plummy - the Cathelin has more fire and potency. Perhaps like a Hermitage of the 19th century.' Three years later he tasted it again: 'Big, wide, peppery bouquet with a little meatiness... A little dampness, gentle coffee, some flowers here too - a real slow-burn bouquet... The wine has a really solid heart, and a lovely, refined texture, grand vin, impressive and very young for its 15 years.'

THE FACTS

Bottles produced
2,500
Composition
100% Syrah
Yield
N/A
Alcohol
13%
Release price
£100 approx
Price today
£3,392-£4,499

DOMAINE J-P & J-L JAMET, CÔTE-RÔTIE 1990

Rhône, France

A LEGEND BECAUSE...

Jamet's Côte-Rôtie had already attracted attention with the 1985 vintage, but with the superb 1990 there was a major leap forward. In previous decades Côte-Rôtie in general could be very extracted, requiring long bottle-ageing, and that didn't always occur. By 1990 the Jamet wine had become far more fruit-forward and although enjoyable on release, the balance was good enough to ensure it could continue to evolve over a further two decades.

LOOKING BACK

Joseph Jamet's first vintage was in 1976. In the 1980s he began expanding his property near Ampuis, though it remained small with just 6ha planted. His sons Jean-Luc and Jean-Paul helped ensure that the right kind of vines were planted in the right spot with the appropriate rootstocks, the estate consisting of 19 parcels on terroirs ranging from near the top of the slopes to the lower sector. The brothers shared the farming and winemaking tasks, and had no hesitation in implementing strict regimes to keep yields below 40hl/ha. By 2010, the brothers were producing three different Côte-Rôties and then introduced a Condrieu, but in 2013 they agreed to split and go their separate ways.

THE VINTAGE

This was an excellent year throughout the Rhône valley. A mild spring led to an early flowering, and the summer was very warm and dry. The harvest began in mid-September, resulting in wines of tension and considerable power.

THE TERROIR

Côte-Rôtie is diverse, as vines are planted on two very steep slopes, the Côte Brune and the Côte Blonde. Most of the Jamet vines are on the brown schist soils of the Côte Brune that usually gives more structured wines than the granitic Côte Blonde. Some vines are planted on the plateau at the top of the slopes. The Jamets had vines in various sectors, and in 1990 most of the vines were still young, but Syrah plants can produce excellent wine at a young age.

THE WINE

After harvest the grapes were lightly crushed but not destemmed, yet greenness was rarely commented on in assessments of their wines, and certainly not in ripe years such as 1990. The wine was aged in 228-litre *pieces* and 600-litre demi-muids, as well as larger casks. Only about 20% of the barrels were new. The ageing period was about 18 months, sometimes a little longer, and the wine was bottled without filtration and generally without fining either.

THE REACTION

Robert Parker in 1994 clearly preferred both the 1989 and the underrated 1991: 'Although the 1990 is dense and tannic, it does not have the flavour dimension or aromatic profile of the 1991. While deep, rich and successful for the vintage, it ranks behind the Côte-Rôties Jamet produced in 1988, 1989 and 1991.'

John Livingstone-Learmonth assessed the wine is 2003: 'Very stewed, stone fruit aroma. Ripe, sappy flavour: has direction, though. Quite a "thick" wine *à l'ancienne*.'

Richard Hemming on Jancis Robinson's website wrote in 2014: 'Mushroom, earth, bracken, black fruit still intact. Dark chocolate character and that wonderful musty evolution. Smoked meat and pepper. Just sublime.' In the same year, *Wine Spectator* also enthused: 'Try this rich and luscious wine with roast lamb studded with rosemary; the flavours will marry beautifully. It's big and expressive, but still needs time to open.'

In 2016, Rajat Parr confided to *Wine & Spirits*: '...the quintessential expression of Côte-Rôtie. It's not always the best wine of the vintage, but it sets the tone... The wine is savoury and peppery with some wild, gamey notes, but it's also got a big, round, soft core of fruit.'

THE FACTS

Bottles produced
N/A
Composition
100% Syrah
Yield
35hl/ha
Alcohol
12.5%
Release price
N/A
Price today
Approx £1,200

E GUIGAL, LA MOULINE 1969

Côte-Rôtie, Rhône, France

A LEGEND BECAUSE...

Marcel Guigal has long been renowned for his magnificent trio of single-vineyard Côte-Rôtie wines: La Mouline, La Landonne and La Turque. La Mouline was the first, its debut vintage being 1966, just five years after he took the helm at the family domaine. It was followed by La Landonne in 1978 and La Turque in 1985. La Mouline was acquired in 1965, and as it was already planted with some very old vines, he was able to make the wine from 1966. The wine also attracted attention because it was aged in mostly new French oak, for 42 months. Such a method was almost unheard of in a region where Côte-Rôtie at that time was still aged mostly or entirely in large old casks (*foudres*) or even in chestnut barrels.

LOOKING BACK

La Mouline had been the property of the Dervieux family and was already a celebrated site before its purchase by Guigal. It also contained a proportion of Viognier, which was gradually increased to its present level of about 11%. This was not a formulaic approach on the part of Guigal - La Landonne, for example, is pure Syrah.

The aim was to produce a wine of exceptional elegance, in contrast to the denser, more powerful style of La Landonne. The early vintages of the single-vineyard wines were directed primarily at the wine lists of the many superb restaurants in the Rhône, but their quality was swiftly recognised and their fame and thus distribution spread.

THE VINTAGE

1969 produced a small crop in Côte Rôtie, but quality was exceptional. This combination of meagre quality with tremendous quality was reminiscent of the even more celebrated 1961 vintage.

THE TERROIR

The vines at La Mouline are on average about 70 years old, although some plants from 1893 still survive. They are grown on soil within the sector of Côte-Rôtie known as the Côte Blonde. Here there is a higher limestone content than in most other sites, although the primary soil types are still gneiss and granite. The 1.5-hectare site is entirely owned by Guigal, unlike La Landonne which has a number of different owners. Guigal has always been a late harvester, aiming for maximum concentration, although never risking overripeness. But, with its southerly exposition in a kind of amphitheatre, La Mouline is a precocious vineyard, and its grapes are picked before most of Guigal's other top sites.

THE WINE

On arrival at the winery in Ampuis, the grapes are crushed and destemmed, and fermented at relatively high temperatures, with pumpovers but no punching down of the cap, as Guigal does not want to extract too much tannin. Vinification of the three single-vineyard wines varies, being adapted to the nature and quality of the fruit. From the start La Mouline was aged entirely in new oak, and reports that the 1969 was partly aged in older casks are erroneous. The racking of the wine varies according to the vintage, but the wine is neither fined nor filtered.

'It was aged in mostly new French oak for 42 months, almost unheard of at the time'

THE REACTION

In 1995, Tom Matthews in *The Wine Spectator* noted: 'Extraordinary life and intensity for its age, offering plum, chocolate and spice flavours, round and firm.' *Decanter*'s John Livingstone- Learmonth had a few reservations in 1997: 'Bouquet rather precarious – ripe fruits, though dusty, dry top notes – and is dense, a little volatile. Warmth and roundness on the palate, chocolate-style flavours. Dense wine, but is a little edgy now. Rather forced black cherries on the finish. Soft sweetness throughout.'

THE FACTS

Bottles produced
4,800
Composition
89% Syrah, 11% Viognier
Yield
35hl/ha
Alcohol
13.5%
Release price
N/A
Price today
£3,960

OTHER WINES OF FRANCE

Alsace, the Loire Valley and Languedoc provided the legendary wines from the rest of France, which may have suggested that omitted areas such as the southwest couldn't match them when it came to quality and longevity. But choices needed to be made, and probably areas such as Madiran, Bandol, or Banyuls simply lacked sufficient prestige.

CLOS ROUGEARD, LE BOURG 1990

Saumur-Champigny, Loire, France

A LEGEND BECAUSE...

Based in the village of Chacé, southeast of Saumur, Nady Foucault and his brother Charly make wines from their 20 hectares of vines that have acquired cult status. Of their two main vineyards, Poyeux and Bourg, it is the latter which has become most prized. While some vintages can be enjoyed in their youth, top years are best cellared for 10 years or more to reveal their aromatic complexity, silky texture and finesse. In 1993 a bottle of Le Bourg 1990 was surreptitiously included in a blind tasting of top 1990 Pomerols, including Pétrus, Le Pin and Trotanoy, and it received the highest average score. A cult was born.

LOOKING BACK

In 1990 the Foucault brothers, the eighth generation of their family to farm in Saumur- Champigny, stood out thanks to their regular use of barriques to age their wines, at a time when many of their neighbours were ageing their Cabernet Franc in large casks or stainless steel tanks so as to produce a less structured wine. The very concentrated Le Bourg is far from the stereotype of Saumur-Champigny as a light wine to quaff in bars and bistros.

THE VINTAGE

This was an extremely hot, dry year. Some rain towards the end of summer proved beneficial and allowed the grapes to ripen fully, although in some generously cropped vineyards this caused dilution. The best wines are proving to be long-lived.

THE TERROIR

The single hectare of Cabernet Franc vines in Le Bourg, located just behind the domaine's cellars, are about 70 years old. The soils are a thin clay with limestone and are organically farmed. (Le Poyeux is on sandier soils and the 3ha of vines are 45 years old.) As rare as Le Bourg is Clos Rougeard's white, made from 1ha of old-vine Chenin Blanc. The vineyards, replanted using massal selections, are ploughed and manually harvested. Yields are kept very low to ensure that the wines have sufficient concentration to withstand and benefit from prolonged barrel ageing.

THE WINE

After destemming, the grapes are fermented with indigenous yeasts in oak vats with either punchdowns or pumpovers, depending on the character of the fruit. Le Bourg goes through its malolactic fermentation in air-dried new barrels, in which it remains for between 18 and 24 months. The wine is unfiltered, and spends a further year in bottle before release. The Foucaults' cold cellars, tunnelled into the rock, ensure that the wines' evolution is slow.

THE REACTION

In March 2015, Antoine Gerbelle of *La Revue du Vins de France* noted: 'On opening, it appeared corked, but no. The aromas of damp mushroom vanished after 10 minutes. The nose opened to reveal a bouquet of cooked red fruits, cherries and spices. On the palate the wine still had breadth, weight and a Pinot-like tone that reminded me of a Volnay with more body: again, this balance of a basket of cherries, small red fruits and spices. Still youthful!'

'It was stunning. The nose reminded me of a great Cheval Blanc'

Rajat Parr

California-based winemaker and sommelier Rajat Parr tasted the 1990 Bourg in mid-2014. 'It was stunning,' he recalls. 'The nose reminded me of a great Cheval Blanc. Intense notes of blackcurrant compote, coffee and cedar with hints of violets. The wine seemed very young and has 20 or more years of ageing potential.'

Richard Bernard, sommelier at the renowned Bordeaux restaurant Le St-James, said in a 2014 interview with *Decanter* that it was the best wine he had ever drunk.

THE FACTS

Bottles produced
2,500
Composition
100% Cabernet Franc
Yield
N/A
Alcohol
12.5%
Release price
N/A
Price today
N/A, though the wine has fetched €450 at auction in the recent past

DIDIER DAGUENEAU, SILEX POUILLY-FUMÉ 2002

Loire Valley, France

A LEGEND BECAUSE...

In the 1980s, a young Didier Dagueneau overturned conventional practice in Pouilly-Fumé. The son of the grower Jean-Claude Dagueneau, his first vintage was in 1982. Until then Pouilly-Fumé had often been a thin and weedy white wine with grassy flavours and trenchant acidity. Dagueneau learned how to make wines that were drinkable on release but also capable of ageing in bottle for many years. Though seen as a wild radical, Dagueneau was conservative in the sense of seeking to return to a time when serious, long-lived Sauvignons were made in the appellation. He created cuvées such as Silex and Pur Sang that were oak-aged yet always elegant. Since his death in a flying accident in 2008, the domaine has been run by his son Louis-Benjamin.

LOOKING BACK

On my first visit in 1988, Dagueneau took me to the vineyards to show me how the majority of producers were overcropping, with potential yields well over the legal maximum. He believed about 50hl/ha was ideal. Moreover, clones were being planted that were far too productive. He deplored the fact that most vineyards were machine-picked, believing in selective hand-harvesting. At a time when almost all wines from Pouilly were aged in stainless steel tanks and bottled early, he matured his top wines, such as Silex, in a high proportion of new oak barrels, which, he believed, would give them the structure for long ageing.

THE VINTAGE

Spring was fine with no frost, but the flowering in June was uneven, reducing the crop by up to 20%. Summer was hot, though there were cooler, wetter spells. Rain in early September persuaded some growers to pick too soon, but the patient were rewarded with an Indian summer and ideal ripeness.

THE TERROIR

There are different soil types in Pouilly, as in neighbouring Sancerre. 'Silex' means flint, and this soil type is mostly found around St-Andelain, where the Dagueneaus are based. The flint is mixed with clay, so it's crucial that vines are planted in places that enjoy very good drainage. Didier Dagueneau was convinced this was the greatest terroir in the appellation, capable of producing wines that can age for decades.

THE WINE

Silex was just one of a number of Sauvignon wines made by Dagueneau, each with a different vinification and ageing. After harvest, the grapes were destemmed and given up to 24 hours' skin contact, although Dagueneau later stopped the maceration as it lowered the acidity and could give wines that were too fat. Half the must was fermented in new oak barrels of 500L and 600L – as the years went by, the proportion of new wood was reduced; by 2002 it stood at about 25%.

THE REACTION

In 2004, *Wine Spectator*'s James Suckling said: 'The aromas of white flowers, fresh earth and straw plume from the glass like chalk dust, while a taut, racy palate provides flint-driven citrus, herb, smoke and lime flavours that just won't quit. Amazing precision and cut.'

Stephen Brook tasted it in 2006: 'The nose is dumb, but there's a terrific attack, fine acidity and concentration. The finish is spicy and exceptionally long.'

In 2013, Sarah Ahmed noted '...vanilla, spice and honey on a weighty but poised palate... deliciously long, spicy and lingering, with absolutely no sign of fading', while in 2015 Julia Harding MW found the wine very much alive: '...honeyed quince and cedar... just the most incredible balance on the palate between fruit intensity and tertiary complexity. Deep and long and so fresh it is almost tart on the finish, but... the whole is in magnificent balance.'

THE FACTS

Bottles produced
About 8,000
Composition
100% Sauvignon Blanc
Yield
40hl/ha
Alcohol
13%
Release price
US$75
Price today
£200

HUGEL, RIESLING SGN 1976

Alsace, France

A LEGEND BECAUSE...

Sweet wines from Alsace had probably been made for decades, if not centuries, but it was the Hugels who from 1865 developed the styles that later became known as Vendange Tardive and Sélection de Grains Nobles. The latter is produced solely from grapes affected by noble rot and with a potential alcohol of 15.2%, although in practice the sugar levels are considerably higher. The 1976 vintage proved ideal for these styles, and the Hugels produced quite substantial quantities of them, from Pinot Gris and Gewurztraminer as well as Riesling, and made them commercially available, rather than keeping them as wines for special occasions within the family. They were rapidly recognised for their outstanding quality, and the SGN style was well and truly established.

LOOKING BACK

Hugel was founded in 1639 in Riquewihr and has remained in family hands ever since. In 1976 the company was run by the much admired Johnny Hugel, who in addition to maintaining high standards at the firm, acted less formally as a kind of ambassador for the region as a whole. As the major producer of Vendange Tardive and SGN styles, Hugel played a major role in laying down the regulations for these styles. These were promulgated in 1984, though subsequently revised on two occasions. Until 1971 what is now known as SGN was labelled, German-style, as Beerenauslese. Riesling was, and remains, the scarcest of SGN wines, as the variety succumbs to botrytis less easily than Pinot Gris or Gewurztraminer. Thus in 1985 Hugel produced a mere 250 litres of Riesling SGN, and subsequent vintages were 1988, 1995, and 1996, as the company only releases such wines when its own high standards are met. At Hugel and indeed many other producers, the legal minimum must weight for SGN is rarely considered sufficient.

THE VINTAGE

As in the rest of France, 1976 produced an exceptionally hot summer, but Alsace's mostly white grapes benefited from occasional storms that refreshed the fruit and aided ripening. The harvest began on 20 September, and Riesling enjoyed particular success in this year. Hugel picked this SGN on 20 October.

THE TERROIR

Like Trimbach and some other Alsace producers, Hugel has never played the grand cru card, even though it owns substantial vineyards within two of them, Sporen and Schoenenbourg. The Riesling SGN generally comes from its best parcels within Schoenenbourg, which has a soil mostly composed of marl and gypsum, plus gravel, sandstone, and fossil limestone. This is a very large site for a grand cru, with 53 hectares in Riquewihr, and is inevitably uneven in quality. (This is the main reason the Hugels are reluctant to identify the site on the label, since they don't want to validate lesser wines produced by other growers from parcels inferior to their own.)

THE WINE

The art of making great SGN is practised almost entirely in the vineyard, where individual berries with the right amount of concentration by botrytis are picked one by one. The baskets are then taken to the winery for pressing, and after settling for a

'Every time Johnny Hugel walked past the cask he removed his hat'

few hours, this must is fermented in either vats or barrels at a temperature no higher than 24°C. The 1976 fermented quietly until 26 July 1977, when it was racked. Every time Johnny Hugel walked past the cask where the wine was stored, recalls Etienne Hugel, he removed his hat. Once the wine was bottled, his good-humoured reverence was seen to be fully justified.

THE REACTION

In 1989 James Suckling wrote of the wine: 'Very youthful and exciting. Deep gold, with wax, petrol and apricot aromas; full-bodied, with developed fruit flavours, good acidity, and a long finish.' In the same year Michael Broadbent described the wine as 'buttercup yellow; grapey, ripe, fragrant; medium-sweet though rich with a marvellous uplift of acidity'. By 2002 his assessment was: 'now a brassy touch to its old gold, but very bright; perfectly harmonious, creamy nose; very sweet, lovely texture, peachy flavour, complete, well balanced.' Steven Spurrier recalls: 'Johnny Hugel told me that each year he "placed the bar a little higher" in what the profile of an SGN should be. With the 1976 he surpassed substantially even his own high standards.'

THE FACTS

Bottles produced	Alcohol
5,500	**12.8%**
Composition	Release price
100% Riesling	**130 French francs**
Yield	Price today
15 hl/ha	**£209 (on a Dutch restaurant wine list)**

MAS DE DAUMAS GASSAC 1982

Languedoc, France

A LEGEND BECAUSE...

This wine burst onto the international wine world with amazing suddenness. In a sense, it was an accidental discovery. In 1971 Aimé Guibert, a glove maker, and his wife, Véronique Guibert de la Vaissière, purchased an abandoned farmhouse near the village of Aniane northwest of Montpellier, as a family home. Their friend, Henri Enjalbert, a celebrated geology professor from Bordeaux University, visited the property and was astonished by the quality of its terroir. Guibert called in the foremost wine expert of the time, Emile Peynaud, who recommended planting the site with a majority of Cabernet Sauvignon. Guibert also planted a range of other varieties, including many from Italy and the Caucasus region, albeit in small quantities.

LOOKING BACK

The 40ha vineyard was planted in 1974 and the first vintage was 1978. Guibert, who died in 2016, was keen to maintain biodiversity by planting vines in small blocks among the scrub and wildlife. However, the wine was slow to win recognition – especially within France. It first received great international acclaim in 1982, and its stature became assured. Over time the vineyard was expanded and new wines were created. Today the estate is run by Guibert's sons.

THE VINTAGE

After a hot summer, the harvest began on 16 September and continued until 1 October. Despite its southerly location in the Languedoc, Daumas Gassac is a cool site and doesn't produce super-rich wines. Harvest can be three weeks later than elsewhere in the area. A large proportion of Cabernet Sauvignon, which ripens without excessive sugar levels, gives the wine a lean structure and remarkable ageability. Although 1982 was riper than most years, the wine was never overblown.

THE TERROIR

The Gassac Valley rises from 250m on the valley floor to 550m at the top of the flanking hills. A stream that traverses the property before joining the River Hérault, and the proximity of the Mediterranean, help to create the estate's microclimate. These attributes first excited Enjalbert, as well as a soil dominated by glacial deposits and rich in iron and minerals. Farming has long been organic. Leaf removal is avoided, as a generous canopy protects the vines from the southern sun.

THE WINE

The winery is gravity-operated and located within a structure whose walls date back to Roman times. The grapes are destemmed, then fermented in steel tanks and given a cuvaison of at least three weeks. The wine is aged for 12 to 14 months in barriques, but no more than 15% of the barrels are new. There is a light fining but no filtration.

THE REACTION

Jane MacQuitty, writing in *The Times*, hailed the wine in 1985: 'Blessed with an inky purple-black colour and grassy blackberry fruit on the palate, and obviously needs at least a decade or two in the cellar yet.'

In 1986, Clive Coates MW, comparing this vintage with the

1983, wrote: 'More tannic, dense, masculine. Slightly spicier and more tarry. Needs a lot of time.'

Michael Broadbent has followed the wine since 1986, when he found it 'immensely impressive'.

Stephen Brook noted in 1994: 'Rich, sumptuous and concentrated, this shows great depth of flavour, and the edge of acidity keeps it lively. Far from mature...'

In 2014 Richard Hemming MW, writing on *jancisrobinson.com*, found the wine had not aged well: 'Black cherry, dry tannins, somewhat hard texture.'

THE FACTS

Bottles produced
32,000
Composition
73% Cabernet Sauvigon, 7% Merlot, 7% Tannat, 5% Syrah, 4% Malbec, 3% Cabernet Franc, 1% Nebbiolo, Dolcetto and Barbera
Yield
37hl/ha
Alcohol
13.2%
Release price
10 French francs
Price today
£120

TRIMBACH, CLOS STE-HUNE 1990

Alsace, France

A LEGEND BECAUSE...

Single-vineyard wines, other than those from grand cru sites, are not that common in Alsace, and over the decades Clos Ste-Hune has won a reputation as the finest of them all. It is only produced in good vintages; thus in 1980 and 1984 no Clos Ste-Hune was bottled. 1990, by contrast, is recognised as one of the greatest years in Alsace. The reputation of the Clos is not restricted to Alsace; many critics and sommeliers regard it as one of the greatest white wines in the world.

LOOKING BACK

The Trimbachs have been producing wine in Alsace since the early 17th century, and have owned the Clos for more than two centuries, although the first vintage to be released commercially was the 1919. In 1990 the winemaker would have been Pierre Trimbach and this was his first vintage after taking over from his father Bernard.

THE VINTAGE

Like its predecessor 1989, 1990 was an outstanding vintage in Alsace, although the crop was reduced by about 25% after poor weather at flowering. But the aromatic varieties were more troubled by these problems than Riesling. The winter was mild and dry, so in spring the vines experienced a growth spurt that was brought to a halt by miserable weather in June, just before flowering. Thereafter the growing season was fine and the harvest took place in early October in perfect conditions; sugar levels were abnormally high.

THE TERROIR

The Clos is a 1.67-hectare parcel within the 26ha Rosacker Grand Cru, but the Trimbachs (like the firms of Hugel and Beyer) have always been firmly opposed to the grand cru system in Alsace. Since the existing grands crus have been generously defined, they feel it would be a disservice to this great wine to place it on the same level as other Rieslings from this site. There is no doubt that Clos Ste-Hune is easily the finest wine to be produced from Rosacker, and the Trimbachs wish to protect that renown. The site faces southeast on a gentle slope, and has rather heavy marl and clay soils over a limestone subsoil. The average age of the vines is about 50 years. Yields are generally about 50 hectolitres per hectare – low but not especially so, given that Riesling can reach a potential alcohol level of 13.5% at such a yield. It is the small size of the Clos that ensures production rarely exceeds 8,000 bottles in any year, a rarity factor that, in addition to its quality, justifies a very high price. Despite this very limited production, the Trimbachs have occasionally, as in 1989, produced an even scarcer Vendange Tardive (late harvest) from the Clos.

THE WINE

The Trimbachs have long produced Rieslings that are among the most severe and uncompromising from Alsace. These include not only Clos Ste-Hune but the magnificent Cuvée Frédéric Emile as well. They have never followed, indeed have always opposed, the trend to leave some residual sugar in the wine. (That said, the 1990 did have 5.6 grams of residual sugar, so rich was the fruit, but there is no perceptible sweetness.) To preserve the acidity so key for the longevity of their wines, the Rieslings do not go through malolactic fermentation. Although fermented in stainless steel, the

'1990 is one of the greatest years in Alsace and this one of the greatest whites in the world'

wine is aged for about six months in large old casks. It is bottled relatively young, but then spends five years in the Trimbach cellars before release. Clos Ste-Hune does not seek to charm, and the initial impression given by a young vintage is often one of ruthless austerity. It's a wine that demands bottle age and should not be broached until it is at least seven years old.

THE REACTION

The response of *The Wine Spectator* in 1996 was a trifle tepid: 'A fine example of traditional Alsace Riesling that shows finesse and sophistication.' By contrast, in 2005 US wine auctioneer John Kapon, having tasted 13 vintages from the Clos, described the 1990 in extravagant terms: 'A fabulous nose, full of musk, rainwater, citrus, nut and sweet Asian spice. Flavours of tender, juicy white meat, rain, citrus dust and oil. Rich, exotic and incredible.' In 2002, I wrote: 'Reserved, nutty apricot and apple nose. Very rich and full-bodied on the palate, supple yet nutty and mineral, a touch alcoholic but has splendid persistence.' Jancis Robinson MW found a more evolved wine in 2012: 'Very deep copper. Huge, intense, very concentrated. Very big and beefy...Very powerful. Almost sweet on the finish because of that massive alcohol but not hot.'

THE FACTS

Bottles produced	Alcohol
8,300	**14.2%**
Composition	Release price
100% Riesling	**N/A**
Yield	Price today
59 hl/ha	**£389**

ZIND-HUMBRECHT, CLOS ST-URBAIN PINOT GRIS SGN 1989

Rangen, Alsace, France

A LEGEND BECAUSE...

The Clos St-Urbain has always been one of Zind-Humbrecht's most prized sites, excelling with Pinot Gris. Even the more basic Pinot Gris bottlings are rich and spicy, while the Sélection de Grains Nobles (SGN) wines from here are off the charts in terms of richness and opulence.

Léonard Humbrecht was a campaigner for low yields, and this conviction, as well as the quality of the estate vineyards, accounts for the superb quality of his top wines. His son Olivier always seeks maximum ripeness in the vineyards, and prefers not to intervene in the fermentation process. If the yeasts stumble to a halt and leave residual sugar in a wine, he is untroubled so long as the wine is balanced. With an SGN, residual sugar (in this case 172 grams per litre) is of course sought after, but the wine must be harmonious if it is to avoid being clumsy. He has no interest in producing ultra-ripe SGNs for the sake of richness alone, and in 1994 created a further category called Trie Spéciale to denote wines made from grapes with a potential alcohol of about 30%.

LOOKING BACK

The Humbrechts have been wine growers in Alsace since the 17th century. Léonard Humbrecht, who was born in 1935, put the estate on the map, but it was his son Olivier who won its wines international recognition. By the end of the 1980s he was in charge of the winemaking, and yet managed to scoop up a Master of Wine qualification in his spare time, becoming the first French MW in 1989.

THE VINTAGE

Other than localised hail in mid-July, the summer was sensational, and yields were generous. Sugar levels were very high and a potential alcohol level of 15% was far from unusual; in some cases the grapes were as high as 26% in potential alcohol. This caused problems for estates focusing on dry wines, but it was a glorious vintage for the production of sweet wines. Zind-Humbrecht produced a number of SGNs from different varieties, of which the Clos St-Urbain Pinot Gris is the most spectacular.

THE TERROIR

Rangen is the most southerly Alsatian grand cru, and unquestionably one of its greatest, as well as one of the steepest. The elevation ranges from 320m to 470m. The soil is volcanic and easily retains heat, and the south-facing aspect usually gives grapes of exceptional ripeness. It comprises 19ha of vines, including two monopole sites: the 4.5ha Clos St-Théobald, belonging to Schoffit, and the 5.5ha Clos St-Urbain, which was planted (half with Pinot Gris) by Léonard Humbrecht in the 1970s. The site lies not far from the river Thur, and this proximity to water accounts for the ease with which the bunches can attract noble rot.

THE WINE

Winemaking at Zind-Humbrecht has generally been non-interventionist. After a pressing of whole clusters, vinification takes place with indigenous yeasts in large casks. This wine was

fermented in a new, carved, 900-litre barrel given to Olivier as a wedding present by his parents. 'I was so worried that it might leak,' recalls Olivier, 'that I slept next to it for the first night.' The wine stays on its fine lees until bottling after a light filtration.

THE REACTION

In 1993 Robert Parker described this as 'celestial', adding: 'The bouquet almost fills the room with its smoky, paraffin-scented, rich fruit. In the mouth, there is mind-boggling richness, extraordinary balance, and a finish that must last several minutes.'

Thierry Meyer in 2007 wrote, of the mature wine: 'If the wine has the complexity of its 18 years of age, the long dried apricot aftertaste is still very fresh. A monumental wine that will keep another half century.'

THE FACTS

Bottles produced	Alcohol
1,140	**11.6%**
Composition	Release price
100% Pinot Gris	**N/A**
Yield	Price today
N/A	**£189**

GERMANY

The nobly sweet wines of Germany – BAs and TBAs – can last a century or more, in my experience, so it's regrettable that only two such wines made the cut. Numerous estates, such as Kloster Eberbach, Weil, and Keller, would have been worthy of inclusion, but our list reflects, sadly, the widespread lack of interest in great German wines.

EGON MÜLLER-SCHARZHOF TBA 1976

Scharzhofberger, Mosel-Saar-Ruwer, Germany

A LEGEND BECAUSE...

This Wiltingen estate has long had an extraordinary reputation, especially for its sweet wines. Some dry wines were made from 1980 to 1997, but Egon Müller never found their quality exciting, so production was halted. Scharzhof was one of the first German estates to make eiswein. The first commercial vintage was 1961, though some earlier vintages were sold as auslesen. Despite the acclaim given to the eiswein, the greatest of the Scharzhof wines is surely the Riesling trockenbeerenauslese (TBA), which has been rewarded by collectors with record high prices at auction.

LOOKING BACK

The estate, and its exquisite manor house, were acquired in 1797 by the ancestors of the present owners. The slopes of the Scharzhofberg had been known for the quality of its wines for centuries, but it was the Müller family that assured the estate's place among the great white wines of the world from the 1950s onwards. Uncompromising selection in the vineyard allowed Scharzhof to produce great sweet wines in years when other properties failed to do so.

It was Egon Müller III, the father of the present Egon Müller, who oversaw the production of this wine. His cellarmaster, and thus winemaker, was Horst Frank, who worked here for decades before his retirement in 2000. Visitors were invited to stand by a round table, while Müller disappeared from time to time to fetch bottles of ever greater antiquity and rarity. The nobly sweet wines were usually tasted in the greater comfort of the Scharzhof library. His son has inherited his courtesy and generosity, if not his formality.

THE VINTAGE

This was a great vintage in the Mosel-Saar- Ruwer. The summer was hot and very dry, and this led to grapes with perfect ripeness. Noble rot followed, and most estates were able to produce beerenauslese (BA) and TBA styles of great opulence and charm. If there was a drawback to 1976, it was the relatively low acidity. This favoured regions such as the Saar, with their naturally high acidity. Lower-quality wines are now probably past their best, but the top BAs and TBAs are still glorious.

THE TERROIR

The steep hill that rises behind the Scharzhof manor is the Scharzhofberg, today some 28 hectares in extent, though until 1971 it was limited to 18ha. The soil is deep, weathered, blue and grey slate that gives wines of the greatest finesse. Scharzhof owns 8.5ha, and other proprietors include Kesselstatt, van Volxem and von Hövel. The site is exceptionally well drained, but water stress is rare. Müller is the sole owner of very old vines – a 2ha block behind the house was planted on ungrafted vines in circa 1900.

THE WINE

Pickers are equipped with two baskets, one for healthy berries, the other for berries with noble rot. Acidity also plays a crucial part in the structure of the wine, but Müller insists he always seeks to pick at optimal ripeness, and avoids berries with any sign of greenness, even though botrytis can settle on grapes that are not yet fully ripe. Müller usually selects only two to three days for the harvesting of heavily botrytised berries, as the need for constant selection can be very tiring for the pickers. He accompanies them to ensure they know what to look for when seeking out potential TBA grapes.

'Müller accompanies pickers to ensure they know what to look for in potential TBA grapes'

Once at the winery, the grapes are pressed without any period of skin contact. After pressing, the juice is settled and then tipped into casks, small steel tanks or demi-johns – the vessel often dependent on the quantity produced – for fermentation and ageing. It is not unusual for the TBA to ferment very slowly, so decisions about lees-ageing and bottling dates have to be made on a pragmatic basis. Müller recalls that the 1976 fermented so slowly that it couldn't be bottled till 1981.

THE REACTION

Michael Broadbent, tasting the wine in 2000, was ecstatic: 'Deep tawny, orange highlights, apple-green rim and rich "legs"; an indescribably lovely bouquet, slightly raisiny, lime honey and acidity (Hugh Johnson just said "Turkish Delight"); tremendously rich, concentrated, dry finish, good length.' He awarded the wine six stars rather than his usual maximum five. More recently, Russian wine writer Eleanora Scholes noted: 'Aromas of minerals, crème brûlée and buckwheat honey; notes of burnt sugar, oranges, spices, with a final touch of freshness, can be found on a complex, nearly viscous, palate.'

THE FACTS

Bottles produced
N/A
Composition
100% Riesling
Yield
N/A
Alcohol
5.5%

Release price
DM1,510 (at Grosser Ring auction, Trier)
Price today
N/A (1989 TBA is £2,621 per half bottle)

JJ PRÜM, WEHLENER SONNENUHR RIESLING AUSLESE GOLDKAPSEL 1971

Mosel, Germany

A LEGEND BECAUSE...

A dream combination of vintage, variety, vineyard and winemaker resulted in this great wine, one of a set of magnificent expressions of the Prüm holdings in Wehlener Sonnenuhr, from Kabinett to Trockenbeerenauslese. All were wonderful, but this top Auslese struck a particular chord with all who tasted it. The hallmark of the JJ Prüm wines is a filigree delicacy wedded to a firm acidic and slate-derived mineral structure.

LOOKING BACK

Dr Manfred Prüm took over from his recently deceased father in 1969, so this was the first outstanding vintage he oversaw. Although he has always been the public face of the estate, until his daughter Katharina took over, he was assisted by his barely visible brother Wolfgang and since 1978 supported by his wife Amei. (The holdings have increased from 12 hectares to 22ha.) JJ Prüm has been a bastion of conservatism. The wine style has barely altered in half a century. Why change a winning formula?

THE VINTAGE

By any account, this was a great vintage in Germany, comparable to the glorious 1953. Flowering was early and the summer was sunny right into the autumn. Dry weather meant that the fruit was perfectly healthy at harvest. Quality was high throughout Germany but at its peak in the Mosel, and many of the top wines are still drinking well, though the majority are fully mature.Dr Prüm recalls: '1971 is a vintage that possesses a beautiful ripe acidity, a fine minerality, and consequently great structure and a good harmony.'

THE TERROIR

The Sonnenuhr, a steep, 45ha site that faces the village of Wehlen on the other side of the river and is named after the sundial in its centre, is one of the most revered vineyards of the Mosel region. It is composed of blue Devonian slate. Underground streams provide sufficient moisture to protect the vineyards from water stress in very hot years. Consequently, the wines always have freshness and a balance that allow them to age for decades. Rieslings would have been selected from the Sonennuhr at various stages of the 1971 harvest, and the Auslese Goldkapsel would have been from botrytised grapes that are not considered fully worthy of being released as Beerenaulese.

THE WINE

The winemaking at JJ Prüm is not an open book. I have never laid eyes on the cellars, and know of no one who has. It is virtually certain that wines are fermented slowly in traditional large casks. The wines can be awkward when very young, as they retain a good amount of natural carbon dioxide that gives them a slight petillance, and long ageing on the lees gives them what can strike inexperienced Prüm tasters as off-flavours. However, that leesy character vanishes a year or two after bottling and permits the wine to age splendidly.

THE REACTION

Michael Broadbent was bowled over in 1999: 'Fragrant, creamy, harmonious bouquet; medium-sweet, lovely flavour, balance, length and fragrant finish.' In 2003 Jancis Robinson MW was equally thrilled: 'Wonderful, and reminiscent of 2001s. This combination of intense ripeness and acidity.' In 2008 Stephen Brook noted: A rich, flowery, flamboyant nose of stone fruit... Amazing finesse and poise.' Linden Wilkie tasted the wine in Hong Kong in 2015: 'Ripe botrytis and mint nose, mature. Juicy, beautifully refreshing style, honeyed touch of decadence on mid-palate, botrytis and mineral on the long, very complex, aromatic finish. Everything in balance. In another league. Exceptional. One of the absolute greatest.'

THE FACTS

Bottles produced
N/A

Composition
100% Riesling

Yield
Selective harvesting used, so unknown

Alcohol
7.5%

Release price
DM30 (equivalent to £35 in today's money)

Price today
£581

ITALY

Italy offers such diversity that it was simple enough to find outstanding wines with personality and great track records. Tuscany and Piedmont dominated, predictably, but there were also wines from Campania, Lombardy and Friuli. And there was a sense that many more potentially legendary wines are waiting in the wings.

BIONDI-SANTI, TENUTA IL GREPPO 1975

Brunello di Montalcino, Tuscany, Italy

A LEGEND BECAUSE...

Biondi-Santi is a truly iconic estate: in the late 19th century it was the first in Montalcino to select the most appropriate Sangiovese plants from its own vineyards and then bottle the finished wine under the name of Brunello. Some of the vintages from the 1880s and 1890s, tasted in the 1990s, were still in fine condition. The wines are no heavyweights, but have floral aromas, and in their youth can be dominated by the firm tannins and pungent acidity that allow them to age so well.

LOOKING BACK

In 1970 the late Franco Biondi-Santi took over running the estate from his father Tancredi. He maintained the traditions set down by his father and grandfather, insisting on very low yields of about half the authorised maximum, and was resolutely opposed to the use of barriques to age the wine. Although the quality of the riservas from years such as 1964 and 1975 is indeed the stuff of legend, the wines of the following decades would prove more controversial. Light in colour and ethereal in aromas and flavour, they were denounced by many wine critics for their lightness. This coincided with the rise of rich, full-flavoured and powerful Brunellos - a style that found favour with many critics. Biondi- Santi remained true to its historic style, and it is still unclear whether there was indeed a lapse in quality in the 1980s and 1990s or whether the wines simply slipped from fashion until fashion came full circle again.

THE VINTAGE

The year was not exceptional in the rest of Tuscany but happened to be outstanding in Montalcino and Montepulciano. The harvest took place in early October.

THE TERROIR

The vineyards are unusually high for Montalcino, rising from about 360m to 500m. The main vineyard is called Il Greppo, which lies just south of Montalcino and has marl soil and some schist, but there are other sites north of the town, with rocky clay soils. All the vines are massal selections produced from existing vines at the estate. Indeed, half the vineyard is planted with BBS 11, a clone specially developed by Florence University from old vines at Biondi-Santi. The contrast between hot temperatures by day and far cooler temperatures at night help to account for the refined and complex perfume of these Brunellos. No herbicides or pesticides have been used at the estate. The vineyards registered for Brunello have a surface area of 23ha but only vines at least 25 years old are used for the riservas.

THE WINE

On arrival at the winery, the grapes are destemmed and crushed. Only indigenous yeasts are used for fermentation of the riserva. This takes place in oak vats, unlike the regular Brunello, which ferments in concrete vats. Temperature control was only introduced in 1983, so the 1975 would have been vinified without it. It was then aged in wooden casks for three years. Total acidity in this vintage was unusually high at 7.5 grams per litre.

THE REACTION

In 1995, *Decanter*'s Michael Broadbent tasted the wine at the estate: 'After 1955 [this is] the best of all the riservas, impressive, plummy; rich appearance, immediately fragrant, spicy, with good fruit, holding back then accelerating with fabulous bouquet, more fig-like, great depth; a gloriously rich mouthfiller. Perfect structure

'A gloriously rich mouthfiller. Perfect structure and balance'

Michael Broadbent

and balance.' In the same year Italian wine specialist Nicolas Belfrage MW reported in *Decanter* on a vertical tasting of the riservas back to 1888: 'Relatively deep colour, still youthful, hint of orange on the rim. Distinct change of character on nose... mushroomy, gamey, some *goudron* [tarmac]. Muscular, strong and tannic, but with plenty of fruit to back it up.' In 2004 Belfrage attended another vertical tasting of the riservas: 'The 1975, still boasting a youthful hue, a forceful aroma of tea leaf, rose petal, and dried fig, plenty of concentration, yet subtle, very long and capable of several more decades if kept well.' American writer Kerin O'Keefe, author of a book on Biondi-Santi, tasted this wine most recently in 2011: 'Still magnificent, with an intense bouquet of spice, flint, pepper and tobacco. Rich berry and fig flavours are balanced by still fresh acidity and supple, silky tannins. Incredibly youthful and focused. Will continue to age smoothly for decades. A gorgeous, glorious wine.'

THE FACTS

Bottles produced
14,646
Composition
100% Sangiovese Grosso
Yield
N/A
Alcohol
14%
Release price
N/A
Price today
£600

Bruno Giacosa, Asili Barbaresco Riserva 2004

Piedmont, Italy

A legend because...

Born in 1929, Bruno Giacosa began working with his winemaker father Mario – his grandfather Carlo had also produced and bottled wines in their home town of Neive. His initial career was as a merchant, sourcing the best grapes for other producers, but inevitably Giacosa wanted to produce wines under his own label, which he began doing in 1961. He was able to identify what he considered the finest plot and his portfolio grew – the most highly esteemed vineyards, including Asili, were the source of his celebrated red-label riservas. Giacosa, unhappy with the treatment-heavy farming practices of the 1970s, started buying outstanding vineyards to give himself maximum control over the entire production process. A perfectionist, he refused to bottle or release wines that he considered even slightly below the standard he set.

Looking back

Giacosa bought his best parcel of Asili in 1996, and other Barbaresco vineyards in Rabajà; the wine from the latter ceased to be made from 2007 on, after boundary changes allowed the Rabajà grapes to be used in the Asili wine. In 2013, Giacosa bought 0.5ha of Rabajà, so in that year a limited production of the wine resumed. Asili, however, remains one of the most sought-after wines in the range. Giacosa made the 2004, but a stroke in 2006 required a very long convalescence. Some vintages that followed were made by other winemakers hired by Giacosa and his daughter Bruna, notably Dante Scaglione, who had worked at Giacosa's side for many years. Giacosa still kept an eye on wine production until his death in 2018.

The vintage

A mild summer followed a wet spring, and the end of the season in September and early October was dry. Growers in both Barbaresco and Barolo were thrilled with a vintage that delivered an abundant crop as well as exceptional quality. Voluptuous on release, the wines had sufficient acidity to give them finesse, while bold tannins gave some structure. However, 10 years later doubts had arisen, and both critics and producers noted that many wines were ageing more quickly than expected.

The terroir

Sheltered and warm, the 14ha Asili vineyard lies at 200m-280m in the commune of Barbaresco. Silty loam and sand as well as clay are important components in the vineyard, and Giacosa believed they accounted for the wine's incomparable perfume and finesse.

The wine

Giacosa tried, whenever possible, to ferment his grapes using indigenous yeasts, although specially selected yeasts were employed when natural fermentations proved tricky. Vinification took two to three weeks in stainless steel tanks, while ageing took place in large casks of French oak: up to 18 months for the regular Asili, 24 for the riserva.

The reaction

James Suckling admired the wine in 2008: 'Full-bodied, with chewy tannins and lots of fruit. Focused and very well done, but really tight at the moment.' Stephen Brook wrote in 2010:

'Sweet, intense, mint and raspberry nose, showing a light smokiness. Supple yet rich and full-bodied, this is very concentrated and still youthful, with fine acidity and spiciness. Very long.'

In 2016, Antonio Galloni reviewed the wine: 'Easily one of the greatest wines Bruno Giacosa made during his long and distinguished career... the Asili Riserva is defined by its stunning inner sweetness, soaring aromatics and silky tannins. One of the attributes all great wines share is their ability to stimulate all the senses, from the intellectual to the hedonistic. The 2004 Asili riserva hits all the right spots and then some. This is just about as good as it gets.'

THE FACTS

Bottles produced
14,040

Composition
100% Nebbiolo

Yield
40hl/ha

Alcohol
14.5%

Release price
US$210

Price today
£570

CONTERNO, MONFORTINO BAROLO 1978

Piedmont, Italy

A LEGEND BECAUSE...

Conterno's Monfortino has long been among the most celebrated Barolos. Its hallmark is the very long ageing it receives. The 1970 vintage was aged for a decade in large casks before being bottled, and the 1978 was aged for eight years. Despite the fact that the vines were only four years old, the wine proved to be remarkable and won wide acclaim. In the 1970s there were far fewer bottles of Barolo produced than there are today. Monfortino was regarded as the ultimate 'traditional' Barolo, eschewing any use of barriques or other non-local practices. When Giacomo Conterno established the Monfortino brand, all producers in Barolo were 'traditional'. However, the estate has never wavered in its adherence to the style it has practised for many decades. Today the minimum cask-ageing for Monfortino is seven years.

LOOKING BACK

Giovanni Conterno was the son of Giacomo Conterno, who was born in 1895 and after whom the estate is named. Giacomo had been producing and bottling Monfortino since the 1920s, and Giovanni succeeded him at the helm. Giovanni died in 2004 and was followed by his son Roberto, who was born in 1968 and had worked with his father since the age of 20. In all this time the house style has not altered. Before 1974 the wines were made from grapes purchased from growers in Monforte and Serralunga. Giovanni was always willing to pay the highest prices to ensure the best grapes. Then in 1974 he bought the fallow Cascina Francia property in Serralunga, a 14-hectare block. Giovanni was finding it harder to source grapes of the quality he required, and decided it was sensible to guarantee his own supply. As the Cascina Francia needed to be replanted, the first vintage made from its grapes was 1978.

THE VINTAGE

This was an outstanding year, although it didn't seem so at the outset. Spring and early summer were damp and cool, but autumn was warm and dry, bringing the grapes to full ripeness. Yields were fairly small, and tannin levels high, so that Barolo in particular benefited from long ageing in bottle.

THE TERROIR

Cascina Francia, the source of all the grapes for Monfortino, lies at up to 450 metres in the village of Serralunga along the border with Monforte, and opposite the celebrated Ginestra vineyard in the latter. The soils are calcareous and the vines face southwest; they are planted to a density of around 4,000 per hectare.

THE WINE

Monfortino is not a selection of the best barrels, but a parcel selection made shortly before harvest. The best parcels can vary from year to year. Only when their quality is significantly superior to the rest of Cascina Francia is the selection vinified separately, in open-top vats. There is no temperature control, thus running the risk of a stuck fermentation, and the maceration period is long, at up to five weeks. Monfortino is then aged in large casks of 2,000 to 7,500 litres. When the regular Barolo has aged in cask for a year or two, the final decision is taken on whether to blend the Monfortino selection with the regular wine, or whether to designate it as Monfortino.

'If I was given the choice of one bottle of Barolo before I die, I'd choose Monfortino'

Nicolas Belfrage

If the decision is to produce Monfortino, it is aged for at least seven years, compared to four for the regular Barolo. Only a wine of great natural concentration and structure can withstand the potential drying effect of such long ageing in wood. The wine is bottled without fining or filtration. Between 7,000 and 10,000 bottles are produced.

THE REACTION

In 2005 Antonio Galloni, in *The Wine Advocate*, wrote: 'One of the greatest Barolos ever made. It offers complex sensation of spice, cocoa, leather, liquorice and menthol, followed by layers of dark fruit that coat the palate with incredible persistence and length... Its ageing potential appears to be virtually limitless.' He scored it 98/100. Nicolas Belfrage MW wrote in 1999: 'If I was given the choice of one bottle of Barolo before I die, I'd choose Monfortino.' Kelly Walker, of the Grand Jury Européen, tasted the wine in 2010, noting 'A benchmark for great Barolo, this was similar to the 1947 on the nose. Broad and lush on the palate, with a mineral spine under copious sweet tannins. Amazingly complex and balanced.' (19.5+).

THE FACTS

Bottles produced	Alcohol
N/A	**14%**
Composition	Release price
100% Nebbiolo	**N/A**
Yield	Price today
N/A	**£1,650**

ISOLE E OLENA, CEPPARELLO 1982

Tuscany, Italy

A LEGEND BECAUSE...

First produced in 1980, Cepparello was one of the original SuperTuscans. Unlike most of the others, it was made entirely from Sangiovese (although a dash of Cabernet Sauvignon was added in a very few vintages). Paolo de Marchi, owner and winemaker of the Isole e Olena estate, was not opposed to international varieties, and became known for his single-varietal Chardonnay, Syrah and Cabernet Sauvignon bottlings, but he also wanted to demonstrate the potential of pure Sangiovese at a time when the Chianti Classico regulations required the inclusion of other grape varieties.

LOOKING BACK

In the 1980s Chianti Classico producers were supposed to include (white) Trebbiano grapes in the blend, although many growers, including De Marchi, simply ignored the requirement. From 1996 it became possible, through new rules connected to Chianti Classico's promotion from DOC to DOCG status, to make the wine solely from Sangiovese. Previously Sangiovese was not held in highest regard, even though it could deliver superlative results in the hillier zones of Tuscany. Cepparello, which takes its name from a stream on the property, validated the variety.

THE VINTAGE

1982 was the first vintage of Cepparello that De Marchi was satisfied with. May hailstorms resulted in the loss of half the crop, but gave better-quality fruit. Summer was sunny and hot with some rain. A fine autumn brought the grapes to full ripeness, and the harvest was early.

THE TERROIR

Until World War II, Isole e Olena was mostly home to sharecroppers. It lost most of its inhabitants at the end of that war and De Marchi's father bought the estate in 1956. The 50 hectares of vineyards are scattered among various sites up to 470m. The soil is galestro: thin and quite rocky, with sandstone and schistous clay beneath the topsoil. The highest vineyards are breezy, benefit from day-long sunshine and often ripen up to 12 days later than lower sites. Cepparello is made from grapes selected from the best parcels and, usually, the oldest vines. Yields rarely exceed 35hl/ha. It is not made in weaker vintages such as 1992.

THE WINE

The winemaking has evolved over the years. The very first vintage, 1980, was aged in chestnut casks, but in 1982 De Marchi switched to French and Slavonian oak, the traditional container for Chianti Classico. After destemming, the must was fermented for over three weeks at temperatures up to 34°C, with regular pumpovers. The wine spent 18 months in barrels, of which two-thirds were French, and one-third Slavonian. A third of the barrels were new. The wine was given a year's bottle age before being released.

THE REACTION

I first tasted the wine in 1989, finding a sweet 'Californian' tone on the nose, while on the palate 'rich tannins still mask the fruit, which is sweetish and dense'. In 1993 I noted: 'Concentrated and impressive but austere. Good length.'

In 1993, James Suckling reviewed the wine from magnum: 'dark coloured and exuberantly fruity... A violet and cherry character emanates from the glass. It also has tannins to back it up.'

Ian D'Agata tasted the wine in 2009: 'Dense, bright and seamless, with lively acidity providing backbone and support to the delicate red cherry and dark plum flavours. Good to go right now and with a short life expectancy ahead of it... so I'm not sure I'll hold on to this much longer.'

In 2012 Antonio Galloni wrote: 'Still deep in colour, it boasts stunning depth and concentration. Sweet roses, mint and liquorice wrap around the deep, intense finish. This is a dazzling showing. Today's Cepparellos are unquestionably more refined, but the 1982 is a monumental and historically significant wine.'

THE FACTS

Bottles produced
14,490 plus 765 magnums
Composition
100% Sangiovese
Yield
28hl/ha
Alcohol
13.5%
Release price
8,800 lire (about £3.56 in 1985)
Price today
N/A

JERMANN, VINTAGE TUNINA 1997

Collio, Friuli-Venezia Giulia, Italy

A LEGEND BECAUSE...

Silvio Jermann has always been inventive. Although he has produced varietal wines typical of the Collio region in Friuli, he created blends from the outset. Easily the most famous of his wines is the blend Vintage Tunina, which was first made in 1975. All the varieties used for Tunina are picked together. Yields are kept well below the generous Friuli average, and grapes are picked about two weeks later than other white varieties, to give additional richness. The wine takes its name from both a previous owner of the property called Antonia, known by the local diminutive Tunina, and a Venetian governess of the same name who was one of Casanova's lovers.

LOOKING BACK

The property was founded in 1881, by Jermann's ancestors from Austria and Slovenia. Jermann is always thought of as a trendy moderniser; after completing his studies in oenology, he took a job in Canada when his father opposed changes he proposed making at the winery. Tunina, however, is a reinterpretation of a traditional blend. Austrian growers had long produced field blends, but they were often heavy and lacked freshness. Jermann's challenge was to retain the richness and complexity without producing a wine that would turn flabby or be prone to oxidation. He was influenced by the celebrated Friuli winemaker, Mario Schiopetto, whose wines signalled a return to purer, cleaner styles of winemaking.

THE VINTAGE

This was an excellent vintage throughout Friuli. Frost in April reduced the crop, but the summer was very dry, leading to a late harvest of very healthy grapes.

THE TERROIR

Vintage Tunina is produced from a field blend in a vineyard that occupies 16ha on Ronco del Fortino, planted on a soil that is mostly marl and sandstone. The density is high at between 6,000 and 7,000 vines per hectare.

THE WINE

Sauvignon Blanc and Chardonnay are the major components, as well as varying doses of Ribolla Gialla, Malvasia and Picolit. The grapes are all picked together, late in the season, pressed in whole clusters, and fermented together as an authentic field blend. Temperature control is aimed at prolonging the fermentation and extracting maximum flavour. Although there has been some discreet oak-ageing in recent years, in the 1990s Vintage Tunina was unwooded; it received a longer than usual ageing on fine lees and was bottled without cold stabilisation some months after Jermann's other whites.

THE REACTION

Tunina was acclaimed by Italian wine guide *Gambero Rosso* as the best wine of the year, which cemented Jermann's reputation. The 1999 edition said: 'The 1997 confirms the greatness of this outstanding wine: a splendid nose, complex with hints of tomato leaf and mixed fruits... A comparable palate and an inexhaustible symphony of fruit flavours on a plump but elegant textural base.'

In 1999 *Wine Enthusiast* commented: 'Musky, melon-like nose. Full in the mouth, lightly spicy and long on the finish. Tight now, needs time to open up and reveal its charms.'

After a vertical tasting of 30 vintages of Tunina in 2017, Jermann noted during a YouTube interview that 1979 and 1997 had particularly impressed him. Richard Baudains, also present at the tasting, was enthusiastic: 'Nose with acacia honey, touch of sultana, tropical fruit, pressed flowers, hint of Riesling-like petrol... Big impact on the palate, ripe fleshy fruit, great progression, long complex finish.'

THE FACTS

Bottles produced
50,000
Composition
25% Chardonnay, 25% Sauvignon Blanc, 22% Ribolla Gialla, 23% Malvasia, 5% Picolit
Yield
30HL/HA
Alcohol
13%
Release price
27,800 lire
Price today
£85.40

MASCARELLO, MONPRIVATO, BAROLO 1970

Piedmont, Italy

A LEGEND BECAUSE...

Single-vineyard or cru wines are a relatively new concept in Barolo, although growers must have known for decades which were the finest sites that consistently gave the best wines. Monprivato, the jewel among the holdings of Mauro Mascarello, was one of the early cru wines. First documented in 1566, the vineyard was hailed as one of Barolo's top sites in Renato Ratti's classification of 1985. It has also become celebrated because of Mascarello's unwavering espousal of traditional rather than modernist winemaking: long maceration and a preference for large casks over barriques.

LOOKING BACK

The estate of Giuseppe Mascarello acquired vines in Monprivato in 1904, and came to own more than 90% of the cru. The vineyard name first appeared on the bottle in 1970. Mauro Mascarello took over from his father Giuseppe in 1967, and in the 1970s he experimented with methods like varying maceration times, but was never tempted to introduce barrique-ageing as he remained unpersuaded that this yielded better results. Above all he did not want to compromise the subtle aromas that contribute to Barolo's complexity.

THE VINTAGE

The growing season was excellent, resulting in a generous crop of high-quality wines. However, its reputation has been slighted by the fact that the 1971 vintage was even more splendid.

THE TERROIR

Monprivato occupies 7ha in the commune of Castiglione Falletto. The site faces southwest and lies at an elevation of 280m. The soils are silty and calcareous, and the vines have an average age of 55 years. A sector planted with a massal selection of Michet clones in 1963 is used to produce the rare Riserva called Ca' d'Morissio, named after his grandfather Maurizio. First made commercially in 1993, this is only made in top vintages, and in other years the wine is blended into the Monprivato. Mascarello believes in low yields, which rarely exceed 40hl/ha and can be far lower. Although always picked late, Monprivato never shows overripe notes.

THE WINE

Mascarello is fanatical about picking only the healthiest fruit, allowing him to give the must a maceration of three to four weeks. Although the fermentation vats, which today are made from cement and steel, are temperature controlled, Mascarello prefers the grapes to ferment slowly and evenly, extracting colour and tannin with pumpovers, only intervening if temperatures rise to a dangerous level. He initially used indigenous yeasts, but today prefers selected yeasts. Despite the long maceration, the tannins of Monprivato are supple. This can be deceptive, suggesting a wine that might not age well, whereas the reverse is the case. A pneumatic press is used after the maceration is completed. The wine spends about 36 months in large oval Slavonian oak casks. There are up to three rackings in the first year, reduced to a single racking in subsequent years.

THE REACTION

In 2009 Antonio Galloni, writing in *The Wine Advocate*, noted:

'Another of Piedmont's legendary, icon wines. Amazingly, it remains incredibly dense, primary and full of fruit. It may very well prove to be immortal. Today all of the elements are in perfect place. The only thing the wine might need is more time!

In 2016 Eric Guido, writing for the Morrell Wine Bar newsletter in New York, said: 'In gorgeous form and still with many years left. Dark, earthy and perfectly mature Barolo. The bouquet was an earthy mix of moist soil, animal musk, parchment, worn leather and dried strawberry. On the palate, silky textures and a perfect balance of acid and still-lively tannin. Dried cherry, minerals and a hint of tart citrus lasted into the long finish, along with a hint of inner dried florals.'

THE FACTS

Bottles produced
5,900
Composition
100% Nebbiolo
Yield
40HL/HA
Alcohol
14.2%
Release price
4,600 lire (equivalent to about €25 today)
Price today
N/A

MASTROBERARDINO, TAURASI RISERVA 1968

Campania, Italy

A LEGEND BECAUSE...

Although by 1968 Mastroberardino already enjoyed a high reputation for its Taurasi (the 1958 was widely admired too) this vintage was of such quality that the company produced three special cuvées of Taurasi (based on zonal terroir differences) as well as this riserva, which was a blend from all three. Mastroberardino's Taurasi owes its reputation as an extremely long-lived wine to vintages such as this, which are still in their prime.

LOOKING BACK

The Mastroberardino firm dates back to 1878 but had to be relaunched after all its markets were lost during World War II. It was the late Antonio Mastroberardino who transformed Campanian viticulture by reviving the almost extinct Fiano and Greco di Tufo grape varieties. This was at a time when Italian wine authorities were urging growers in Campania to plant Sangiovese and Montepulciano rather than revive the indigenous varieties. While Taurasi existed as a wine long before, it was thanks to Mastroberardino that it gained an international reputation. (The oldest Taurasi in the Mastroberardino cellars dates from 1928, and vintages from the 1920s are still alive if fully mature.)

THE VINTAGE

The growing season in 1968 was very warm, with only a few millimetres of rainfall in summer. These dry, warm conditions created a generous crop with great concentration of colour and tannin; this concentration ensured the excellent quality of the Aglianico grapes and explains the remarkable longevity of wines from this vintage. The quality of the vintage was immediately apparent, and current president Piero Mastroberardino (who was age two at the time) remembers 1968 being spoken of with reverence ever since.

THE TERROIR

The Aglianico grapes came primarily from the company's 12-hectare vineyard at Montemarano in the southern part of the present DOCG region. Other grapes would have come from sites in Pian d'Angelo and Castelfranci. At Montemarano the vines are planted at an elevation of 500m to 650m and face southeast. The soils are clay and crushed limestone, and planting density is 4,000 vines per hectare. The climate is essentially continental, with hot days and cool nights, which delay maturation and consolidate the acidity and tannins. Grapes are usually harvested in early November, at yields generally between 45hl/ha and 50hl/ha.

THE WINE

Although DOCG regulations allow the inclusion of 15% of other grape varieties, Taurasi at Mastroberardino has always been made entirely from Aglianico. The grapes were picked by hand and destemmed at the winery. The wine remained 10 days on the skins during fermentation. It was given long ageing, up to 36 months, in large casks of Slavonian chestnut wood. In the 1960s the wines were aged for about eight years in the company's cellars in Atripalda before being released.

THE REACTION

Burton Anderson in 2001 remarked in *Best Italian Wines*: 'Admirers of Taurasi will never forget Mastroberardino's riserva from the 1968 vintage.' More recently, Antonio Galloni reported in 2010 for *The Wine Advocate*: 'Marvellously dense and ethereal, this classy,

'It was thanks to Mastroberardino that Taurasi gained an international reputation'

breathtaking Taurasi offers up a mélange of plums, prunes, liquorice, herbs, spices and minerals, showing incredible detail and tons of inner perfume. Amazingly, the 1968 comes across as incredibly youthful and vigorous.' My own appreciation in the same year was similar: 'Sweet, intense nose, still floral and lifted, with charm and freshness. Medium-bodied, completely fresh, concentrated and balanced, still tannic and bright and vigorous, elegant and persistent, with little sign of age.' In 2014, Ian D'Agata wrote in *International Wine Cellar*: 'Vibrant aromas of raspberry, sour red cherry, tobacco and mint are complicated by an intense minerality. Juicy, perfumed and concentrated, with red fruit and chocolate flavours that have wonderful precision and amazing inner-mouth energy. Creamy-sweet but with nicely integrated acids, and with sweet, fine-grained tannins on the extremely long, perfumed and smooth finish. This is still amazingly youthful, and a paragon of balance.'

THE FACTS

Bottles produced
20,000
Composition
100% Aglianico
Yield
40HL/HA
Alcohol
12.25%
Release price
N/A
Price today
£450

Nino Negri, 5 Stelle Sfursat 2001

Valtellina, Lombardy, Italy

A legend because...

This rare style – produced by the same method that results in Amarone but infusing it with the finesse of the Nebbiolo grape – was first bottled by the Nino Negri winery in 1956. The wine is produced from healthy grapes that are dried for many months before vinification. The natural drying process elevates the alcohol and the dry extract, resulting in a wine of intensity and power. The 2001 vintage 5 Stelle, which is the winery's top Sfursat, has long been considered one of the supreme expressions of the style.

Looking back

The Nino Negri estate, based in the village of Chiuro, was founded in 1897 in the Valtellina valley on the southern edge of the Alps, and in 1986 it became part of the large Gruppo Italiano Vini company. For 40 years after his appointment as the estate's oenologist, the wines were made by the revered Casimiro Maule. Negri's holdings consist of more than 30ha, but it supplies most of its needs by purchasing fruit from more than 200 growers. Valtellina's vineyards are small plots of land run mostly by part-time growers, and in 1988 Nino Negri united its suppliers under its own grape producers' association. The winery produces a wide range of wines of high quality, but the 5 Stelle is its most prized release.

The vintage

There was a wet start to the year, with a snowy winter and warm rainy spring. A very hot and dry summer followed, which encouraged a positive vine development, ensuring high sugar levels and good aromatic qualities. September was dry too, but with cool nights that help retain good acidity. There was no pressure to pick early, and the grapes were harvested in fine condition on 6 October.

The terroir

Sfursat is not required to be a single-vineyard wine, and the grapes for this vintage came from outstanding sites within the sub-regions of Inferno and Grumello, and from a monopole vineyard called Fracia. The vines are planted on south-facing terraces at an altitude of up to 450m, on sand and silt soils. After harvest a severe selection took place, and only a quarter of the crop made its way into this wine.

The wine

The drying of the grapes was completed in late January, then the fruit vinified in stainless steel tanks with a maceration of 12 days. It was then aged 16 months in new barriques, specifically from the Allier and Nevers forests. (In contrast, the regular Sfursat is aged only in large casks.) After the barrels were blended, the wine was bottled, left to rest for five months, and then released in December 2003.

The reaction

In 2004 James Suckling wrote: 'Enticing nose, lightly spiced blackberry, vanilla and mineral aromas. Full-bodied, with an intense, fresh palate, well-integrated tannins and a long minerally finish. Rich, almost Port-like.'

In 2014 Daniele Cernilli wrote: 'A regular year with...excellent conditions for raising the grapes. This is the best vintage...

Bouquet is very complex, bottle-aged scents of tar, smoked wood and dried mushrooms together with those of spice and raspberries preserved in alcohol. The mouthfeel is full, rich and defined, velvety and intact tannins, excellent acidity and elegant body. Finish is very long and subtle.'

Stephen Brook first tasted it in its youth in 2004, noting its 'sweet rich oaky nose of stewed tomato, dried plums and cherry pie', while the palate was 'very rich and concentrated, super-ripe and a touch candied'. By 2018 the wine had developed 'a complex nose of wet leaves, sour cherries, vanilla and sweet raisiny fruit. Still fresh and precise on the attack, concentrated and spicy but not discernibly hot, good acidity, and a long, elegant, piquant finish.'

THE FACTS

Bottles produced
21,500
Composition
100% Nebbiolo (Chiavennasca)
Yield
45HL/HA
Alcohol
15.6%
Release price
€30
Price today
€55

Ornellaia Bolgheri Superiore 2001

Tuscany, Italy

A legend because...

Throughout the 1970s and early 1980s, the most admired SuperTuscan wine was Sassicaia, from grapes grown in Bolgheri near the Tuscan coast. Other producers were quick to copy the trend. Piero Antinori launched Tignanello and Solaia, and in 1982 his brother Lodovico planted his own estate, Ornellaia, in Bolgheri, with Michel Rolland as consultant.

Ornellaia differs from Sassicaia in that it contains a significant amount of Merlot, which gives it an opulence contrasting with the more reticent Sassicaia. It is also aged in a greater proportion of new oak. Lodovico Antinori's ebullient personality helped to promote the wine, establishing its reputation. The winery releases small quantities of outstanding back-vintages, labelled Archivio Storico; the 2001 is one of them.

Looking back

By 2000, Ornellaia was in a state of flux. Lodovico Antinori was, according to his winemakers, brilliant at setting up new projects, but less keen on running them. Robert Mondavi took a share in the property, and by 2002 had acquired a joint controlling interest with Frescobaldi. In 2001, winemaker Andrea Giovannini was replaced by Thomas Duroux, later the director of Château Palmer. When Mondavi was acquired by Constellation Brands in 2005, Frescobaldi became the sole owner, which it remains today.

The vintage

A mild, damp winter and spring led to an early flowering. Over the summer, the climate was normal and consistent, allowing the grapes to ripen evenly, assisted by some judicious bunch-thinning. Merlot was harvested from early September, while the Cabernet Sauvignon was picked in good conditions from mid-September to early October.

The terroir

The soil at Ornellaia is varied, but is mostly a mixture of clay, gravel and sand near the winery. The vines are planted to a density of 6,000 vines/ha. The main vineyard, Bellaria, lies to the north. Here, the soil is stonier, although the site is essentially alluvial, with marine and volcanic traces. Planted on gentle slopes, Bellaria's 70ha enjoy excellent drainage. Current winemaker Axel Heinz finds the grapes here give fresher, more vibrant wines than those closer to the winery.

The wine

Grapes were harvested manually, sorted, destemmed and lightly crushed. Fermentation took place both in steel tanks and in large wooden vats at up to 30°C. After a post-fermentation maceration, the wine was placed in 70% new barriques, where the malolactic fermentation and ageing were completed. After 12 months, the final blend was created, and the wine was aged for a further six months in barrels. Just before bottling, it was fined, then aged a year in bottle before release.

The reaction

In 2005, Jancis Robinson noted: 'Inky, flattering, full and smooth, though it does belong more to Bordeaux than to Tuscany! Great freshness – great intensity – great wine. Still very thick.' And in 2013, Stephen Brook was impressed: 'Spicy, oaky, blackberry nose, with vanilla tones and great intensity. Quite rich and suave, very concentrated and still displaying firm tannins. Fairly youthful, this remains persistent and balanced on the finish.'

In 2015, *Falstaff* editor Peter Moser felt it needed time: 'Seductive cherry fruit, delicate notes of tangerine peel, a floral touch, a hint of mint. At the moment it is quite closed. Juicy and elegant on the palate, showing a fine extract sweetness, silky yet firm tannins and delicate notes of chocolate and nougat. Lean yet with extraordinary length... Lock it up!'

Then, in 2017, Antonio Galloni wrote in *Vinous*: 'Exotic, rich and decidedly flamboyant, the 2001 [Ornellaia Archivio Storico in magnum] is at its peak, where it is likely to remain for a number of years.'

THE FACTS

Bottles produced
150,000
Composition
65% Cabernet Sauvignon, 30% Merlot, 5% Cabernet Franc
Yield
N/A
Alcohol
14.5%
Release price
US$145
Price today
£220

SPAIN

Rioja led the field, as one would expect, although there was also space for Cava, Penedès and Priorat. Surprisingly, there were no wines from Ribera del Duero; not even Vega Sicilia, and none of the great aged sherries made the cut. I suspect this is a reflection of fashion rather than quality. Moreover, Rioja has the stylistic consistency and longevity to justify its position.

ALVARO PALACIOS, L'ERMITA 1993

Priorat, Spain

A LEGEND BECAUSE...

This was the first vintage of what was rapidly to become Priorat's most famous wine. Although the region had been producing wine for many decades, with Carthusian monks in the forefront of vineyard owners, the steep and rocky terrain made it difficult to cultivate profitably, and many vineyards were being abandoned. It took the vision of a handful of winemakers in the late 1980s to recognise the extraordinary potential of the region.

LOOKING BACK

The revival of Priorat began as recently as 1989, when René Barbier recognised the potential of the amazing, steep, schist soils that give Priorat its typicity. By then the area under vine had dwindled to 600 hectares and appeared to be in terminal decline. Barbier was joined by other pioneers, such as José Luis Pérez and Daphne Glorian. They were joined by Alvaro Palacios, who soon began producing exceptional wines from a number of single vineyards such as Finca Dofí, which he acquired in 1990. It soon became clear that the L'Ermita vineyard was the finest of them all.

THE PEOPLE

Palacios was born into a Rioja winemaking family. But as one of nine siblings, he found it prudent to focus on other historically great vineyard regions; in particular he was keen to rediscover abandoned vineyards. After working with Christian Moueix in Bordeaux, he travelled to Priorat in 1989. At the time the region was not well known, but L'Ermita and a handful of other wines soon demonstrated the fabulous quality of which Priorat was capable.

THE VINTAGE

1993 was a fine vintage in Priorat. Growers had a scare in early October when abundant rain fell, but the L'Ermita grapes were still not ripe thanks to an exceptionally dry summer. After another shower on 17 October, Palacios decided that the grapes had reached optimal ripeness, and harvested over the next two days. The 1993 vintage has not had the recognition it deserves, overshadowed by the excellent vintage in 1994.

THE TERROIR

The very steep L'Ermita vineyard, near the village of Gratallops, was planted with bush vines in 1910 and 1940. In 1993 it occupied 1.7ha, and though in 1996 it was expanded to 4.5ha, those newer plantings are still not used in the L'Ermita blend. The soil is schist (known locally as *llicorella*) and the vines grow in an amphitheatre at an elevation of 400m to 520m, facing north and east. The exposition is not ideal, but its relative coolness accounts for the wine's fragrance. Cabernet Sauvignon was a more recent planting here. The blend is 90% Garnacha, 7% Cariñena and 3% white grapes. The vines, now 73 years old, are farmed biodynamically. Horses and mules are used to cultivate the site, due to its extreme steepness.

THE WINE

The grapes are often picked by selective harvesting, with up to three passages through the vines to ensure that only the ripest, best fruit is harvested. There is a further sorting at the winery. The bunches are destemmed by hand, then fermented in wooden vats with punching down of the cap; after 45 to 50 days on the skins the wine is pressed, and malolactic fermentation

'In 1998, the late John Radford enthused that L'Ermita was "arguably Spain's finest red wine'

takes place in barrels. The wine is aged for 18 months in new oak, and is bottled after egg white fining, but there is no filtration. Around 500 to 1,800 bottles are produced today.

THE REACTION

Because of its tiny production and limited renown, reviews on release of L'Ermita's first vintage were scarce. Robert Parker in *The Wine Advocate* gave it a relatively stingy 89 points. Spanish wine expert Jesús Barquín tasted the wine in the late 1990s and was slightly disappointed, probably because of his very high expectations. However, in 2003 he found the wine 'delicious'. In 1998 the late John Radford enthused that L'Ermita was 'arguably Spain's finest red wine, and certainly its most expensive.' US wine critic Jeff Leve noted in 2013: 'Dry, overly oaked, with fresh, bright, wild strawberry, cherry and wet earth characteristics... Perhaps this was better in its youth.' Indeed, Ferran Centelles, former sommelier at El Bulli, which listed the wine, recalls the 1993 as 'very classical, with lots of forest floor, very ripe fruit, a mature nose, already at its peak'.

THE FACTS

Bottles produced
500

Composition
90% Garnacha, 7% Cariñena and 3% white grapes

Yield
5hl/ha

Alcohol
14%

Release price
N/A

Price today
£203

Bodegas Roda, Roda I Reserva 1994

Rioja, Spain

A legend because...

Roda was founded in 1987 by drinks distributors Mario Rotllant and Carmen Daurell, after a long search for the ideal base for their winemaking project. They eventually settled on the Rioja Alta region. They located their winery in the historic Haro Station District, and it soon made an impact with modern-style wines. The focus was on old vines, especially those cultivated as bush vines. Roda also differentiated between wines with a predominantly red-fruit character – labelled simply as Roda – and those with more balsamic black-fruit character, which were released as Roda I. This is a stylistic choice on the part of the winery, the goal being to create two different interpretations of Rioja.

Looking back

Although the company was established in 1987, the winery in Haro wasn't completed until 2001. By then it had gained its reputation as one of the top producers in the region. Rotllant had deliberately assembled a viticultural and winemaking team that had extensive experience outside Rioja and very little within it. The idea was to approach the region with a clean slate and no preconceptions, hence the release of cuvées based on style rather than location.

The vintage

The 1994 growing season in Rioja was very dry, and the grapes matured in perfectly healthy conditions. Rainfall was low, but a downpour in late September refreshed the grapes and allowed them to complete the maturation cycle without too much stress. The harvest took place from 1-25 October.

The terroir

Roda owns 70ha of vines, but controls a further 50ha through agreements with trusted local growers. The 20 vineyards from which grapes are sourced are located at elevations between 380m-650m, and the vines are all more than 30 years old. They are dry-farmed, and although the viticulture is sustainable, Roda does not claim to farm organically, as the climate makes that approach too risky.

The wine

The fermentation took place with indigenous yeasts in oak vats at temperatures no higher than 30°C, and malolactic fermentation was completed in barriques. Then the wine continued its ageing in 33% new French oak for 24 months. The toasting was light to medium, to ensure that the oak did not dominate the wine – recent vintages are only aged for about 16 months, but in 50% new oak. Before bottling, the wine was fined with egg whites, but not filtered. After bottling it was left undisturbed for a further 12 months before release.

The reaction

In 1998, Thomas Matthews noted in *The Wine Spectator*: 'This polished red marries extraction and elegance, with a firm structure and well-balanced flavours of plum, toast and spice that linger on the clean, fresh finish. Drink now through 2005.'

In 2017, Sarah Jane Evans MW attended a vertical tasting of Roda wines in Rioja and noted: 'It's a fresh, linear wine with a firm and lively palate. It may not be fleshy, but it is bold and intense, with black plums, dark chocolate and tobacco. Its age has endowed it with a silky texture. The finish is very long, with spicy notes and a hint of black pepper. There's plenty of life in this. The only Roda with any Garnacha.'

In 2018, Tom Cannavan reported on the same tasting on *www.wine-pages.com*: 'Lovely edge of brick to the colour. Dry, mineral, a touch of iron oxide, a touch of dried blood. Beautiful fruit on the palate, very dry, the tannins coating the mouth, but such a delightful cherry and blackcurrant intensity of fruit. Racing acidity adds to the wiry, tense feel of the wine. Fabulous length.'

THE FACTS

Bottles produced
83,000
Composition
83% Tempranillo, 17% Garnacha
Yield
40hl/h
Alcohol
13.5%
Release price
£45
Price today
£100 approx

DOMINIO DE PINGUS, PINGUS 1995

Ribera del Duero, Spain

A LEGEND BECAUSE...

Pingus came out of nowhere. The 1995, the debut vintage, was sold through the Bordeaux market by American négociant Jeffrey Davies. Its winemaker, Peter Sisseck, took samples with him when he went to Bordeaux to stay with his uncle, winemaker Peter Vinding-Diers. Adam Brett-Smith of Corney & Barrow in London tasted the wine with Vinding-Diers and told Robert Parker about it. The US critic waxed lyrical, and its reputation was made. With Pingus, Sisseck had created a legendary and very profitable wine. Its status was only enhanced when in 1997 a quarter of the vintage was lost in a shipwreck in the Atlantic.

LOOKING BACK

Sisseck trained in his native Denmark and then worked with his uncle Vinding-Diers in Bordeaux. He moved to Spain in 1990 to seek out vineyards for his uncle, but those he found were in poor shape. They were bought instead by a Spanish group that created Hacienda Monasterio and hired Sisseck as manager. In 1994, he was winemaker at Hacienda Monasterio in Ribera del Duero, but the company was ailing and Sisseck left to pursue his own project.

THE VINTAGE

Ribera del Duero suffered from heavy frost in late April, but damage was limited and the vintage was saved by a very hot summer, which helped bring the vines to full and even maturity.

THE TERROIR

Pingus is sourced from five organically farmed parcels in La Horra, four of them contiguous. The soil is clay-gravel over limestone. The 4.5 hectares of vineyards are well drained but also water-retentive, which is essential, as the vines are dry-farmed. As they were planted in 1929, yields are between 9hl/ha and 20hl/ha. The grapes are picked at high ripeness, and though the final alcohol levels can be very high, Sisseck finds it rarely detectable thanks to the wine's natural balance.

THE WINE

Sisseck has always adapted vinification and oak-ageing regimes to suit the nature of the vintage, and his own evolving ideas. In 1995, two-thirds of the crop was hand-destemmed, the remainder vinified as whole bunches; of the hand-destemmed segment, half was crushed, half left as whole bunches. The juice is fermented with native yeasts. Malolactic fermentation takes place in new barrels, and in the 1990s 20% of the wine was decanted after racking into another set of new oak barrels. The idea was to expose the young wine to the most natural oxidation possible and avoid reduction. By 2008 Sissek was no longer using entirely new oak barrels, so the ageing regime has evolved. The wine stayed in barrel for almost two years, and bottled without fining or filtration.

THE REACTION

US critics Stephen Tanzer and Robert Parker both reported on the wine shortly before it was bottled. Tanzer wrote: 'Incredibly sexy aromas...and an utterly seamless, suave finish that goes on and on.' And Parker: 'One of the greatest and most exciting young red wines I have ever tasted... Extremely

'One of the greatest and most exciting young reds I have ever tasted'

Robert Parker

rich and full-bodied, with exceptionally well-integrated acidity and tannins...Impeccably balanced wine that has a level of concentration that must be tasted to be believed.'

In 2004, Jancis Robinson wrote: 'Intensely gamey, meaty nose with whiffs of blackberry. Significant acidity and tannins quite amazingly recessed. Lovely mellow mouthfeel. Very, very, slightly short?' In 2012 Jeff Leve was dazzled: 'Layers of sweet, ripe, black fruits, liquorice, espresso bean, earth, smoke, jam and spice. Rich, deep and concentrated, with opulent, lush textures.'

THE FACTS

Bottles produced
3,900
Composition
100% Tinto Fino (Tempranillo)
Yield
12hl/ha
Alcohol
14.5%
Release price
N/A
Price today
£878

R López de Heredia, Viña Tondonia Blanco 1964

Rioja, Spain

A legend because...

This famous producer, one of the most traditional in Spain, was founded in Rioja in 1877. Its wines, white as well as red, are given prolonged ageing in casks and released later than most modern Riojas. They are renowned for their ageability, and the slight oxidation inherent in the ageing process gives the wines remarkable stability. 1964 was an outstanding vintage for both red and white Rioja.

Looking back

The 150ha property is owned by the López de Heredia family, represented since the 1990s by María José, her winemaker sister Mercedes and brother Julio César, all fourth generation. Their father Pedro, born in 1928, ran the company from 1955 onwards without help from his four siblings. Money was tight, so there was little investment in the cellars, and up to 20 vintages would have been ageing there at any one time. The wines were adored by fans for their individual style, but they weren't widely accepted. However, in recent years they have soared into fashion and María José now has to sell certain vintages on allocation.

The vintage

For many, 1964 is the finest vintage of the 20th century for Rioja. It was a dry year with no risk of disease and proved a fine vintage for both quantity and quality. The harvest at Tondonia took place in one month starting with the whites grapes on 25 September. Weather was exceptional throughout the harvest period.

The terroir

This vineyard of over 100ha is the family's pride and joy. Planted on the right bank of the Ebro river on clay-limestone soils, the yields are very low due to the old vines. There are 6ha of white vines; the white Tondonia is 90% Viura and 10% Malvasia. The site is planted with bush vines, though there are some trellised rows that belong to other growers who have refused to sell their vines to López de Heredia.

The wine

Grapes are basket-pressed and fermented in large wooden vats a century old, without temperature control. The indigenous yeasts are powerful, so there's little risk of a blocked fermentation. Pedro's motto was: 'Don't worry.' He reassured his chidren that if fermentation stopped, it would always resume. The 1964 was aged for 10 years in neutral American oak casks coopered at the winery. Because rules establishing the reserva and gran reserva categories were not finalised until 1981, there is confusion about the labelling of this wine. Before 1981 all López de Heredia wines were released as crianza. But given its long ageing, this wine easily qualifies as a gran reserva.

The reaction

In 2009, John Gilman declared this to be: 'The single greatest white Rioja that I have ever had the pleasure to taste. Full-bodied, complex and still very racy, with stunning cut and grip for a dry white wine at its age, brilliant focus and balance, and a nearly endless, complex and profound finish.'

In the same year Hugh Johnson remembered the 1964 vintage: 'López de Heredia made famous wines that year, including a white that could be Haut-Brion – still pale, waxy, pungent and vital.'

In 2006, Stephen Brook relished the wine's 'wonderful honeyed, peachy nose, with its touch of burnt toast. It's quite austere, but retains some sweet fruit, and keen acidity should keep it going.'

In 2018, Pedro Ballesteros Torres MW wrote: 'Mature aromas of lemon peel, dried apricots, wax and cedar. It has a lovely classic structure that's so typical of this house. Great.'

THE FACTS

Bottles produced
16,000
Composition
90% Viura, 10% Malvasia
Yield
28hl/ha
Alcohol
12%
Release price
2,000 pesetas (€12)
Price today
£900

MARQUÉS DE GRIÑÓN, CABERNET SAUVIGNON 1982

Castilla-La Mancha, Spain

A LEGEND BECAUSE...

When this wine was launched on international markets in the mid-1980s, it caused a sensation. This was not just because of its quality but because wine lovers were not accustomed to tasting high-quality Cabernet Sauvignons from Spain. Moreover, this was the first vintage of this wine. True, the Torres Black Label wine already had a high reputation, but it came from Penedès in Catalonia. Carlos Falcó, the Marqués de Griñón, established his estate further south, in central Spain, in the town of Malpica de Tajo in the Toledo province of Castilla-La Mancha, which was hardly known as a centre for fine wine. This single estate, the Dominio de Valdepusa, would become the first recognised 'pago', paving the way for the Grandes Pagos group of high-quality private wine estates which Falcó helped to establish 20 years later in 2003.

LOOKING BACK

Carlos Falcó was already established as a gastronomic expert, with an enviable appetite and a determination to demonstrate the full potential of Spanish viticulture. At his own estate in La Mancha he was a pioneer of drip irrigation, which he had seen installed at Israeli orange groves in the early 1980s. He also employed the great Bordelais oenologist Professor Emile Peynaud as his consultant for this wine and for subsequent vintages until 1991, when Michel Rolland took his place. He never rested on his laurels, and in the early 1990s hired Australian viticulturist Richard Smart to advise on canopy management and irrigation controls. Moreover, he was keen to share his knowledge of advances in grape-farming with other growers and estates.

THE VINTAGE

1982 was a classic year across Spain. A dry, mild spring continued into a hot and dry summer with some drought stress that reduced yields. Red wines from top estates were structured and long-lived.

THE TERROIR

Cabernet Sauvignon was first planted at Valdepusa in 1974 on 14ha, and those vines were the source of this wine. The soil is clay over fractured limestone with good drainage. Falcó took advice not only from Richard Smart but from the distinguished viticultural consultants Claude and Lydia Bourguignon. Irrigation proved beneficial as this is a dry site, with an average annual rainfall of 450mm. Although the district receives 3,000 hours of sunshine per year, nights are cold and the overall climate continental, and the vineyard lies at an elevation of 490m.

THE WINE

Ageing took place in French barriques for a period of 26 months, presumably with traditional racking. The final blend was assembled under the supervision of both Emile Peynaud and Alexis Lichine.

THE REACTION

Perhaps due to the fact that Spanish still wines, other than Rioja and Vega Sicilia, were very much under the radar in the 1980s, there was an absence of reviews when the Marqués de Griñón 1982 was launched. However, this author tasted the wine at a now defunct wine shop in Clerkenwell and bought a case. In 1986, I recorded: 'Splendid deep red. Sweet blackcurrant nose, with some classy oak and considerable intensity. Excellent fruit but not yet knit, and its austerity still warring with the minty fruit. New World in style but with good depth. Medium weight and perhaps lacks some grip, but quite long, with a firm finish.'

Tasted again in 1992, it remained 'deep in colour, with some maturity. Sweet and smoky on the nose, with elegant damson fruit. Soft but concentrated, this is now ready to drink, and the prominent oak gives an austere, slightly woody structure with a touch of astringency. But spicy and long, with a ripe finish.' Sadly it will be in decline now, even if you could find a bottle. Mine have long gone.

THE FACTS

Bottles produced
75,628

Composition
90% Cabernet Sauvignon, 10% Merlot

Yield
35hl/ha

Alcohol
12.5%

Release price
N/A

Price today
N/A

MARQUÉS DE RISCAL 1964

Rioja, Spain

A LEGEND BECAUSE…

The long-lived wines from Marqués de Riscal have long been benchmarks for traditional oak-aged Rioja, and certain vintages have survived in drinkable condition for a century or more. The 1964 vintage was a great one in Rioja, and Riscal was still at the top of its form. In the 1970s and 1980s the winery opted for swift expansion and thus an increase in production, which unfortunately led to a decline in quality. However, over the past two decades quality has soared again, aided by the advice of high-powered consultants from Bordeaux. The dazzling new winery built by Canadian architect Frank Gehry has returned Riscal to the centre of attention, both for wine tourism and for the quality of its wines.

LOOKING BACK

Established in 1858, the Riscal bodega soon became the last word in modernism. Built from stone, it was modelled on the cellars of Bordeaux, and the equipment was the most up-to-date imaginable at that time. The French influence was also evident in the vineyard, which has always included a substantial proportion of Cabernet Sauvignon, although Tempranillo was of course the dominant variety. Riscal has always had just over 200 hectares of its own vineyards, although its crop is supplemented by purchases from growers on long-term contracts.

THE VINTAGE

The 1964 vintage has long been widely acclaimed as one of the finest of the 20th century in the Rioja region. June was unusually chilly, and although the overall rainfall was low, there was sufficient rain during the hot summer months of July and August to prevent hydric stress. As well as being exceptional in quality, 1964 was also an abundant vintage.

THE TERROIR

The grapes would have been sourced from some of Riscal's older vineyards in Rioja Alavesa, planted on clay-limestone soils. Alavesa is the smallest of the three Rioja sub-regions, and its vineyards lie at an elevation of up to 700 metres.

THE WINE

Like almost all Rioja houses, Riscal produces a range of wines. The gran reserva was made entirely from Tempranillo, but this *cosecha* (meaning vintage) reflects Riscal's Francophile origin by containing 25% Cabernet Sauvignon. The juice was fermented in temperature-controlled, epoxy-lined cement vats. Oak of various origins has been used to age the wines, but American oak dominates here. This wine spent four years in wood before being bottled.

THE REACTION

Jancis Robinson MW tasted a recorked bottle of this wine in 2014, writing: 'Strong French oak on the nose. Sweet and spicy with smooth tannins and a lot of spicy oak. Just a hint of sweetness and brie on the nose. Impressive delicacy. Very refined.' *Decanter*'s Stephen Brook reported from the same tasting: 'Still deep red with some slight evolution on the rim, but looks very healthy. Rich, oaky vanilla nose, still has depth of fruit and power, with forthright cherry fruit. Full-bodied, quite tannic and concentrated, spicy and lively, still taut and showing freshness and drive. Mature but not tiring, and has good length.'

After a vertical tasting in 2015 of Riscal wines from 1860 onwards, Australia's Andrew Caillard MW noted: 'Medium to deep colour. Fresh red cherry, cola, praline aromas with herb notes. Round and supple with sweet red cherry and plum, sweet fruit flavours, underlying tobacco notes, rich iron-fisted tannins and marked acidity. Finishes firm and tight. Still holding well.' At the same tasting, *Decanter*'s Steven Spurrier wrote: 'Explosive yet controlled power. The oak, richness of fruit and tannins are blended together almost perfectly; a highlight in the entire tasting.'

THE FACTS

Bottles produced
74,000
Composition
75% Tempranillo, 25% Cabernet Sauvignon
Yield
26hl/ha
Alcohol
12.2%
Release price
275 pesetas
(equivalent to about €38/£32 today)
Price today
€1,750/£1,495

MARQUÉS DE MURRIETA, CASTILLO YGAY GRAN RESERVA ESPECIAL 1925

Rioja, Spain

A LEGEND BECAUSE…

Marqués de Murrieta, established by Luciano de Murrieta y Garcia-Lemoine in 1852, was the first Rioja estate to export its wines. Garcia-Lemoine bought the Ygay vineyard and built the castle of the same name. The Ygay wines became renowned for their elegance and longevity. The Gran Reserva Especial is only produced in outstanding vintages. The former King of Spain Juan Carlos I, who abdicated in June 2014, often chose Ygay wines to mark major events in his life, and this 1925 Gran Reserva Especial was selected for presentation on the day he passed the crown to his son Felipe VI.

LOOKING BACK

In 1925 the estate was still owned by the Murrieta family – it was bought by current owner Vincente Cabrián, the Conde de Creixel, in 1983. French wines were still the models for the finest Riojas, although no French estate would have contemplated the decades-long barrel-ageing characteristic of the most traditional Rioja estates. Even at Ygay, this lengthy barrel-ageing period began to be reduced from the end of the 1950s, and the 1925 represents a style of winemaking that is unlikely ever to be practised again. (Indeed, the 1917 Gran Reserva Especial spent 45 years in barrel.) Nonetheless the Cabrián family seeks to maintain the character and quality of the top Ygay bottlings without asking that consumers wait half a century before enjoying them.

THE VINTAGE

Curiously, 1925, unlike 1924, was not rated an outstanding vintage in Rioja, but produced exceptional quality at Ygay. The rainfall was no more than 400mm that year.

THE TERROIR

The vineyard sits at 485m altitude, at the southern end of Rioja Alta, close to the boundary with Rioja Baja. The total estate is 300 hectares, but the historic Ygay vineyard is smaller and today has 80-year-old vines. Its terroir is characterised by large, reddish stones. The vineyards of Rioja, and its wines, are today dominated by Tempranillo, so it's interesting that this celebrated vineyard was planted with a wide range of local varieties – with Tempranillo in the majority but still representing only half the blend. By the 1980s Tempranillo would account for almost 80% of the blend. In 1925 it is likely that the wine would have been a selection of the best lots. More recent vintages have been sourced from specific plots that, in the words of the Murrieta winemaker, give 'the most elegance, purity, longevity, complexity and depth'.

THE WINE

After harvest the grapes were fermented for 13 days in American oak vats, and the new wine remained here for a further eight months. It was then transferred to fairly new American oak barrels, where it stayed for five years. The wine was then moved into older barrels, neutralised by tartaric acid deposits on the inside, and aged for an astonishing 32 years more, before being bottled in 1964. Even at this stage the wine was not considered ready, and was given considerable bottle age before finally coming onto the market in 1973. Its longevity is partly explained by its high acidity

'The 1925 represents a style of winemaking that is unlikely ever to be practised again'

and a pH of 2.96, a figure more commonly associated with a racy white wine.

THE REACTION

A decade ago, Spanish wine expert Jesús Barquin found the wine 'delicious and appearing much younger, fruitier and tighter than anyone would expect from a wine of this age'. In 2013 an overexcited but appreciative Jeff Leve recorded: 'Served double blind, I was willing to bet it was a 1947 Right Bank Bordeaux, due to its insane, jammy, liqueur, VA, earthy, floral, liquorice, truffle, brown sugar, ripe, riper and overripe berry, plum, fig and raisin profile. It was definitely among the most incredible wines I have ever tasted – exotic, sexy and decadent in all the right ways, finishing with sensuous, pure, cherry liqueur flavours.'

THE FACTS

Bottles produced
N/A
Composition
49% Tempranillo, 19% Garnacha, 17% Mazuelo, 15% Graciano
Yield
N/A
Alcohol
13%
Release price
N/A
Price today
£608

Recaredo, Turó d'en Mota 1999

Sant Sadurní d'Anoia, Alt Penedès, Spain

A legend because...

Cava has never had a great reputation, perhaps because most consumers expect a wine of middling quality given its modest price. Over the years some top producers have attempted more serious and ageworthy bottlings, but it was Turó d'en Mota in 1999 that broke through the barrier when released in October 2008. It was the first single-vineyard Cava, cropped at very low yields, and took its name from the Mota hill, *turó* being a Catalan word for hill. Its quality was swiftly recognised, and some maintain it is the region's finest Cava.

Looking back

Recaredo was founded in 1924 by Josep Mata Capellades and specialises in single-vintage, brut nature Cavas. Its 65ha of vineyards are 40km from Barcelona in the Bitlles Valley, which experiences mild winters and hot, dry summers. Southerly breezes from the coast also help to moderate temperatures. The average annual rainfall is 530mm, most of which falls during autumn. More than half the vines are of the Xarel-lo variety. Some still wines are also produced separately under the Celler Credo label, so as to maintain the individuality of the Recaredo cavas. Today the company is run by Ton Mata, the third generation of the family, who is responsible for the innovations of recent years.

The vintage

1999 was marginally cooler than average but, more significantly, it was considerably drier, with an annual rainfall of only 393mm. The grapes were picked on 11 September.

The terroir

This single vineyard of just under 1ha was planted in 1940 on limestone soils near the village of Sant Sadurní d'Anoia. These are bush vines, trained up a stick. Since 2011, the vineyard, as well as others in the Recaredo portfolio, has been ploughed by horse to reduce compaction. All were converted to biodynamic farming in 2006, but the 1999 was made from an organically cultivated vineyard. The harvest is manual, as for all Recaredo's vineyards.

The wine

This sparkling wine spends almost 10 years on its lees (some subsequent vintages have spent 130 months on the lees) and is closed with cork. The bottles are riddled by hand. More unusually, they are disgorged by hand, after the freezing of the neck of the bottle.

The reaction

The prestigious Spanish wine guide edited by José Peñin gave this debut vintage a cautious welcome with 90 points, but more recent vintages (produced biodynamically and made in a less oxidative style) have scored far higher; Peñin himself rates this wine as one of the two top Cavas ever produced. Another Spanish wine guide, *Guía Proensa*, rated it more highly on debut: noting: 'A new dimension in the world of Cava. Shows complexity and elegance with pronounced mineral nuances. Harmonious and vigorous.'

In 2008, Joan Roca of El Celler de Can Roca (three Michelin stars; *Restaurant magazine* World's Best Restaurant 2013 and 2015) in Girona, stated: 'It is the first grand-cru Cava in history.

It's like a great white wine, but with bubbles. In spite of the 100-months-long ageing, it keeps the vividness, the intensity and the freshness of a great Cava.'

The Wine Advocate's Jay Miller reviewed the wine in 2011 and gave it a score of 96, but did not provide a tasting note. In 2014, Tom Stevenson wrote that 'the 1999 is fully mature with great concentration and muscularity'.

Margaret Rand, writing in 2016 in *The World of Fine Wine*, said: 'Ton Mata was 28 when this wine was made, and 38 when it was released – a long wait. It tastes chalky and fine, with fennel and grapefruit on the nose and honey on the palate. Lean, structured and precise; weighty, concentrated and very long.'

THE FACTS

Bottles produced
2,973
Composition
100% Xarel-lo
Yield
23hl/ha
Alcohol
12%
Release price
€95
Price today
£213

Torres, Gran Coronas Reserva Cabernet Sauvignon 1970

Penedès, Catalonia, Spain

A legend because...

In 1979, a blind-tasting in Paris, the Gault-Millau Wine Olympics, placed great French classic Cabernets such as Châteaux Latour and La Mission Haut-Brion alongside newcomers such as this wine from Torres. Known as Black Label, the 1970 was made from young vines, but the wine still triumphed, launching Torres onto the international stage.

Looking back

The firm of Torres was founded in 1870, and in 1962 a youthful Miguel A Torres took over the winery. Forward-looking and open-minded, in 1964 he planted international varieties in some of the Penedès vineyards. The Cabernet Sauvignon cuttings came from Jean Leon, another Penedès pioneer, and it's rumoured that its source was the Médoc: Châteaux Lafite and La Lagune. Moreover, some cuttings came from a nursery in Montpellier. Planting French varieties was a controversial decision, and even Torres' father had strong reservations about the wisdom of planting Cabernet. 1970 was the first vintage of the Black Label, which from the 1995 vintage on was renamed after the vineyard, Mas La Plana.

Now fourth-generation president of Familia Torres, Miguel A Torres recalls: 'The wine was so different, it immediately gained a reputation, especially by triumphing over some of the best French wines. What a lot of people don't know is that it was my mother's idea to send Mas La Plana to the 1979 tasting.'

The vintage

An outstanding year in Penedès as well as Rioja, 1970 offered an ideal growing season, although the crop was small.

The terroir

29ha of Cabernet Sauvignon are planted in the Pacs sub-region of central Penedès. The original plantings were on deep, yellowish grey-brown alluvial soils that are well drained and have a moderate water holding capacity. The soil is made up of layers of gravel, sand and clay. The elevation of 225m ensures relatively cool night-time temperatures.

The wine

The grapes were fermented in stainless steel tanks; indeed Torres was almost certainly the first Spanish wine producer to install them. The wine was then aged six months in new American oak, then in older barrels for a year more. It was not until the 1990 vintage that Torres decided to age the wine entirely in French barriques.

The reaction

Stephen Brook tasted the wine in 1993: 'Fairly deep red but becoming pale and russet on the rim. Light liquorice nose, becoming attenuated but still attractive... still powerful but perhaps the fruit is in retreat.'

In 2008, Tom Cannavan noted: 'Lovely old wine vegetal sweetness on the nose, notes of dried blood, truffle, prune and that echo of very sweet black fruit. On the palate lovely sweetness still, masses of clove and spice, and still a fine core of redcurrant and cherry acidity. Lovely soft, truffly finish.'

In 2015 in Beijing, Edward Ragg wrote: 'Tertiary aromas of roasted meats, mushroom, leather, combining with barrel-matured notes of coffee, cocoa, chocolate, now caramelised with age... complex. On the palate a profound tannic structure, but still with this wonderful core of fruit coming through... Lively acidity, quite vibrant fruit – this wine is not "dried out" in any sense – with mellowing chewy tannins and a long, layered finish.'

THE FACTS

Bottles produced
54,000

Composition
70% Cabernet Sauvignon, 20% Tempranillo, 10% Monastrell

Yield
55HL/HA

Alcohol
12.4%

Release price
1,650 pesetas

Price today
€85

OTHER OLD WORLD WINES

A mixed bag, with so many regions and styles from which to choose, but each of the wines selected fully justifies its inclusion. Perhaps Musar lacks the polish of the best Bordeaux and Rhônes, but it has personality in spades and has been a firm favourite of wine drinkers for decades. And mature Tokaj has a reputation going back for centuries.

CASA FERREIRINHA, BARCA VELHA 1966

Douro, Portugal

A LEGEND BECAUSE...

The late technical director of Port producer Ferreira, Fernando Nicolau de Almeida, long aspired to create a top red wine from the Douro Valley, so he went to Bordeaux to see how it could be done. The result was Barca Velha, and the first vintage was in 1952. It was soon recognised as an outstanding red wine – arguably Portugal's finest – though there was little competition at the time. Barca Velha is only released in top vintages, and until 1966 the only years released were 1952, 1954, 1957, 1958, 1964 and 1965.

LOOKING BACK

Almeida knew that he had to source his grapes from the Douro Superior, not far from the Spanish border, but in the 1950s and 1960s vineyards in this torrid zone were scarce. At the time, wine from the Douro meant a fortified wine. There was production of table wines, too, often from cooperatives based far from the prestigious quintas flanking the river, but most were mediocre. Barca Velha and its second wine, Casa Ferreirinha Reserva Especial, were the shining exceptions.

THE VINTAGE

Twenty shippers declared 1966 as a Port vintage. The winter was normal, with sufficient rainfall, and between April and September the weather was dry. The summer was hot, but not so hot that the fruit became raisined, and some rain in September probably aided maturation. However, declared Port vintages are not necessarily great vintages for Barca Velha, as a different quality of fruit is required for a balanced dry wine.

THE TERROIR

The grapes for Barca Velha were always grown on schist soils in the Douro Superior, initially mostly at Quinta do Vale do Meão, near Pocinho. In the 1970s, this source was replaced by Quinta da Leda and other sites. The main variety used for Barca Velha was Tinta Roriz, though small quantities of wine from other traditional Douro varieties, such as Touriga Franca or Touriga Nacional, were blended in. The grapes were picked at dawn, before the heat of the day peaked at around 40°C.

THE WINE

Although the wine is fermented today in modern stainless steel tanks, in the 1960s the grapes were vinified in wooden vats. There was no temperature control during the early vintages, so the must had to be cooled using blocks of ice bought from a fisherman's village close to Oporto. The new wine was transported to the Ferreira lodges in Vila Nova de Gaia, across from Porto, and there aged in new, mostly Portuguese oak. No immediate decision was made on whether any vintage was worthy of being released as Barca Velha. The wine was given prolonged bottle age before its eventual release in 1977, giving the winemakers ample time to assess its quality as it slowly evolved. If it was not deemed worthy of the top label, it was released under the name of Reserva Especial at a lower price.

THE REACTION

Sogrape's head winemaker Luis Sottomayor, who has worked at Casa Ferreirinha since 1989, selected the 1966 vintage as probably the finest Barca Velha after drinking the wine in a vertical tasting in Brazil in 2008. He found the colour immensely deep, and the wine both structured and fresh. In 1998, *Decanter*'s Port expert Richard Mayson declared the 1966 to be 'an extraordinary wine, still upright and concentrated, with a touch of tobacco box and the long sinewy finish that has become Barca Velha's hallmark'. More recently, in 2014 he wrote: 'Still relatively youthful in appearance... a little hollow (or just closed) initially on the nose, a hint of tar and tobacco, a touch rustic in style with the alcohol evident, but some finesse underlying; wonderful sinewy, leathery fruit, gravelly tannins underlying, still quite tough and holding together very well.'

THE FACTS

Bottles produced
N/A
Composition
50% Tinta Roriz, 40% Touriga Nacional and Touriga Franca, and 10% Tinta Barroca, Tinto Cão and Tinta Amarela
Yield
40hl/ha
Alcohol
12%
Release price
N/A
Price today
£395

CHATEAU MUSAR 1964

Bekaa Valley, Lebanon

A LEGEND BECAUSE…

Chateau Musar is a distinctive wine, for many years the only one that could demonstrate the potential of the vineyards of Lebanon. It also, in certain vintages, has a remarkable capacity to age. But the vineyards lie within the Bekaa Valley, which frequently became a war zone during Lebanon's seemingly endless civil strife. With its imperfect infrastructure and relative isolation, Lebanon can never have been an easy place to produce a wine with an eye on the international market, and military and terrorist action between the vineyards and Beirut offered an unwelcome complication. In 1983, the harvest had to be postponed for a month because of fighting in the valley. Only one vintage (1976) had to be abandoned.

LOOKING BACK

Gaston Hochar founded Musar in the 1930s, and in 1959 handed the reins to his son Serge, who had studied with Emile Peynaud in Bordeaux and ran the estate until his accidental death on New Year's Eve in 2014. The Hochars were not dependent on the winery for their living, as they had a thriving construction business. But Serge was no dilettante, and wine for him was a consuming passion. Nor was he a formulaic winemaker, with each vintage a variation on the theme provided by the grape varieties and terroir. In 1984 he was named the first Decanter Man of the Year.

THE VINTAGE

Civil war broke out in 1975, so the 1964 vintage was produced in less traumatic times. Musar was the only producer of Lebanese wine then, so few records of climatic conditions exist. But it appears that the Bekaa Valley enjoyed a very good summer that allowed all three varieties planted to reach full maturation.

THE TERROIR

The organic vineyards, both owned and leased, are planted in three villages in the Bekaa Valley: Aana, Ammiq and Kefraya. Soils are rocky and vary in fertility and richness; Ammiq has more gravelly soil. Then as now, Musar is an unusual blend of bush-vine Cabernet Sauvignon, Cinsault and Carignan. Elevation (about 915m) and cool nights are key factors in the wine's balance and ageability. Cabernet usually forms its backbone, with exact proportions in the final blend varying from year to year.

THE WINE

The grapes are transported, gunfire permitting, to the winery 70km away in Ghazir, a village perched high above Beirut. The fruit from each vineyard is fermented separately with wild yeasts in cement tanks for five weeks or so. After fermentation the wine is aged, still separately, in those vats for about nine months before being aged in Nevers barriques for 10 to 14 months. The wines are then returned to vats, blended and further aged in cement before being bottled at the end of the third year. There is no fining or filtration. Bottles are stored for up to three years before release. A great vintage, such as the 1964, often has a baked character reflecting the climate, but also great complexity in the form of herbal and truffley aromas and flavours. The wines can be

'A great year often has a baked character as well as herbal, truffley complexity'

deceptively pale, and can display high levels of volatile acidity and traces of oxidation, which admirers easily overlook.

THE REACTION

Tasting notes on the 1964 are scarce, probably because a decade or two would go by before Musar attracted the attention of wine writers and collectors. It was tasted in 1986 by Michael Broadbent, who recalls: 'Nose like Turkish Delight, delicious flavour. Impressive, Bordeaux-style, fleshy.' In 2013, an avid New York collector of 1964 vintages from around the world declared it to be 'the youngest 1964 vintage I have ever tasted'.

THE FACTS

Bottles produced
About 72,000

Composition
N/A

Yield
N/A

Alcohol
19%

Release price
45p

Price today
£302–£951 per bottle

ROYAL TOKAJI, NYULÁSZÓ ASZÚ 6 PUTTONYOS 1993

Tokaj, Hungary

A LEGEND BECAUSE...

After decades of Communist state monopoly, the Hungarian wine industry underwent gradual privatisation after 1990. Royal Tokaji was one of the very first to benefit from international investment. Initial vintages of that decade were not exceptional, but ideal conditions in 1993 allowed new producers to make Tokaji of high quality. Although vintages of the early 1990s have not aged particularly well, 1993 has stood the test of time.

LOOKING BACK

Royal Tokaji was founded by Hugh Johnson, Peter Vinding-Diers and other investors, who acquired some outstanding vineyards and hired István Szepsy as consultant winemaker. Szepsy was profoundly knowledgeable about traditional techniques for the production of Tokaji Aszú. From the outset there was a conflict between an oxidative style of winemaking, misleadingly thought of as 'traditional', and a more modern approach that ignored the rulebook and permitted experimentation with fermentation techniques as well as ageing in newer barrels. Royal Tokaji would prove innovative without pursuing an oxidative style.

THE VINTAGE

Warm weather at flowering ensured a good crop, and the balmy summer that followed brought the vines to full maturity. Autumnal mists brought an early onset of botrytis, allowing the production of exceptional aszú wines.

THE TERROIR

The Royal Tokaji founders relied on historic vineyard classification maps from the late 17th century when buying or leasing parcels of vines. Nyulászó had been classified as first growth, and the company acquired 12ha (today expanded to 18ha) of southeast-facing vines at an elevation of 200m. The topsoils are volcanic, and below lies a complex blend of clay, calcareous loam, tufa and quartz.

THE WINE

Aszú means a wine made from hand-picked botrytised grapes. A paste is made from compressed aszú grapes and added to a base wine, which re-ferments. This results in a wine with high residual sugar, acidity and extract. The puttonyos number reflects how many 20kg hods of berries are added, and the higher the number the greater the intensity and sweetness of the finished wine. In recent decades the system has simply reflected the proportion of berries, rather than a counting of hods. After fermentation, the wine was aged for three years in small casks of Hungarian oak. At bottling the wine had 218g/L of residual sugar and an acidity level of 10.3g/L.

THE REACTION

In a 1997 review, *The Wine Spectator* found the wine 'complex and multilayered... clean and pure, with loads of tropical, dried apricot and dried fig, vanilla bean, ginger snaps and curry... Bravo!' A year later, Stephen Brook relished the wine's 'lovely racy honeyed nose, smoky, dried-fruit aromas. Lean, firm, robust, voluptuous, with fine acidity giving tangy citric tones. Creamy, complex and very long.'

Richard Hemming MW reported in 2017: 'Caramel, milk

chocolate, mint, pear and ginger – the list goes on. Fractal complexity and endless persistence... Captivating, profound, extraordinary.' In the same year, Peter Richards MW wrote in *World of Fine Wine*: '...the palate explodes in a burst of vigour and juicy energy, full of tangy acidity and bittersweet candied fruit... somewhat old-school, but with plenty of life and swagger in the bones.'

In 2019, Neal Martin said in *Vinous*: 'Floral nose features yellow plum, dried honey and quince notes that blossom in the glass... well balanced, offering quince, marmalade and dried orange peel toward the finish. This significantly improves with aeration. Perhaps the first really great post-1990 Tokaji.'

THE FACTS

Bottles produced
12,007
Composition
Furmint-Hárslevelű
Yield
0.5hl/ha
Alcohol
10.7%
Release price
US $77
Price today
£234/50cl

SZEPSY, TOKAJI ASZÚ 6 PUTTONYOS 1999

Tokaj, Hungary

A LEGEND BECAUSE...

In 1989, István Szepsy became the winemaker for Royal Tokaji, one of the first foreign-investor companies to produce Tokaji after Hungary threw off Communist rule. The wines were highly acclaimed, but in 1992 Szepsy left to focus on his own label. Even during the Soviet era, he had been able to make small quantities of Tokaji, but he was keen to expand. By 1997 he had about 9ha in some of the region's best sites. 1999 was an excellent year, and those who tasted it were dazzled.

LOOKING BACK

After privatisation of the vineyards in Tokaj, it was hard for the early investors to find qualified winemakers. Many of the region's traditional production methods were no longer understood, let alone practised. Szepsy explains: 'We all knew that new methods had to be found, but there was no fund of knowledge and experience from the past. We were starting from scratch.' One of his 17th-century ancestors had been credited with 'discovering' how Tokaji Aszú should be made and Szepsy realised that mass-produced wines, sweetened with concentrated must, were false to the authentic style of Aszú. Royal Tokaji's Hugh Johnson and Peter Vinding-Diers encouraged Szepsy to recover those methods and try to restore the region's lost reputation. Everything had to be revised, from identifying top vineyards, to farming to vinification and ageing.

THE VINTAGE

A fine growing season led to very ripe grapes, and harvest took place during the second half of October. Botrytis came in stages, so conscientious growers had to pick selectively. The wines showed not only exemplary richness, but purity of fruit and balance. Szepsy was initially cautious about the quality of the vintage, but his own wines proved him wrong.

THE TERROIR

Most of Szepsy's vineyards are close to Mád, with parcels in outstanding sites such as Nyúlászó, Király, Szent Tamás and Betsek. However, in 1993 Szepsy stopped producing single-vineyard wines, and blended the aszú berries. When planting or replanting, he favoured massal selections of old-vine Furmint to ensure small bunches. In 1992 he began green-harvesting. No fertilisers are used and he prunes short to manage yields, which, for aszú wines, are around 4hl/ha. The grapes are picked berry by berry. Each vine yields roughly half a glass of aszú wine.

THE WINE

To make aszú wines, a paste of botrytised berries is added to a dry base wine for a second fermentation. Szepsy uses late-picked (but not botrytised) berries to produce his base wine, as he wants a high level of ripeness. The grapes are crushed, given brief skin contact, then fermented with natural yeasts in Hungarian oak barrels, 25% new. The wine is aged for 28-34 months in barrel. The 1999 was released with 228g/l of residual sugar.

THE REACTION

In 2003 Stephen Tanzer wrote: 'Apricot, orange rind and

smoky botrytis aromas and flavours dominate, but with fascinating floral, spicy and carnal notes... the most intense acidity, ravishing complexity, and ultimately the most refinement and delicacy.'

Jancis Robinson MW tasted the wine in 2010. 'Deep reddish tawny. It's losing the protective reductive elements and looks a bit old. Still tastes very fresh with massive acidity. Not massively sweet. Dried, candied apricots! Tingly.'

In 2018 Stephen Brook found the wine still radiant: 'The nose is intense, with complex aromas of crème brûlée and marmalade. The attack is lean thanks to its high acidity, but it has a silky texture. Pungent and spicy flavours of oranges and barley sugar. It's surprisingly fresh and citric without losing its caramel character. Amazingly persistent.'

THE FACTS

Bottles produced
8,000
Composition
70% Furmint, 30% Hárslevelű
Yield
4hl/h
Alcohol
10.5%
Release price
£80
Price today
£200/50cl

PORT AND MADEIRA

When it comes to vintage port, we are spoilt for choice, given the very high standards maintained over centuries by the top shippers. All these ports fully merit their inclusion. The only regret is that there wasn't space for more vintage Madeiras, given their amazing longevity and scarcity, and varied styles from saline and dry to unctuously sweet.

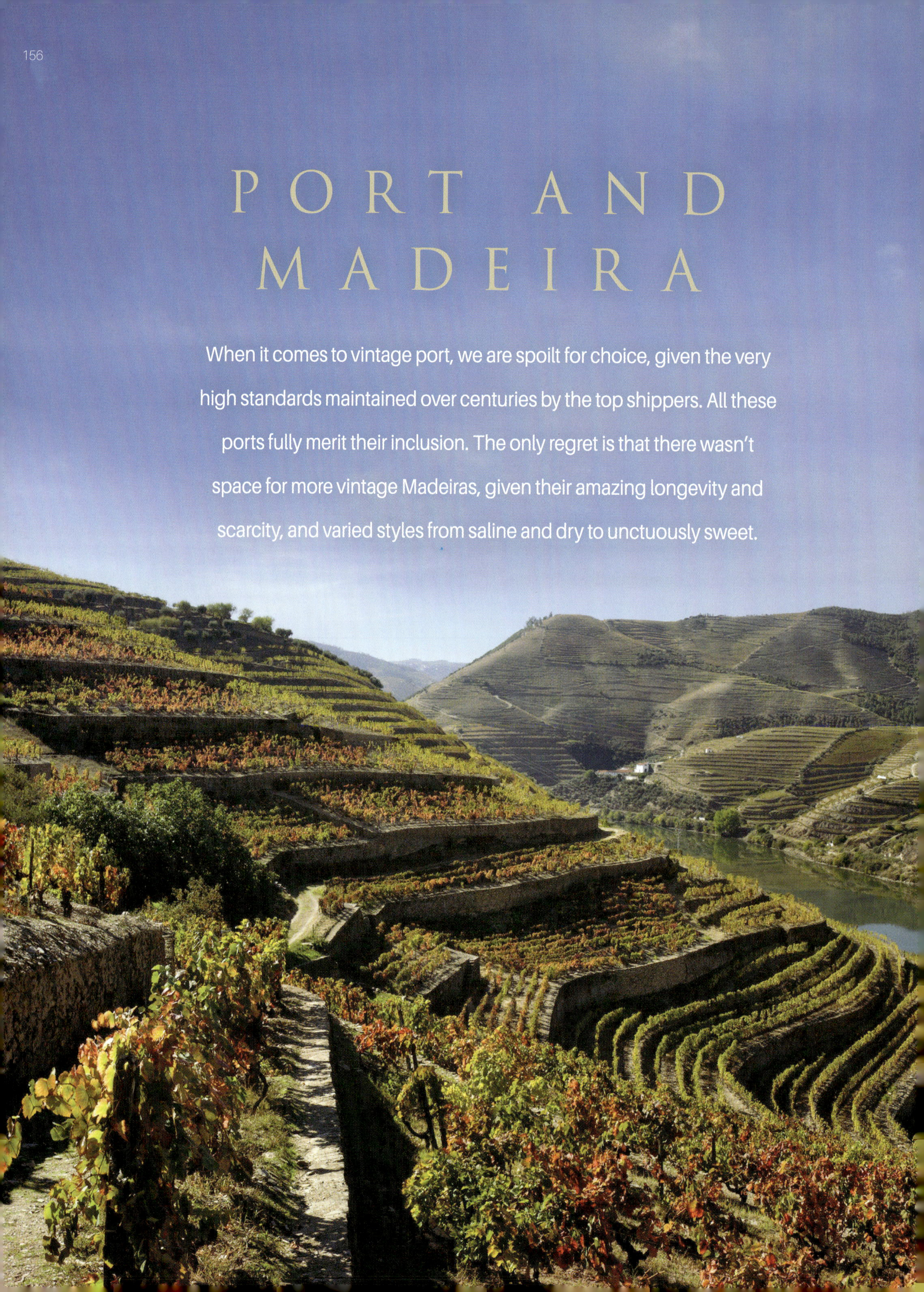

HM BORGES, TERRANTEZ 1862

Madeira, Portugal

A LEGEND BECAUSE...

Michael Broadbent says the 1862 was not only the best vintage of Terrantez ever made but 'the greatest of all Madeiras'. Scarcity has always given wines from Terrantez a high reputation, but few examples have proved more persuasive than this. Given the near extinction of the variety in the 20th century, remaining bottles from the 19th century have been especially prized.

LOOKING BACK

This wine was not originally made by Borges as the firm was only founded in 1877, by Henrique Menezes Borges. Like other firms on the island, Borges bought up stocks of old wines from other companies and from private collectors – this Terrantez was sourced from TT De Camara Lomelino. One of Borges' activities was to supply other shippers with these wines, and many bottles of the 1862 are from stocks bought by the firm Leacock. The Borges company still exists and is run by the fourth generation of the founding family.

THE VINTAGE

In 1851 Madeira's vineyards were devastated by oidium (powdery mildew), which destroyed most of the island's vines. By the early 1860s the vineyards were just beginning to recover but production in 1862 was still very low.

THE TERROIR

The vineyards from which this wine was made belonged to João Alexandrino Santos, but he owned many properties so the precise origin is not known. It was not unusual for wine companies to buy old stocks of finished wine, either to blend them or to age them further as vintage wines. This was no exception.

Terrantez, which combines high acidity with richness of fruit, is a tricky variety to grow, but was acclaimed in the 18th and 19th centuries as the source for some of the greatest Madeiras. It was originally grown near Lamego in the Douro valley but phylloxera led to its virtual disappearance, so 20th-century Terrantez wines are exceedingly rare. The variety is gradually being replanted, but it is unlikely that, even today, more than a few hectares are under vine.

THE WINE

Like all vintage Madeiras this would have spent decades in casks, subject to extremes of summer and winter temperatures to give an even oxidation. The wine would eventually be transferred to demijohns and bottled on demand, or at a slow pace so as to maintain stocks for decades. Borges' 1877 Terrantez was still in demijohns in 2014, but the 1862 was moved to demijohns in 1905, bottled in 1936.

THE REACTION

Michael Broadbent in 1994 recalled he had tasted the wine five times, noting 'an almost overwhelming bouquet and flavour, high toned, tangy, scented, power and delicacy magically combined... Sweeter than some Terrantez, with slight touch of singed caramel and chocolate.' Retasting the wine in 2010, he found his earlier note still valid. This was also one of the very few wines to which he awarded 'At best six stars' in *Vintage Wine*.

Richard Mayson in his 2015 book *Madeira*, has a note from 2009:

'The greatest of all Madeiras'

Michael Broadbent

'Like a good old amontillado but without the tang, candied peel with a touch of coffee and butterscotch; a slightly cask finish.'

Peter Reutter, reporting on a tasting in 2012 on *Madeirawineguide.com*, noted: 'Misleadingly harmonious at first, but quickly a bitter Terrantez backbone and lots of acidity burst through, together with caramel and hints of coffee.' In his book on Madeira (2014 edition), Alex Liddell was captivated: 'Astonishingly full and assertive bouquet [of] candied peel, coconut and kiwi fruit; immensely weighty on the palate... but behind the opulence, a steely backbone of acidity; almost medicinally dry, with a bitter finish and length which goes on and on... Sensational. A giant among giants.'

THE FACTS

Bottles produced
N/A
Composition
100% Terrantez
Yield
N/A
Alcohol
20%
Release price
N/A
Price today
Expect to pay at least £1,800

COCKBURN'S VINTAGE PORT 1947

Douro Valley, Portugal

A LEGEND BECAUSE...

Although the 1947 vintage was not that widely declared, it was one in which the Cockburn's team had the highest confidence. The 1948, recalls family member Peter Cobb, was a bigger wine but the 1947, although relatively light in body, had just the elegance and breed that were most sought after by the blending team. In his 1978 book, *Port: An Introduction to its History and Delights*, Wyndham Fletcher, who worked at Cockburn's from 1930 to 1975, wrote: 'Possibly because the [1947] wines were light in colour and body they have never quite achieved their due recognition. The fine, delicate quality reminiscent of the 1900s has tended to be overlooked.' Yet the 'light' 1947 has stood the test of time and is still drinking well, if with inevitable bottle variation.

LOOKING BACK

The company was founded in 1815 by Robert Cockburn and, as it evolved, other partners were taken into the firm. It continued as a family enterprise until 1962, when it was bought by Harvey's of Bristol, which in turn was bought by Allied-Lyons and later renamed Allied-Domecq. These weren't the best decades for Cockburn's, but in the 1940s it was still a name to be reckoned with. Later, the company would show little interest in vintage declarations, focusing instead on the high-volume Special Reserve Ruby. Cockburn's decided to skip both 1977 and 1980, though it returned to the market with its 1983. In 2010 the somewhat moribund company was bought by the Symington family.

In the 1940s there were four partners: Reggie Cobb, his cousins John Smithes and Felix Vigne, and Trevor Heath. Vigne and Heath were the principal blenders for the vintage Ports, but it was Smithes – one of the great Port tasters of his generation – who would have had the final say on the blend. It is ironic, given the later decline of the brand, that in the 1940s Cockburn's was the highest-priced vintage Port.

THE VINTAGE

The spring was wet but followed by a hot summer. A little rain shortly before harvest brought the grapes to full ripeness. The grapes were picked from late September onwards. Eleven shippers declared the vintage.

THE TERROIR

The principal source for Cockburn's vintage Ports was Quinta dos Canais, a 96-hectare, south-facing property that stands directly opposite Taylor's famous Vargellas vineyard. Peter Cobb, the nephew of Reggie Cobb, believes it is likely that the 1947 would also have included fruit from Quinta do Tua (today part of the Graham's holdings) and from Quinta da Gricha, a property in the Rio Torto Valley now owned by Churchill Graham. It is highly likely that most if not all the plantings in these quintas would have been field blends, making it impossible to determine the proportion used of the principal Port varieties.

THE WINE

The grapes would have been trodden and then fermented in lagares. There was no temperature control. Then the wine was run off into oak vats, and the fermentation arrested by the

> 'The light, delicate 1947s have never achieved due recognition'
>
> Wyndham Fletcher

addition of pure grape spirit. Michael Broadbent confirms that at the time of declaration, the 1947 was regarded as a relatively light wine. The trade found the wine very attractive but doubted that it had great ageing potential. However, the vintage has lasted well, though most wines are probably by now at or just past their peak.

THE REACTION

In 2002, Broadbent recorded: 'Fairly pale, little red though pink/red highlights; pure liquorice, harmonious, well evolved, firm, good flavour and flesh, smooth texture, dry finish, delicious aftertaste.' After the wine was poured at a retrospective tasting in 2012, Jancis Robinson MW commented: 'Pale tawny with definite yellow at the rim. Prunes and strong dried-fruit notes. Dried citrus peel. Appetising. A tiny bit of spirit on the finish.' At the same tasting, Steven Spurrier noted: 'Fragrant, dried red fruits, slightly "burnt" from the heat at harvest, but with remarkable sweetness. Still holding well.' Port expert Richard Mayson was more critical: 'Lime marmalade aromas, fragrant yet mellow. Sweet and honeyed, retaining some peppery tannins, with length and elegance though drying out on the finish.'

THE FACTS

Bottles produced
About 72,000

Alcohol
19%

Composition
N/A

Release price
45p

Yield
N/A

Price today
£302-£951 per bottle

Dow's Vintage Port 1955

Douro, Portugal

A legend because...

There was a plethora of excellent Ports made in this vintage, but Dow's has long stood out for its elegance as well as richness. William Warre, who sold these wines for many years, described them as 'rather more delicate, feminine wines' that 'seldom let anyone down in quality'. They age well, even if in their youth they seem less structured and powerful than some other well-known Ports. They are also a touch drier than some of the more sumptuous Ports, but that doesn't impede their ageing ability.

Looking back

Silva & Cosens, an Anglo-Portuguese shipper, bought the established Dow's brand in 1877, and one of the shareholders was a member of the Warre family. Warre's own Port was owned by the Symington family, who invested in Silva & Cosens, and by 1961 had become the sole owner. There were no significant changes in the wine's style during this period.

The vintage

This was the most widely declared vintage since 1927, so consistent was the evaluation of the wines by 26 shippers. The spring months were unusually hot and led to a good flowering. The summer was slightly warmer than average, and the little rain that fell sporadically proved beneficial as it quenched the thirst of dehydrating berries. The fine weather continued into the autumn. The resulting wines were rich but so well balanced that a long life in the cellar seemed certain.

The terroir

Like all vintage Ports, the Dow's is a blend of different grape varieties from different vineyards. However, the mainstay of the blend is fruit from the Symington family's Quinta do Bomfim, close to Pinhão, and Quinta da Senhora da Ribeira in the isolated Douro Superior sub-region, farther upstream. The proportions of each vineyard's contribution varied from vintage to vintage. The grape varieties were then field-blended and would have included Touriga Franca, Tinta Barroca, Tinta Roriz, Tinta Amarela, Tinta Francisca, Tinto Cão and a small proportion of Touriga Nacional, which was then much less widely planted than it is today.

The wine

At this time virtually all of the wine would have been foot-trodden in lagares, the stone tanks traditionally used to crush the grapes and begin their fermentation. The fermentation period would have been slightly longer than for most other vintage Ports, and this accounts for the slightly drier style of Dow's, as the yeasts would have consumed more sugar. After 18 months of storage in large wooden vats (to minimise the wood's influence), the wine was bottled without fining or filtration.

The reaction

Michael Broadbent frequently tasted Dow's Ports between the mid-1960s and 1998. In 1994 he noted that the 1955 had 'a silkily tannic texture' but in later years bottles were 'tending to dry out although very flavoury, with a lingering finish. Vanilla and liquorice noted, then a touch of acidity creeping up.'

In 1990, James Suckling recorded: 'Plenty of fruit and a solid backbone. Brilliant ruby-garnet, with a rich tomato and cassis nose, full-bodied, with tons of fruit flavours, medium tannins and a rich finish.' Nine years later he tasted it again: 'I have always loved this wine. Dark ruby in color, with a brick rim and lovely aromas of cherry, blackberry and flowers. Full-bodied and sweet, with loads of fruit and a long, long finish. Still in a holding pattern.'

Richard Mayson adored the wine in 2008: 'Still very deep in colour, only just browning on the rim; extraordinarily fresh, powerful, tight-knit bitter chocolate aromas, minty fruit; very fine and focused, dry in characteristic Dow style, remarkably fresh, ripe, minty fruit. Absolutely delicious. Just about as good as it gets.'

THE FACTS

Bottles produced
N/A
Composition
Principally Quinta do Bomfim, with an important Senhora da Ribeira component and possibly a very small contribution from Quinta do Zimbro
Yield
N/A
Alcohol
20%
Release price
£1
Price today
£360

FONSECA 1963

Douro, Portugal

A LEGEND BECAUSE...

This excellent and abundant vintage produced wines that immediately attracted the interest of Port lovers worldwide, and Fonseca was soon recognised as one of the finest wines of the vintage. Almost all shippers declared the vintage. Michael Broadbent describes the 1963 as 'consistently beautiful... one of the top '63s, and one of the best-ever Fonsecas'.

LOOKING BACK

Fonseca was founded in 1815 and declared its first vintage in 1840. There followed a stream of magnificent vintage Ports such as the 1868 and the 1927, one of the finest ports ever made. In 1949 Taylor, Fladgate & Yeatman bought Fonseca. The stylistic consistency of Fonseca Ports is often attributed to the fact that they have been made by six successive generations of the Guimaraens family, currently represented by winemaker David Guimaraens. His father, Bruce Guimaraens, a much respected, larger-than-life personality, was the winemaker from 1960 onwards.

THE VINTAGE

A frigid winter preceded a very dry summer, with light rain refreshing the crop in September. All this guaranteed an excellent harvest, and a copious one too. Summer was relatively cool, delivering a late-flowering and slow-ripening season that gave the wines an exceptional elegance, although they are less conspicuously fruity than the 1970s. Harvest was late, taking place in the second week of October, when hot weather had returned.

THE TERROIR

In the 1960s grapes would have been sourced from properties with a long association with Fonseca. The most important was Quinta do Cruzeiro on the east bank of the Pinhão river, which has supplied the firm since the late 19th century; it was subsequently purchased by the house in 1973. Quinta Santo Antônio, also in the Pinhão valley, often provided more aromatic and vibrant wines to balance the richly fruity character of the Cruzeiro grapes.

THE WINE

Fonseca vintage Ports are made in much the same way as all other vintage Ports, the significant difference being the source of the grapes. Fruit is foot-trodden in lagares in the traditional way, fortified, and then aged in large old vats in the lodges in Gaia, across from Oporto, before a relatively early bottling and release the second year after the harvest.

THE REACTION

In 1989 James Suckling acclaimed the wine: 'A grand slam. Masses of fruit, full tannins and an extremely long finish.' In the same year Robert Parker wrote: 'The 1963, one of the great modern-day classics of vintage Port, is an incredibly aromatic, sublime, majestic Port that simply defines Fonseca's style perfectly.'

In 1998 Michael Broadbent found the wine 'medium-deep, richly coloured, cinnamon and cress fragrance; still sweet, fairly assertive, shapely, lissom.'

Stephen Brook in 2012 noted, 'Prunes and wood on the nose, which is also orangey and floral. Very sweet and intense, with a silky texture, fine acidity... and an evolved character.'

In 2013 Neal Martin assessed a bottle from the Fonseca cellars and declared: 'This is a sublime Fonseca that will last another two or three decades with ease.'

In 2015 Richard Mayson compared two bottles side by side: 'The first, brick red, fragrant and floral, soft, sweet and elegant with gentle tannic grip, but soft and redolent of a nutty tawny on the finish. The second, seemingly identical in colour but with the wonderful focus and dark chocolate intensity that I would expect from this great vintage. Spellbinding depth, like a black hole, with bitter chocolate and thick-cut marmalade in perfect balance.'

THE FACTS

Bottles produced
N/A
Composition
N/A
Yield
Around 20hl/ha
Alcohol
21%
Release price
N/A
Price today
£260-£341

QUINTA DE NOVAL, NACIONAL 1931

Douro, Portugal

A LEGEND BECAUSE...

There is no shortage of great Port-producing houses, although most of the best known, such as Graham's or Taylor's, have always been in British hands. Quinta da Noval is the great exception. This beautifully located property has always made memorable Ports, but it's the rare Nacional bottlings – from a small parcel of ungrafted vines – that set the pulses of Port lovers and collectors racing. Nacional 1931 has entered the history books as the most prized of all vintage Ports. Its supreme quality defies the notion that the oldest vines give the greatest wines, as in 1931 the vines were a mere five or six years old.

LOOKING BACK

When António José da Silva bought Quinta da Noval in 1894, the vineyards had been almost destroyed by phylloxera, and had to be replanted. However, da Silva retained 1.8 hectares of vines on their own roots, and the wines produced here were kept apart from the regular bottlings and released, in exceptional vintages, as Nacional. By the time the 1931 vintage was ready to be declared, da Silva was handing over the property to his son-in-law Luis Vasconcelos Porto. Vasconcelos Porto was impressed by the wine's quality but unsure that he could sell it, since sales of the great 1927 vintage had been sluggish, but it was one of his British importers who convinced him to declare it. Family disputes later led to the sale of the estate to its present owners, AXA Millésimes of France, in 1993.

THE VINTAGE

1931 was not an acclaimed vintage for Port; only two other shippers declared it. The reason had little to do with the quality of the wines: it was the shippers' misfortune that the vintage came in the middle of the worldwide economic slump.

THE TERROIR

The Nacional vines – no more than 5,000 – were planted on northwest-facing terraces along the drive leading to the house. And although they are ungrafted, they are not ancient: there are vines over 60 years old in the parcel, but the average age is around 35 years. When they are no longer productive, they are replaced. Unlike the rest of the Noval vines, they are not replanted on American rootstocks, but remain on their own roots. The fruit character is very different from the grapes used for the regular Noval vintage Port, as the foliage growth is less vigorous and the berries are far smaller, giving very low yields – about half those for the main Noval vineyards – and thus intense concentration of flavour and higher tannin levels.

THE WINE

After harvest the grapes are foot-trodden in a small lagar. The Nacional grapes are vinified separately every year, but the wine is rarely released. During its traditional ageing in used pipes for about two years, the wine is continuously assessed. If it fails to measure up to Nacional standards, it is not declared.

THE REACTION

For Michael Broadbent, this is 'the Everest of vintage Ports'. In 1982 he said: 'I noted its amazing high-toned bouquet which reminded me of eau de cologne, Armagnac, and a sort of ultra-refined liquorice. Although only medium-sweet, it was incredibly full-bodied, a rich, bittersweet wine, spicy, of great

'Its supreme quality defies the notion that the oldest vines give the greatest wines'

length.' James Suckling in 1989 noted: 'The Port is still incredibly rich and youthful... with a focused chocolate and cherry nose, medium-bodied, with great balance, a superb concentration of fruit and a neverending finish.' In 2002 Clive Coates MW summarised his six encounters with the wine over the previous decade: 'The colour is still an intense black-purple. The nose is creamy rich, crammed with very high quality fruit, and on the palate there is an intensity coupled with a class which seems effortless. But the finish! Few wines have this length and this complexity. A really very great wine.' In 2004 Port blogger Roy Hersh wrote: 'Amazing depth of flavours prevailed... overwhelming intensity to the sweetness of the juice.' Wine collector Cary Feibleman wrote, in an article on his favourite wines in *The Underground Wineletter*: 'One of those 21-out-of-20 point wines for incredible richness, concentration, complexity and a finish that goes on for five minutes.'

THE FACTS

Bottles produced
About 2,500

Composition
Touriga Francesa, Touriga Nacional, Tinta Roriz, Sousão

Yield
13 hl/ha

Alcohol
20%

Release price
N/A

Price today
An English-bottled example sold at Christie's in 2006 for £4,840

Sandeman Vintage Port 1945

Douro Valley, Portugal

A legend because...

With its brilliantly memorable logo of a don in a wide-brimmed hat and cape, Sandeman has long been one of the drinks industry's most recognised brands. Quality has not always matched the dashing image, yet there were some magnificent wines produced in the first half of the 20th century. Sandeman certainly triumphed in 1945. Well-stored bottles remain vibrant and drinkable to this day.

Looking back

Shipping its wines to Britain since 1790, Sandeman was family-owned until 1980 when it was acquired by Seagram, and since 2001 it has been owned by Portugal's Sogrape. The 1960s to 1980s were a tricky period, probably because of excessive production and a loss of contracts with some exceptional quintas. However, in the 1940s and as recently as 1963 some exceptional wines were produced. Recent vintages such as 2011 and 2016 show a welcome return to form. Earlier this year George Sandeman recalled: 'The 1945 vintage has a special place in my heart. It was the vintage my father contributed to the Factory House when he joined.'

The vintage

The growing season was outstanding, and although the second half of August was cool and wet, hot weather returned in time for harvest, which Sandeman began on 10 September. The grapes were small and thick-skinned. The second week of September was torrid, and Sandeman recorded slow fermentations, delivering deeply coloured and rich wines of very high quality and immense concentration.

The terroir

As with most vintage Ports, the grapes are sourced from company-owned vineyards as well as other quintas with which the firm has long-term contracts. Sandeman generally acquires fruit from vineyards around Pinhão and in the Rio Torto area.

The wine

The just-picked bunches were foot-trodden in traditional lagares (shallow stone troughs), ensuring a thorough and relatively swift extraction of colour, tannin and flavour. The fermenting must was run off the skins and fortified with grape spirit, to arrest the fermentation. The wine then rested for a month or so before being racked into storage tanks and subsequently transported to Oporto for ageing in casks, known as pipes, for up to two years – vintage Port is intended to be aged in bottle. As was common at that time, some of the wines were bottled in Oporto, while others were shipped in cask to British importers to be bottled in their cellars. There is usually no significant difference in quality between the two sources.

The reaction

In 1990 James Suckling exclaimed: 'It can't get much more enjoyable than this... Full-bodied, with very focused, sweet fruit flavours, great concentration and a silky mouthfeel.' In 2000, Michael Broadbent commented on an Oporto-bottled example: 'Protruding cork and level into neck: fairly pale but lovely colour; sweet and equally lovely bouquet and flavour.'

In 2002, Serena Sutcliffe wrote: 'A real smell of smoky roses.

Amazing power and punch on the middle palate and finish, great fruit and impact. So frank and foursquare. The greatest Sandeman with the heavenly 1912.'

Richard Mayson described the wine in 2011 as: 'Ripe yet restrained and gentle on the nose, touch of dark chocolate; rich, ripe, tight-knit, bitter-sweet fruit, very fine, firm and still very fresh with lovely length and depth.' And Austrian wine critic Peter Moser tasted the wine in 2014: 'Very restrained in aroma and still needs a lot of time to reveal itself. Subtle red-berry nuances... immense sweetness on the palate, which has liquorice and spice notes and hints of dried orange-peel. Fine and well-handled length.'

THE FACTS

Bottles produced
N/A
Composition
A field blend of Touriga Nacional and other indigenous varieties
Yield
N/A
Alcohol
20%
Release price
£1 approx.
Price today
£792

TAYLOR'S VINTAGE PORT 1927

Douro, Portugal

A LEGEND BECAUSE...

Other than the rare Nacional bottling from Quinta do Noval, Taylor's vintage is the most sought-after and expensive of all vintage Ports, and this wine, from an acclaimed vintage, is the epitome of the style. Ironically, the 1927 vintage was released at the height of the worldwide economic slump. Consequently sales were sluggish for many years.

LOOKING BACK

Taylor's can trace its history back to the end of the 17th century, although it subsequently had numerous owners, of whom the best known were the Bearsley family. By the 1830s John Fladgate and Morgan Yeatman were among the major shareholders, and the business remained in their hands until 1921, when Frank Yeatman became the sole proprietor. It was not until the end of World War II that the company began its expansion by buying Fonseca. In the 1920s Taylor's was a far more modest concern, though always with an emphasis on quality. It was in 1927 that the Yeatmans planted blocks of individual varieties at Quinta de Vargellas, but the usual custom at the time was to plant field blends, and the 1927 vintage would certainly have been produced from the latter.

THE VINTAGE

This is widely accepted as one of the great vintage Port years of the 20th century, declared by about 30 shippers. The climatic conditions allowed a relatively early harvest, well before any threat of inclement weather could materialise. Moreover, the harvest was copious and most Port houses declared a far larger quantity than was usual in vintage years.

Despite the large volumes released, quality was extremely high, with admirably concentrated fruit and fine structure, which has allowed the wines to age extremely well. Because the market, hit by economic crisis, could not absorb so much vintage Port, much of the wine ended up being blended with standard ruby Ports.

THE TERROIR

Quinta de Vargellas has long been the company's flagship estate, and its wines, then as now, form the core of the vintage blend. It was bought in 1893, though its grapes had supplied Taylor's for many previous decades. Wines from Vargellas are known for their floral aromas, often described as violets, and for concentration allied to great elegance. Vargellas's top wines would almost certainly have been blended with wines purchased from other quintas, such as Terra Feita. This vineyard had been supplying Taylor's since the 1890s, and would subsequently be bought by the firm in 1974.

THE WINE

All the grapes would have been foot-trodden in stone lagares, a method that ensures gentle but complete extraction of colour and tannins. After a few months of ageing in vats, the wine would have been transferred to the Taylor's lodge in Vila Nova de Gaia, across the river from Oporto. There it would have been kept in wood for about two years before being bottled. The Taylor's style is one of great concentration and depth, and is marked by a long, tannic finish that promises a very long life in bottle.

'Because of the economic crisis, much of the wine ended up being blended with standard ruby Ports'

THE REACTION

In 1989, US critic James Suckling described the wine as 'incredibly concentrated yet superbly balanced... with intense raspberry and blackberry aromas, full-bodied, with rich, velvety, ripe raspberry flavours and a long, thick, rich finish'. DWWA Regional Chair for Port, Richard Mayson, tasted the wine in the same year, alongside Niepoort and Fonseca, and found it 'still incredibly powerful and concentrated, retaining the bitter chocolate and liquorice-like intensity that is the hallmark of a really fine vintage Port'. *Decanter* columnist Michael Broadbent's most recent recorded tastings were in 1993 and 1997 – 'magnificent' on both occasions.

Adrian Bridge, Taylor's current managing director, recalls: 'The 1927 is a sublime vintage Port that I rarely get to taste these days, but when I do, I am always amazed by its incredible structure, vigour, and elegance. True hallmarks of a great Taylor's vintage Port.'

THE FACTS

Bottles produced
N/A

Composition
N/A

Yield
N/A

Alcohol
21%

Release price
£0.20 a bottle (in today's money)

Price today
Auction £773 a bottle

AUSTRALIA AND NEW ZEALAND

The sheer versatility of the Antipodean vineyards meant there was no shortage of candidates for legendary status, with entries from all over Australia, even if New Zealand's far more recent embrace of wine production limited us to just one selection.

CAPE MENTELLE, CABERNET SAUVIGNON 1983

Margaret River, Western Australia

A LEGEND BECAUSE...

David Hohnen was the winemaking wizard behind Cape Mentelle from 1976 and founded Cloudy Bay in New Zealand. Cape Mentelle was to become quite a large estate, with vineyards in different areas of Margaret River, but the Cabernet Sauvignon is sourced primarily from its 16ha vineyard in Wallcliffe, which was planted in 1970. The most prestigious award in the Australian wine show circuit is the Jimmy Watson Trophy, which Cape Mentelle won not only for this 1983 Cabernet but also for the preceding vintage.

LOOKING BACK

Cape Mentelle was founded in Margaret River in 1970, making it one of the first estates to be established in the region. Its wines, Hohnen admitted, were initially seen as too expensive, which hampered domestic sales in particular, but international distribution was boosted by its partnership with LVMH-owned Veuve Clicquot from 1990, in a deal that included Cloudy Bay. Hohnen sold his remaining interest in 2000, and Cape Mentelle and Cloudy Bay were fully absorbed into the LVMH luxury group. Cape Mentelle's white wines were highly rated, but it was the outstanding Cabernets that captivated wine lovers, aided by the International Cabernet Tasting, established by Cape Mentelle in 1982. In 2003, David Hohnen ended his association with Cape Mentelle, and moved on to create his own brand, McHenry Hohnen.

THE VINTAGE

It was a very hot year in Western Australia, with drought conditions, but Cape Mentelle claims to have fared better than most, thanks to cool ocean breezes. The Cabernet grapes ripened two weeks earlier than on average, and were picked over a five-day period.

THE TERROIR

The Wallcliffe Vineyard is planted midway between the town of Margaret River and the Indian ocean just 5km to the west, making it one of the cooler sectors of Margaret River. In 1983, 4.8ha were devoted to Cabernet Sauvignon. The soils are called ironstone and are granite-derived, with a deep red colour. Gravel and varying degrees of sand give excellent drainage, as well as good water retention.

THE WINE

After harvesting, the grapes were crushed and tipped into large fermenters with daily pumpovers for 10 days. The wine was transferred into large oak vats for the malolactic fermentation, then aged for 20 months in barriques, of which one-third were new. It was filtered shortly before bottling.

THE REACTION

In 1985, James Halliday, in an article about the wine, hailed it as an 'immensely rich, robust and massively structured Cabernet Sauvignon which demands cellaring for a decade or more'. Stephen Brook first tasted the wine in 1988: 'Deep purple-red. Sweet minty nose, quite restrained. Rich and rounded, not too much oak, excellent fruit and length.' And 25 years later, in 2013: 'Lightly herbaceous nose, with black cherry aromas. Supple, ripe, and quite concentrated, with firm tannins. It still has lift and texture and is far from tiring.' Jancis Robinson commented in 2017: 'Deep blackish ruby. Very accomplished harmony and it's easy to see how it wowed the judges way back. It's ageing well, though with a little kiss of tannin that's likely to remain to the end of its days.' Sarah Ahmed attended a vertical tasting in 2018 and noted: 'Spicy oak and perfumed cassis on the nose which follow through on the palate. It still retains fruit power. Classic Margaret River eucalypt and dried herbs, with ripe but sturdy tannins and savoury meat pan juices to the finish.'

THE FACTS

Bottles produced
15,600

Composition
98% Cabernet Sauvignon 2% Malbec (field blend)

Yield
35hl/ha

Alcohol
13%

Release price
A$13

Price today
£210

Clonakilla, Shiraz-Viognier 2001

Canberra District, New South Wales, Australia

A legend because...

The style of Shiraz that blends, and usually co-ferments with Viognier is an established, if not historically accurate, tribute to Syrah from Côte-Rôtie. Not everyone admires the style, but most would agree that no Australian winery makes a better version than Clonakilla. Most vintages through the 1990s received high critical acclaim, from show judges and wine guides, and the 2001 came to be regarded as one of Clonakilla's most outstanding.

Looking back

The Kirk family arrived in Australia from Ireland in 1968, and three years later the biochemist John Kirk planted a vineyard in Murrumbateman, 40km north of Canberra. The property took its name from the family farm in Ireland's County Clare. The first commercial wines (and the first for any in this region) were made in 1976. Viognier was first planted in 1986, when it was still seen as a rare, exotic variety. Throughout the 1980s Clonakilla Shiraz was blended with Cabernet Sauvignon, but after visiting the Rhône in 1991, Tim Kirk resolved to model the wine on Guigal's single-vineyard blends he'd tasted from barrel. The first Clonakilla Shiraz-Viognier was made in 1992.

The vintage

2001 was a warm year that gave a good growing season without disease pressure, and harvest for this wine took place from 31 March to 10 April. Although the crop was large, the wines show rich flavours and good concentration.

The terroir

The soil at Murrumbateman is sandy clay-loam, over a layer of friable red clay, which sits on a subsoil of decomposed dacite. By Australian standards the climate here is cool, as the vineyards lie at 600m. The Kirk family gradually increased the area under vine, planting more Shiraz and Viognier between 1993 and 2007, until it reached today's 13.5ha. The cool climate brings out the spicy red fruit and floral character of Shiraz, though the profile inevitably varies according to vintage conditions.

The wine

In 2001 a third of the Shiraz went into the fermenters as whole bunches. Lightly crushed Viognier grapes were added and then covered with destemmed Shiraz. The gradual release of juice as the bunches broke down through the course of the fermentation prolonged the process and moderated the rising temperatures. There were three punchdowns daily. After a short post-fermentation soak, the wine was run into fine-grained French oak barrels, of which one-third were new, for 12 months. Kirk is aware that an excess of Viognier can impart a blowsy apricot sheen to the blend, which he is keen to avoid, and he also steers clear of a pronounced oaky character to the wine.

The reaction

In the *2002 Penguin Good Australian Wine Guide*, Huon Hooke and Ralph Kyte-Powell named the wine Best Red and Wine of the Year: 'This could be the best yet in a very distinguished line. Tremendously intense and alive, with great elegance and power.'

In the same year Max Allen in *Decanter* declared it a 'new benchmark for cooler-climate Australian Shiraz, and a serious rival for the classiest Côte-Rôtie'.

In 2009 on *www.JancisRobinson.com*, Julia Harding wrote: 'Apricots on the palate as well as on the nose. Fine and tight and superbly structured. Scented, floral, peppery aftertaste with beautiful finesse and length.'

In 2014 Lisa Perroti-Brown of *The Wine Advocate* wrote: 'Lovely crème de cassis, prune and pot pourri notes allied to hints of dried Provence herbs, tobacco and game. Crisp and structured by medium-level, chewy tannins... a stemmy character to the fleshy palate and finishes long, earthy and savoury. Drink now.'

THE FACTS

Bottles produced
10,700
Composition
93% Shiraz, 7% Viognier
Yield
50hl/ha
Alcohol
14.1%
Release price
A$48
Price today
£70-£80

De Bortoli, Noble One 1982

Riverina, New South Wales, Australia

A legend because...

Although Australia has a long tradition of sweet wine production (mostly fortified), Noble One, first made in 1982 and labelled as 'Sauternes' until 1990, was a new departure. In 2016 Jancis Robinson MW described it as 'perhaps the greatest southern hemisphere challenge to Sauternes and Barsac'. Placed as a ringer among a few dozen 1983 Sauternes in a blind tasting in 1987, I was one of the tasters who, while puzzled by the wine, acclaimed its quality. It was, I noted, 'worryingly mature for a 1983 Sauternes', but its plump, unctuous character gave it immediate appeal.

Looking back

De Bortoli is a family winery, founded in 1928. In the early 1980s it was run by the late Deen De Bortoli. His son Darren had been enchanted by the 1975 Château Coutet he'd had drunk while a student at Adelaide's Roseworthy College; moreover, Deen had already experimented with botrytis wines in the 1970s, though with little success. Their decision to embark on a significant production of a botrytis-affected Semillon did not meet with universal approval within the family, but they were vindicated. The 1982 Noble One has gone on to win (on the Australian wine show circuit) more than 11 trophies and 46 gold medals. As the wine was re-entered into subsequent wine shows, it garnered 138 trophies and 425 golds. The De Bortolis have since made the wine every year except in washed-out 1989 and 2012.

The vintage

Preceding years in Riverina had been hit by drought, but in 1982 there was abundant rain, and growers were confronted with lots of botrytised fruit. Initially abject at having to discard part of their crop, the growers were delighted when the De Bortolis offered to buy the best of it. This was something of a gamble on their part, as it was not immediately clear whether the mould was the noble botrytis cinerea or the less desirable brown rot. Fortunately it was mostly the former.

The terroir

The grapes came mostly from the De Bortoli vineyards in Griffith, an area within the Riverina region that has won a reputation for botrytis-affected wines, especially Semillon. Although the grapes were grown on differing soil types, there were some factors in common: moisture-retentive clay soils and regular morning dews that helped to provoke botrytis infection; while warm sunny days helped to concentrate and ripen the fruit. The use of flood irrigation also contributes to the necessary humidity for noble rot.

The wine

After a manual harvest, the juice is settled overnight, then clarified before being inoculated with yeasts to start fermentation, which can take up to three months. The 1982 was picked at a potential alcohol of more than 23%. Early vintages of what became Noble One were unoaked, but from 1990 the wine was aged mostly in tight-grained Seguin-Moreau barriques, although about 10% to 15% remains in tanks to preserve freshness.

THE REACTION

In 1986 Stephen Brook noted: 'Lush, stylish botrytis nose. Plump, rounded, but very intense with delicious peachy fruit, and the botrytis bringing viscosity. Good length, but there's a slight lack of acidity on the finish. Excellent.' In 2009 Sarah Ahmed admired the wine: 'The nose shows a spicy marmalade/orange-peel character with a barley sugar twist. Quite warm, with flavours of barley sugar, apricot and buttery bruléed apple tart. Good acidity still, with texture, tannin and a spicy marmalade finish.' In the same year Australian wine writer Jeremy Oliver found it very evolved: 'Now very mature with a complex, dusty and nutty bouquet suggestive of herbal and citrussy notes. It's beginning to break down and dry out towards the finish but delivers charming intensity and elegance, finishing with savoury and vanilla aspects.'

THE FACTS

Bottles produced
48,000
Composition
100% Semillon
Yield
N/A
Alcohol
12.8%
Release price
A$25 (about A$81/£35 in today's money)
Price today
£150

JIM BARRY, THE ARMAGH 1999

Clare Valley, South Australia

A LEGEND BECAUSE...

The heartland of Australian Shiraz is usually considered to be the Barossa Valley, but other regions have shown they can also produce outstanding wines from this variety. Jim Barry, a Clare Valley pioneer, established his winery in 1959. In 1968 he planted Shiraz vines in the Armagh region, which led to the creation of The Armagh 17 years later. The name is a tribute to the place and to the Irish settlers who came here from 1849 onwards. Barry intended the wine to be a challenger to the iconic Penfolds Grange and Henschke Hill of Grace, and it was priced between them on release. The Armagh has been made in most vintages, but there were years when none was bottled under that label: 1986, 2003, 2011.

LOOKING BACK

By 1999, the Armagh style was well established, though with less reliance on American oak, and the wine was already considered an exceptional Shiraz with a worldwide reputation. The Barry property had expanded from its early days to consist of 260ha over 11 sites, as well as vineyards in Coonawarra. Jim Barry had by then retired and handed over to his children Nancy and Peter, who became managing director in 1985. Jim died in 2004, and the estate remains in the hands of second-generation Peter Barry and his children.

THE VINTAGE

Conditions were patchy in Australia's wine regions in 1999, but the climate was ideal in Clare Valley, with a dry summer and just enough rain before harvest to bring the grapes to full ripeness. When picked, the bunches were entirely healthy.

THE TERROIR

Clare Valley has cooler nights than regions such as Barossa, and this contributes to a level of acidity that gives wines freshness as well as power. The Armagh vineyard is a mere 3.3ha of sandy clay over alluvial pebbles and clay. Rainfall is modest, with an annual average of 600mm.

THE WINE

After harvesting, the grapes are crushed and vinified using pumpovers and délestage (rack and return) for a period of 7-10 days. Fermentation takes place at no more than 23°C, with the grapes submerged under boards. In many vintages all the press wine is added to the blend, as the grapes are picked at high ripeness levels that deliver supple tannins and no green flavours. The oak regime has varied over the years; the 1999 spent 15 months in 50% new French oak and 50% new American oak. This vintage was sealed with natural cork, as screwcap closures were only introduced for The Armagh in 2010.

THE REACTION

Jeremy Oliver was impressed: 'Ultraconcentrated spicy aromas of cassis, plum, raspberry and redcurrant, with musky, spirity, gamey undertones of animal hide and asphalt. Powerful and velvety; a particularly vibrant expression... Seductively smooth and seamless, dripping with flavours of ripe crushed raspberry, blackberry and tarry red plum, and handsomely coated in spicy oak tones of vanilla and chocolate.'

In 2015, Huon Hooke noted: 'The bouquet is restrained and quietly complex, while the palate is rich and concentrated, intense and penetrating, with layers of black fruit and espresso coffee, chocolate and toffee flavours all nicely integrated. A big, solid, powerful wine that serves up all the things that we expect in a top Armagh.' Tasting at the winery in the same year, Andrew Graham was less enthusiastic: 'Oak kicks off the nose and palate. I think this is still very backward – in time it might follow the path of the 1995, but for the moment it's just big, oaky and awkwardly bulky.'

In 2016, Lisa Perrotti-Brown MW reviewed the wine for *The Wine Advocate*: 'Very deep garnet-brick coloured, the 1999 The Armagh has a touch of balsamic over a gorgeous core of liquorice, prunes, baked blackberries and crème de cassis, plus an invigorating waft of espresso. Big, rich, concentrated and ripe in the mouth, it has a soft, velvety backbone and goes into exotic spice mode in the long finish.'

THE FACTS

Bottles produced
N/A
Composition
100% Shiraz
Yield
32hl/ha
Alcohol
15%
Release price
£60
Price today
£132

LINDEMAN'S, BIN 1590 SHIRAZ 1959

Hunter Valley, New South Wales, Australia

A LEGEND BECAUSE...

In the 1950s and 1960s, winemakers at Australia's leading wineries were allowed to try their hand at small lots of outstanding wines, giving those wines 'bin numbers' to differentiate them from regular and more commercial bottlings. Many of these wines - white as well as red - were soon recognised as classics, especially the series produced by Lindeman's, which was a brand devoted to Hunter Valley wines at that time. The red Burgundies were produced mostly from Shiraz.

LOOKING BACK

Hans Mollenhauer, a food technologist from Germany, was the chief winemaker at Lindeman's Ben Ean winery, and began producing limited-production 'bin' wines in 1953. He was responsible for the celebrated Bin 1590. Ray Kidd was also involved in producing this wine, as was Karl Stockhausen, who was about to succeed Mollenhauer as Lindeman's chief winemaker. This was a time when Hunter Valley wines, produced not only by Lindeman's but by McWilliams, were widely regarded as Australia's finest.

THE VINTAGE

The 1959 harvest in the Hunter Valley was delayed by outbreaks of rain - not an unusual occurrence in this region. Despite this, the vines, though low-yielding in 1959, produced fully ripe fruit, and Hunter growers celebrated what they considered a perfect vintage. The Lindeman's team was not slow to recognise the quality of the Shiraz grown in their Ben Ean vineyard, and a new bin wine was born.

THE TERROIR

The Ben Ean vineyard, like other top sites in the region, is composed of red volcanic soil with clay. It was customary to assess the new wines after vintage, and the best lots were set aside for special treatment, eventually to be released as bin wines. These lots often came from parcels of very old vines - up to 70 years old - that were low-yielding and gave wine of remarkable concentration. In less than outstanding vintages, such as 1955 and 1960, no bin wines were produced.

THE WINE

Bin 1590 was part of the winery's Hunter River Burgundy Series. In those days Australian wineries often referred to their Shiraz blends as Burgundy. Some of the Lindeman's Burgundies did contain a minuscule quantity of Pinot Noir, but the 1959 was pure Shiraz. (Curiously, according to Len Evans, the Bin 1590 was initially labeled as Claret, but eventually released as a Burgundy.) The wine was fermented in open concrete vats, with wild yeast, then aged for around 18 months in barriques, mostly Nevers, before being bottled. Bin 1590 was bottled on 21 October 1960, and James Halliday notes that to signal the quality of the wine, the decision was taken to use an imported Bordeaux bottle. Bin wines were generally given long ageing - as long as 17 years for the 1965 - before commercial release, but Bin 1590 was released much more rapidly. It was also entered into Australian wine shows. Bin 1590's first exposure to the system was in 1963, and it won a number of gold medals over the following decade.

THE REACTION

In 1985 James Halliday, in his *Australian Wine Compendium*,

'Len Evans proclaimed that Bin 1590 was "the greatest Hunter wine of the last 50 years"'

noted the wine's 'light to medium garnet-red colour' and its 'soft but infinitely complex amalgam of leather, earth and vegetative aromas, yet with the fruit to carry all those things. The palate is a logical extension of the bouquet: the velvety softness gives an allusion of lightness, but the wine has both the alcohol and the structure to go on almost indefinitely.' When he tasted the wine again later he said: 'A gloriously fragrant and complex bouquet with a magnificent array of aromas from sweet berry through liquorice to sweet leather.' Hunter Valley Shiraz, he concluded, does 'not come any better than this'. The Australian wine writer Ken Gargett recalls Len Evans proclaiming after a wine dinner in around 2006, at which it was served, that Bin 1590 was 'the greatest Hunter wine of the last 50 years'. Gargett himself found it 'mature and complex, with notes ranging from animal hide to campfire... richly flavoured, a hint of beefstock. Amazingly elegant. Though obviously mature, a very long, complex wine. Extraordinary.'

THE FACTS

Bottles produced	Alcohol
6,000 approx	**N/A**
Composition	Release price
100% Shiraz	**A$26**
Yield	Price today
N/A	**Last sale price (2012) was £1,477**

Moss Wood, Cabernet Sauvignon 1975

Wilyabrup, Margaret River, Western Australia

A legend because...

In the late 1960s and early 1970s there was a rush to make wine in Margaret River, and a number of properties - not only Moss Wood but Vasse Felix and Cullen - were planted. Largely improvised, these early vintages received unexpected acclaim. The 1975 Moss Wood Cabernet was one of those wines, and has long been considered one of the greatest red wines produced in the region.

Looking back

The surge in interest in Margaret River as a wine region can be attributed to the publication in 1966 of a report by Dr John Gladstones. A botanic research scientist with an interest in viticulture, he spotted the suitability of the region for wine production. Frost-free and maritime, the region's climatic conditions were similar to those of Bordeaux. First to respond was Dr Tom Cullity, founding Vasse Felix in 1967. Dr Bill Pannell and his wife Sandra were not far behind with Moss Wood - the original block is Margaret River's second oldest vineyard. Present owner Keith Mugford, winemaker from 1979, recalls how at weekends they would drive down to Margaret River with a shovel in search of the best gravelly loam soils, considered ideal for vineyards by Gladstones. The Moss Wood property looked just right, and was for sale. The Pannells bought it and planted Cabernet Sauvignon in 1969.

The vintage

The 1975 growing season was quite mild, with Cabernet ripening slowly. It was certainly cooler than the very warm 1976 and 1977. There were no problems with disease or bird damage, and yields were moderate. The grapes were hand picked.

The terroir

The soils of the original vineyard, lying on a gentle, sheltered slope, are a reddish gravel loam over a clay subsoil, with a few sandier sectors. The clay contributes a good deal - there is enough to retain water and prevent drought stress, but not so much that the soil becomes waterlogged. The clay also adds to the wine's opulence. Strong coastal winds help to moderate temperatures in summer. The vines are entirely dry-farmed. Minimal pesticides are used, but Moss Wood is not organic.

The wine

After harvest on 15 March, the grapes were fermented in open-top tanks with cultivated yeasts. The cap was plunged by hand three times a day, and temperatures were controlled, never rising above 28°C. Surprisingly, there was no malolactic fermentation. The wine was aged for 15 months in 300-litre barrels, of which 20% were new; 20% American oak was used, the rest being French.

The reaction

One of the first experts to recognise the wine's quality was Edmund Penning-Rowsell, who tasted it while touring Australia on behalf of the Wine Society in the late 1970s. 'To the best of my memory,' says Mugford, 'this was the first international recognition of the quality of Cabernet Sauvignon from the Margaret River region.'

In 1993 Jeremy Oliver was enthusiastic: 'Heady, opulent, smoky aromas of cedar and cigarboxes over lightly meaty suggestions of undergrowth. Superbly preserved, with surprising fruit sweetness and vivaciousness.'

In 2002 Stephen Brook admired its 'sweet, rich, cedary nose, with a touch of mint. Medium-bodied, it's still healthy, with fine acidity and amazing freshness, leading to a long, lean, elegant finish.'

THE FACTS

Bottles produced
6,000
Composition
100% Cabernet Sauvignon
Yield
35hl/ha
Alcohol
13.5%
Release price
A$2
Price today
N/A

TE MATA, COLERAINE 1998

Hawke's Bay, New Zealand

A LEGEND BECAUSE...

Although New Zealand is best known for its cool-climate wines - notably Sauvignon Blanc, Chardonnay and Pinot Noir - it has been recognised for some time that Hawke's Bay is particularly well suited to weightier reds, such as Bordeaux-style blends and Syrah. The development of the Gimblett Gravels zone put these wines on the map, but the Buck family at Te Mata had started to focus on such styles years before that. From 1982, the first vintage, Coleraine has been Te Mata's finest expression of the Bordeaux style and the most avidly collected of New Zealand red wines.

LOOKING BACK

John Buck was still very much in charge of this important estate in 1998, although today his son Nicholas is deeply involved. John bought the property in 1974, as it was already planted with vineyards widely regarded as among the finest in Hawke's Bay. Indeed these sites, known collectively as the Havelock Hills Vineyards, were first established in 1892, and by 1909 it was the country's largest vineyard. In the late 1970s Buck, with experience gained in the British wine trade before returning to his native land, redeveloped the vineyards and winery.

THE VINTAGE

After a wet winter, the growing season was very dry and one of the hottest on record. Flowering in early December delivered a potentially large crop, so bunches had to be thinned. The vineyards had to be attentively managed to avoid dehydration and stress, but the fruit for Coleraine was exemplary, with Cabernet Sauvignon the most impressive of the three component varieties.

THE TERROIR

The soils in Hawke's Bay are varied, but Coleraine is planted on north-facing, sandstone-based alluvial gravel. The first vines were planted in 1979, with the chosen varieties being Cabernet Franc, Cabernet Sauvignon and Merlot. The vineyard is harvested by hand, then the grapes are sorted at the winery, to eliminate any sub-standard fruit. Initially Coleraine was a single-vineyard wine, but since 1989 it has been a selection from the best plots in the Havelock Hills Vineyards.

THE WINE

For 35 years Peter Cowley has been Te Mata's technical director, and thus responsible for overseeing how Coleraine was made. The grapes are destemmed and crushed, before being fermented for up to 21 days in open-top vats at temperatures up to 32°C, with regular punchdowns. After an extended maceration, the wine goes into French barriques, of which 70% are new, for 18-24 months; the 1998 was aged for 20 months. Racking is performed from barrel to barrel. Before bottling, the wine is traditionally fined with egg whites.

THE REACTION

In 2009 Huon Hooke remarked: 'Coleraine is arguably New Zealand's greatest red wine'. Shortly after release Pierre Rovani reviewed the 1998 for *The Wine Advocate*: 'Explosive black-fruit aromas...velvety textured, this impressive wine

coats the palate with blackberries, blackcurrants and freshly laid asphalt.' After a vertical tasting in London in 2007, Steven Spurrier wrote: 'Of the older wines, 1998 was outstanding, fragrant, floral, with a fine future.'

In 2012 James Suckling pronounced: 'This is the legendary Cabernet Sauvignon and Merlot blend of NZ. A lovely combination of fruit, tobacco, liquorice and dried flower. New Zealand's Sassicaia.'

In 2016, Cameron Douglas MS noted: 'A seductive, almost heady perfume: soft violet scents nestled against the residue of the Cabernet with a quiet tobacco and earthy layer. The tannins were fully integrated and the acidity ensured the wine retained some texture and length.'

THE FACTS

Bottles produced
25,000
Composition
60% Cabernet Sauvignon, 32% Merlot, 8% Cabernet Franc
Yield
50hl/ha
Alcohol
13.5%
Release price
NZ$75
Price today
NZ$250 (£138)

TYRRELL'S, VAT 1 SEMILLON 1994

Hunter Valley, New South Wales, Australia

A LEGEND BECAUSE...

Hunter Valley Semillon is one of Australia's miraculous wines. Tasted very young, it can seem anaemic and feeble, notable only for its strident citric character. After five years of bottle age, it is transformed into a honeyed, toasty, complex wine, full of flavour despite its low alcohol. Tyrrell's Vat No 1 is one of the supreme expressions of this underrated wine style. No wine has been awarded more medals on the Australian show circuit.

LOOKING BACK

Tyrrell's is one of Australia's great family wineries. The land was acquired and planted by Edward Tyrrell in 1858 and he produced his first vintage in 1864; the Tyrrell family has been making wines here ever since. Murray Tyrrell, who became head of the family in 1959, was still very active in 1994, but, aged in his 70s, was being assisted both by his son Bruce, the present head of the company, and by winemaker Andrew Spinaze, who still holds that position today. Then as now, Tyrrell's remains hugely committed to Semillon, and produces three single-vineyard bottlings. Nonetheless, Vat 1 has always been conceived as the company's top wine. It was first made in 1962 and known as Hunter Valley Riesling, when European grape and regional names were used with abandon. In 1990 the present name was adopted.

THE VINTAGE

A late bud-burst led the estate to assume the vintage would be fairly late. However, very warm weather in December and January speeded up the ripening, although it also led to bush fires, the smoke from which may have tainted some wines. The fruit for Vat 1 was picked by hand during the last week of February. Although the vintage as a whole was patchy in New South Wales, the Hunter Semillon grapes were in perfect condition.

THE TERROIR

Vat 1 comes from two very old blocks within two vineyards, with a combined area of about six hectares. Short Flat was planted in 1923, while the oldest vines in Johnno's Vineyard date from 1908. The two blocks are separated by just 800m. They flank the same creek and share the same alluvial sandy loam soils. Both blocks are unirrigated.

THE WINE

Australia is renowned (or criticised) for its high-tech approach to winemaking, but Hunter Valley Semillon has always been an exception. Vat 1 follows the usual pattern in being fermented in stainless steel tanks; thereafter it receives minimal lees contact in the tanks and is bottled early. It is bottle-ageing that transforms Semillon from a lightweight, neutral wine to one with extraordinary intensity. This ageing is undertaken by the winery itself, which gives some of its Semillons up to five years' bottle age so as to allow its secondary characteristics to develop before the wine is released.

THE REACTION

The wine certainly pleased Australian judges in the regional and national shows; it garnered no fewer than 32 gold medals and 12 trophies. In 2001, James Halliday lavished praise on the wine: 'An utterly magical combination of complexity and vibrant freshness.' (Today he points out that vintages such as 1994, which were sealed with cork, may suffer from random oxidation.)

'No wine has been awarded so many medals on the Australian show circuit'

In 2007, Huon Hooke and Ralph Kyte-Powell noted: 'The nose is mellow, quietly complex – and only lightly toasty. Melon, wood smoke, earth and honey lead the way. The palate is rich and unusually smoky.' They scored it 95/100. Jeremy Oliver, in 2009, was blown away: 'This complex, deeply layered Semillon has acquired plenty of richness and depth. Its smoky, meaty bouquet reveals nuances of buttered toast and dried flowers over rich notes of melon-like fruit. Its intense, exceptionally long core of assertive flavour drives onwards to a savoury, slightly earthy finish tightly wound around a fabulously taut acidity.'

Australian wine writer Ken Gargett shared his last bottle with friends in June 2014 and reported: 'Refined, elegant, almost delicate. Finely balanced, with hints of spice and lemon and, with time, plenty of mango notes. Excellent length, mature and complex. Why leave it any longer as it is drinking so beautifully now?'

THE FACTS

Bottles produced
30,000
Composition
100% Semillon
Yield
35hl/ha
Alcohol
10.6%

Release price
About A$15
Price today
Not available, but vintages from the late 1990s are listed at £50-£90, so the 1994 would probably fetch more.

WENDOUREE, SHIRAZ 1990 (IN MAGNUM)

Clare Valley, South Australia

A LEGEND BECAUSE...

Tony Brady has been crafting intensely flavoured wines from Shiraz, Cabernet Sauvignon, Malbec and Mourvedre (Mataro) since 1974, when he took over running this small Clare Valley property. He has been aided in his project by carefully preserved Shiraz bush vines planted gradually between 1893 and 1920. These vines are still alive. (The property was planted by Alfred Percy Birks, a gentleman farmer, who named the estate after the aboriginal name for 'place of water'.) As is the case with centenarian vines everywhere, the production is low and generally self-regulating, and yields rarely exceed 30 hectolitres per hectare. This legendary 1990 Shiraz is made from the original Shiraz bush vines (block 24B) and was released only in magnum. Australian critic James Halliday has described Wendouree as a 'living treasure'.

LOOKING BACK

In the 1920s and '30s about half the wine from Wendouree was based on Muscat of Alexandria and fortified, the remainder being red. It was mostly sold locally to restaurants. Birks' son Roly had become the winemaker in 1917, and remained active until 1983. He bottled very little wine, but sold grapes to other wineries. This continued into the 1950s and '60s, although more of the wine was being sent to WJ Seabrook, a Melbourne merchant, where its reputation grew. In 1970 Birks, then in his late 70s, retired. He found a purchaser, but the new owners went bankrupt and the vineyards were all but abandoned, having shrunk from 25ha to 12ha. Then in 1974 businessman Max Liberman bought the decrepit property and entrusted it to his son-in-law, Tony Brady. This saved Wendouree from likely extinction. Brady was a lawyer by training, with no experience of winemaking. Fortunately, his wife Lolita took courses, although it was some years before Wendouree could give up bulk sales and focus on bottling its own wines.

THE VINTAGE

After a wet spring, summer was cool in South Australia. But it remained dry, causing some stress, although ancient vines such as those at Wendouree were largely immune. Yields were average and quality high.

THE TERROIR

The vineyards occupy 12ha. They are planted on reddish-brown loam soils over a limestone subsoil and are dry-farmed. This wine was made from the original bush-vine Shiraz vineyard of 0.75ha with a total of 952 vines.

THE WINE

During harvest the grapes are taken to the stone winery, which was completed in 1903, making it of roughly the same vintage as the venerable vineyard. The grapes are vinified in open-top fermenters of moderate size, and during fermentation it is usual for some of the alcohol to evaporate. An ancient basket press, dating from 1898, is still in use. Malolactic fermentation generally takes place in tanks, while the finished wine is aged in 300-litre barrels, of which no more than 25% are new. This 1990 was released in 900 magnums in 1995 to mark the centenary of the property. (There is another 1990, released in 750ml bottles, but it was made from 1919 trellised Shiraz.) The label, designed in 1900, has been unaltered ever since.

THE REACTION

Andrew Caillard MW of auction house Langton's, which classifies

'It's a window into Australia's colonial past'

Andrew Caillard

Wendouree Shiraz as one of the 21 'exceptional' wines in its Classification of Australian Wine, tasted the 1990 in magnum in 1991. He noted: 'Very complex, ethereal prune/raspberry and slightly salty/rusty aromas. The palate is strongly flavoured and immensely tannic with developed blackberry/raspberry fruit and rusty leather nuances, massive concentration and lock-jawing, iron-like tannins. Needless to say it finishes extremely firm. Will it soften out?' Caillard says Wendouree Shiraz 'offers wine drinkers a window into Australia's colonial past'. In 1992, noted Australian wine writer and Decanter contributor Huon Hooke was impressed: 'Loaded with vanilla/cherry tastes and huge tannins but also huge flavour to match. It's a wine to keep for at least five years and drink for 20 thereafter.' In 2006, UK wine critic Jamie Goode said: 'Earthiness emerging under the smooth, focused, almost liqueur-like fruit. The palate is beautiful and the structure has softened a bit to reveal pure, subtly spicy red fruits.'

THE FACTS

Bottles produced
900 magnums
Composition
100% Shiraz
Yield
19hl/ha
Alcohol
13.8%
Release price
A$100 (about £45 at the time)
Price today
£121

WYNNS, JOHN RIDDOCH CABERNET 1982

Coonawarra, South Australia

A LEGEND BECAUSE...

John Riddoch was a land owner and politician who owned 28,500 hectares across Australia. He first planted vines in Coonawarra in the 1890s, and Wynns' top Cabernet Sauvignon pays homage to him. Today Wynns owns 900ha of vines (about 20% of the region), so winemakers can select the very finest fruit for the John Riddoch bottling. Wynns is now owned by global giant Treasury Wine Estates, but quality has long been consistent. This 1982 was the first John Riddoch bottling.

LOOKING BACK

The 1970s had not been an outstanding period for Wynns, mainly because new plantings were just coming on stream and so those vines were very young. There was a shortage of labour in Coonawarra, which meant that grapes were not always picked at optimal ripeness. John Wade, who made the 1982 John Riddoch, joined Wynns as winemaker in 1978. At the time there was no electricity in the winery, hence no refrigeration, and so fermentations could veer out of control as temperatures mounted. Nor was there a proper lab where the winemaking team could perform detailed analyses. However, a visit to Bordeaux in 1981 inspired Wade to invest in better barrels, and he was able to gain the support of Wynns general manager Robin Moody. This investment allowed Wade to use more new oak to age the best wines.

THE VINTAGE

1982 enjoyed a mild growing season, and was an exceptional vintage in Coonawarra, where the Cabernet Sauvignon in particular was of superlative quality. The autumn was steadily warm, but with lower temperatures than would be common in more recent times.

THE TERROIR

Coonawarra is famously flat; it makes the Médoc look hilly. Yet its special character lies just underground in the form of the famed terra rossa soil. Its red hue derives from the soil's iron content, but equally important is the permeable limestone subsoil that retains moisture and sustains the vines even during very dry periods. Only central Coonawarra (a strip 1km wide and 15km long), has terra rossa soil, and many vineyards are planted on heavier clay and sand. The climate is cooler than Barossa, resulting in Cabernet of great structure and ageing potential. The grapes for this wine were sourced from two terra rossa sites: Johnson Vineyard, planted in 1954, and Majella Vineyard, which had fairly young vines. The fruit for this wine would have been machine-harvested – not the case today.

THE WINE

Only 1% of the Wynns vineyards are used to source John Riddoch. The wines were fermented for about 10 days and about 3g of acidity added, probably at fermentation. Wade would have aimed to keep the temperature no higher than 28°C, but it wasn't always possible without temperature control. The wine stayed in tank for malolactic fermentation, and then transferred to one-year-old barrels for one year, followed by a further year in new oak. Sue Hodder, Wynns' chief winemaker today, reflects: 'In the late-1970s people started talking about New World wines, and Coonawarra winemakers recall endless discussions about what our regional style should be. The 1982 John Riddoch has riper flavours and aromas than many Cabernets of that era.'

'The 1982 vintage has riper flavours and aromas than many Cabernets of that era'

THE REACTION

In 2009, Jancis Robinson MW wrote: 'Leafy and a little minty, cedary oak. Full of fresh cassis leaf. Some coffee. Rich in cassis. Pretty powerful but very fresh and elegant. Lovely balance with integrated light oak spice.'

In 2011 James Halliday and Peter Bourne noted the 'fresh dark cherry and chocolate nose, lifted and inviting. Excellent varietal definition ageing very gracefully. A true Australian benchmark classic'. In the same year, Australian critic Jeremy Oliver described the wine as 'classically elegant, complex and wonderfully structured'. It shows 'a smoky bouquet of cassis, dark plums, coffee and polished leather baked by nuances of camphor, dark chocolates and animal hide... Exemplary.'

In late 2013, in the company of Sue Hodder, I tasted a bottle long stored in the Wynns cellars. The colour was deep, the blackcurrant nose lush and generous. Medium-bodied on the palate, fine acidity gave intensity and freshness. The tannins were fine grained and the finish had charm, purity and persistence

THE FACTS

Bottles produced
24,000

Composition
100% Cab Sauvignon

Yield
about 45hl/ha

Alcohol
12.9% on label (act. 13.4%)

Release price
A$13.50

Price today
£290

CHILE AND ARGENTINA

Lacking a large population, Chile pitched its wine industry at export markets. Very successfully too, but it did not result in very individual or high-quality wines. That soon changed, as producers such as Aurelio Montes and Eduardo Chadwick explored the full potential of Chile's climate and soils. Simultaneously, in Argentina, Nicolas Catena raised standards to the highest international level.

MONTES, ALPHA M 1999

Apalta, Colchagua Valley, Chile

A LEGEND BECAUSE...

It was Aurelio Montes who suspected that the Apalta hillsides had extraordinary potential for exceptional wines. He bought and planted the site in 1989, intending that the area would be the source for his top range. He reduced the yields to levels unheard of in Chile at that time, and gradually launched a range of varietal wines including a Chardonnay, a Syrah and a Cabernet Sauvignon. These made a strong impact on the international market, so Aurelio decided to create an even more special cuvée, which was named Alpha M after his business partner, the late Douglas Murray.

LOOKING BACK

Aurelio worked at a number of Chilean wineries before setting up his own company, Montes, and producing his first vintage in 1987. He was keen to show that Chile could produce not only good value, sound varietal wines but also wines of the highest quality – and he realised that this would require the right site, and the right winemaking and marketing strategies. The outcome was Alpha M. Its first vintage was 1996, but fewer than 10,000 bottles were released.

THE VINTAGE

Outstanding in Chile, being warm and dry until harvest, which took place under ideal conditions. Although there was some regional variation in ripeness and quality, many argue that for Cabernet Sauvignon the 1999 vintage has never been surpassed.

THE TERROIR

Apalta is a small, bowl-shaped region within Colchagua Valley, with a southern exposure. Aurelio has written: 'Some would consider this to be a negative factor, because in Chile a northern exposure is usually preferable. However, the fact that a harsher sun does not hit the vines all day long causes the grapes to ripen more slowly.' Mountains and the nearby Tinguiririca river also have a moderating influence. The high-density vineyards for Alpha M are steep, especially at the top of the slopes, and cool winds at night reduce the average temperature.

THE WINE

After harvest, the grapes were destemmed and given a cold soak. Once the alcoholic fermentation was completed, a post-fermentation maceration was encouraged to add body and structure. The wine was then aged for 18 months in new barriques.

THE REACTION

In 2002, James Molesworth noted in *The Wine Spectator*: 'Racy, pure red, with cassis, suave smoke, mineral and bittersweet chocolate notes, this glides along to an impressively lengthy and stylish finish. Should strut its stuff for some time to come. Clearly part of Chile's elite right now.'

Just over a decade later, in 2013, Jay Miller commented in *The Wine Advocate*: 'The 1999 Alpha M remains opaque purple-coloured with an expressive bouquet of pain grillé, graphite, espresso, blueberry and blackcurrants. This is followed by a mouth-filling wine with layers of blue and black fruits, well-concealed tannins, and a 45-plus second finish.' In the same year, Jancis Robinson MW recorded: 'Dark with a ruby rim. Still very concentrated. Tea-leaf flavours and really concentrated... Lovely freshness.'

In 2015, James Suckling wrote: 'This luscious and silky red shows some bottle age now. Full body, ripe fruit with chocolate, meat, currants and roasted nuts on the palate. Very long and flavourful. I love the depth and decadence to this mature red.'

John Stimpfig reviewed the wine in *Decanter* in 2017: 'A really impressive and very drinkable wine, which is in its pomp right now... There's a real sheen to this generous but not overdone blend, which has a muscular frame but supremely soft and succulent tannins... The wine is mature with sous-bois notes, coffee, leather and tobacco spice. But there's also plenty of primary fruit coming through, making this a generous, voluminous wine to enjoy and savour over the next five years.'

THE FACTS

Bottles produced
25,900
Composition
80% Cabernet Sauvignon, 10% Cabernet Franc, 5% Merlot, 5% Petit Verdot
Yield
28hl/ha
Alcohol
14.2%
Release price
£40
Price today
£75 approx

NICOLÁS CATENA ZAPATA 1997

Mendoza, Argentina

A LEGEND BECAUSE...

It was Nicolás Catena, whose grandfather had left Italy to settle in Argentina in 1902, who thrust Argentinian wine into the modern era. A widely travelled academic economist, he learned from his exposure in the 1970s both to great Bordeaux and the huge promise of Napa wines. In the early 1980s, Catena and his consultants, including Paul Hobbs and Jacques Lurton, agreed the key was to plant the right varieties in the right location, specifically cooler, higher sites where jamminess would not be an issue. Catena had also worked at the family winery and was able to supervise the selection of high-quality plant material. The Nicolás Catena Zapata demonstrated the fruition of his aspiration and hunches.

LOOKING BACK

By the mid-1990s, Catena's experiments were bearing fruit. With her own background in science, his daughter Laura assisted him greatly, helping to bring a specifically Argentinian identity to the Catena wines. Vineyards were planted at different altitudes to produce a hierarchy of wines, but the project's finest achievement was the Nicolás Catena Zapata. The 1997 was the first vintage, vinified by then winemaker José Galante. After its release in 2000 it was entered into blind tastings with other 1997 wines such as Château Latour, Opus One, Caymus Special Selection and Solaia, and the Argentinian wine regularly took first or second place.

THE VINTAGE

A warm dry spring delivered a good crop of healthy grapes, though there was sporadic hail damage in some sites. The summer was hot and prolonged, and despite some storms, careful viticulture ensured good aeration and no rot. The rest of the season was mild and sunny with cool nights. The fruit at harvest was highly concentrated, with ripe tannins and fine acidity to balance the sugars.

THE TERROIR

The Cabernet Sauvignon grapes were grown at 950m in the alluvial loam and clay soils of Catena's La Pirámide vineyard in Luján de Cuyo, cool nights and clay soils helping to preserve acidity. The small Malbec component was sourced from the 60-year-old Angélica vineyard at 920m, where the soil is mostly gravel and loam. This site has some pre-phylloxera vines that are the source of all plantings of Malbec in the Catena vineyards.

THE WINE

On the advice of Tuscan consultant Attilio Pagli, the wine was fermented at a lower temperature than was customary at that time in Argentina. It was aged for 18 months in 80% new barriques – reduced in subsequent vintages to 50%. There were regular rackings, although there are fewer nowadays.

THE REACTION

Robert Parker welcomed the wine in 2000: '...sensational nose of crème de cassis liqueur intermixed with toasty oak. Unevolved and supple, with enormous concentration and richness in addition to a funky, grilled meat flavour.' Patricio Tapia also tasted the wine soon after release, finding 'ripe fruit flavours of a relatively warm vintage,

but also an intense acidity and a firm structure of tannins to support that load. A wine designed for long ageing in bottle'.

In 2001, James Molesworth said: 'Goes for the gusto, and pulls it off. Dense texture, with gobs of cassis, kirsch and blackberry – like the distilled essence of Cabernet fruit... Muscular, yet suave.'

In 2016 Stephen Tanzer found the wine showed 'deep aromas of cassis, black cherry, menthol and chocolate, lifted by a minty nuance. Very smooth and fresh, with its juicy dark fruit flavours enlivened by elements of crushed stone, eucalyptus and spicy oak... Not a powerful style but this sexy Cabernet is full of life...A distinctly claret-like drink.'

THE FACTS

Bottles produced
9,000
Composition
95% Cabernet Sauvignon, 5% Malbec
Alcohol
14.4%
Release price
US$80
Price today
N/A

SANTA RITA, CASA REAL 1989

Alto Maipo, Chile

A LEGEND BECAUSE...

This was the first vintage of Santa Rita's icon wine, and it soon became established as one of Chile's greatest Cabernets. It is only produced in exceptional years in order to retain the quality level set by the 1989 vintage. None was released in 1992, 2000 nor 2006. The winemakers had been aware for some years that Santa Rita's Carneros Viejo vineyard was capable of producing exceptional Cabernet, but it was only in 1989 that they took the decision to offer a separate bottling under the Casa Real label. This vintage is extremely scarce and only five bottles remain in the Santa Rita cellars.

LOOKING BACK

Santa Rita was founded in 1880 and acquired a century later by the late Ricardo Claro, a tycoon with diversified interests. He expanded the company by acquiring other wineries, such as Carmen, and opening the Doña Paula winery in Argentina. In the mid-1980s he launched an export drive, which hugely increased the international availability of Santa Rita wines. Their success has been boosted by the shrewd recruitment of winemakers, such as the consultant Patrick Valette and the veteran in-house winemaker Cecilia Torres Salinas. She was trained at Santa Rita under Ignacio Recabarren and then spent time in the late 1980s at La Rosa and Luis Felipe Edwards before returning to Santa Rita as chief winemaker in 1990. The pair of winemakers had been experimenting with the wine that would eventually become Casa Real for the best part of a decade.

THE PEOPLE

From the first vintage to the present day the winemaker has been Cecilia Torres Salinas, and since 2009 her work within Santa Rita is devoted exclusively to the production of Casa Real. For her, the primary criterion for selection is the quality of the tannins, as she seeks both accessibility and ageability.

THE VINTAGE

Together with 1982, 1989 is regarded as the best vintage of the 1980s in the Maipo region. Yields were quite generous – in more recent vintages they have been far more restricted than they were back then. Torres also picked much earlier than she would today, as she was seeking elegance rather than roundness.

THE TERROIR

The vineyard, called Carneros Viejo, is a single block of around 20ha (hectares) located within the Alto Jahuel zone in Alto Maipo, where the soils are alluvial over a clay subsoil. This vineyard is located quite close to the Santa Rita winery at an elevation of 500 metres, and the vines are now 50 years old and in good condition. The vineyard contains three different selections of Cabernet planted together in a field blend. Alto Maipo is widely considered the finest region in Chile for Cabernet Sauvignon. Yields at Carneros Viejo are low, and today they never exceed 30 hectolitres per hectare.

THE WINE

A pure Cabernet Sauvignon, Casa Real is given a 20-day maceration, then aged in barriques for up to 15 months. In 1989 the wine was fermented in large wooden casks, but today vinification takes place in stainless steel. Torres always preferred a very gentle extraction, with brief pumpovers, the aim being to

'The aim is to retain elegance and velvety character, with tannins present but discreet'

retain the elegance and velvety character of the wine, with tannins that are present but discreet. In the mid-1980s Santa Rita began to import new French barrels, so it was logical that its top red wine should be aged entirely in new oak, although today the proportion has dropped to 90%.

THE REACTION

Written recollections of this wine are scarce. Torres herself regards Casa Real as a work in progress: 'In 1989 we were far less worried about potential greenness in the wines, whereas today we pick at much higher sugar levels to obtain more roundness and softness. In 1989 we vinified in a classic way, but today we are experimenting with barrel fermentation for a small proportion.' In 2013, Peter Richards MW wrote: 'Lovely dried fruit, leather and tobacco nose. Lots of age here. But lovely cogency and fluidity on palate. Still got good juicy acid. Earthy tannins. Not at all decrepit. Roasted green pepper, may have been green and mean when young! But it's a lovely, old school, traditional Chilean Cab, just lovely to drink.

THE FACTS

Bottles produced	Alcohol
12,000	**12.5%**
Composition	Release price
100% Cab Sauvignon	**£9.99**
Yield	Price today
40hl/ha	**N/A**

SEÑA 1997

Aconcagua, Chile

A LEGEND BECAUSE...

Robert Mondavi had a knack for forming distinguished joint ventures far from his native California. During his first trip to Chile in 1991, he met Eduardo Chadwick; the first vintage of their new label, Seña, was in 1995, a year before a comparable joint venture, Almaviva, was created by Concha y Toro and Mouton-Rothschild. However, the first wine from the dedicated Seña vineyard was not produced until 2001. From the beginning the wine showed a more European, indeed French influence and polish than Californian weight and brashness. Because of changes in the Mondavi wineries' structure and ownership, Chadwick bought its 50% share in 2004.

LOOKING BACK

The first vintage of Errazuriz's Don Maximiano Founder's Reserve Cabernet, arguably Chile's first 'icon' wine, was in 1983, so the development of the Seña label was a natural progression. Viñedo Chadwick would follow in 1999. In 2004, Eduardo Chadwick organised a blind tasting in Berlin, pitching his Cabernets against the best-known versions from Europe, including Bordeaux first growths. Seña took an honourable second place to Viñedo Chadwick. Similar tastings would take place in Asia and New York, again with gratifying results. Chadwick's aim was not just to promote his own wines, but to ally Chilean reds with some of the world's most admired wines.

THE VINTAGE

The early part of the growing season was cool, but then it warmed up considerably. Before harvest there were alternating periods of heat and cool, foggy weather, which brought some concerns about rot. However, by the time of harvest the weather was dry, although heat spikes retarded maturation so that the harvest was not completed until mid-April. Yields were moderate because of drought conditions.

THE TERROIR

The Seña vineyard was planted from 1998 and occupies 42ha on a hillside in Ocoa, Aconcagua – home to the Errazuriz estate. The site has been farmed biodynamically since 2005. However, the grapes for this vintage were sourced from various parcels, the oldest vines being 26 years old.

THE WINE

The handpicked grapes were fermented at moderate temperatures in stainless steel tanks with pumpovers. For this vintage the winemakers were Irene Paiva and Edward Flaherty. The wine was aged in 43% new barriques for 16 months, as the team wasn't aiming for a conspicuously oaky style. Later vintages were given longer ageing in entirely new French oak. The 1997 was a blend of Cabernet Sauvignon and Carmenère, although by 2004 some Merlot, Cabernet Franc and Petit Verdot had been added to the blend.

THE REACTION

James Molesworth, in *The Wine Spectator*, assessed the wine in 2000: 'High-toned, stylish Cab that's robed in cedar, mineral, smoke, iron and currant flavours. It's plush yet sophisticated, and the structure is finely grained... showing more elegance than previous vintages of Seña.'

In 2012, *The Wine Advocate*'s Neal Martin said: 'The 1997 Seña... is endowed with more fruit concentration [than the 1996], with baked black cherries, strawberry, orange peel and dried tobacco that attest to a warmer vintage... plenty of mocha-tinged black fruit with a crisp acidic bite on the finish, although it does not have great length or authority. The nose is showing better than the palate here.' Putting it into the context of a vertical tasting, Martin added: 'While I understand that older vintages have their share of plaudits, I discerned more complexity and vitality as well as finer integration of oak on newer vintages, as if more thought had gone into the wines. The result can be seen in the wines themselves, in particular the outstanding 2010.'

In 2018, Jancis Robinson noted: 'Dark blackish garnet. Very mellow mature nose. Warm and welcoming with only the freshness of Carmenère on the palate suggesting Chilean origins. Finishes a little suddenly but very correct and refreshing.'

THE FACTS

Bottles produced
30,000
Composition
84% Cabernet Sauvignon, 16% Carmenère
Yield
35hl/ha
Alcohol
13.5%
Release price
US$60
Price today
£112

VIÑEDO CHADWICK 2000

Alto Maipo, Chile

A LEGEND BECAUSE...

Although the Chadwick vineyard close to the Maipo River was only planted in 1992, the wine was an immediate success from its first vintage (1999) onwards. Subsequent vintages received Robert Parker's highest scores for a Chilean Cabernet Sauvignon for a number of years, ensuring international recognition. In 2004, Eduardo Chadwick, the sixth generation of his family to run Viña Errazuriz, staged a blind tasting in Berlin of 16 Bordeaux and Bordeaux-style wines, including 2000 vintage Château Lafite and other top-scoring first growths – but it was this wine that received the highest average score. Since then Viñedo Chadwick's reputation has been assured.

LOOKING BACK

Eduardo Chadwick wanted to honour his father Alfonso with a top-quality wine originating on the family's home estate in Alto Maipo. The vines for Viñedo Chadwick were planted on Alfonso's former polo ground, where he had trained daily to become Chile's champion at the sport.

THE VINTAGE

After a wet winter, the spring was cool and the summer months delivered moderate temperatures. More cool weather in the autumn slowed ripening, resulting in a late harvest of balanced grapes with intense flavours. Green-harvesting ensured yields were reduced to a level that maintained fruit concentration and maturity.

THE TERROIR

The 15ha vineyard was planted at a height of 650m in Puento Alto in the Alto Maipo valley, right next to one of the blocks used to produce another of Chile's outstanding red wines, Almaviva. The soil is largely gravel, with a top layer of clay and loam over a stony subsoil that ensures excellent drainage. The vines are planted to a density of 4,160 vines/ha. Nights are cool, and morning breezes drift down the slopes of the Andes, moderating the daytime heat.

THE WINE

Vinification varies from parcel to parcel, but there is a clear nod to top-tier Bordeaux. The grapes are lightly crushed then destemmed. Maceration can take up to 25 days, with the frequency and duration of pumpovers adapted to the character of each lot, and the wine is aged for 17 months in new barriques with regular racking. The final blend is assembled towards the end of the ageing process, with no fining but a light filtration before bottling.

THE REACTION

Stephen Brook appraised the wine soon after bottling: 'Rich, smoky, leathery nose. Very rich, plump and concentrated, opulent and spicy, a complex if somewhat broad wine, with good acidity and length.' In 2012, Neal Martin wrote: 'Has a ripe, sumptuous bouquet with forward black cherries, burnt toast and kirsch aromas that offer dried rose petal notes with time... a little coarse and rustic towards the savoury finish, although it displays admirable length.' In the same year, Jancis Robinson MW noted: 'Fully evolved but very clean and fresh... the fruit is just starting to fade and the alcohol insists just slightly, but it's a very unforced wine.' James Suckling judged: 'A round and savoury red with chocolate, plums and hazelnut. Hints of rose petal and tobacco too. Full body plus round and soft tannins. Attractive mouthfeel.'

In 2015, Jeannie Cho Lee MW wrote: 'A beautiful expression of Cabernet fruit – layers of cassis, cedar and tobacco with supple tannins... tightly knit and a bit reserved but opens up with time in the glass.' Steven Spurrier, long a fan of this wine, recorded in 2016: 'Still a wonderful nose with hints of rose petal and seductively aromatic. Extraordinary warmth and depth from just eight-year-old vines, almost "southern" richness with the spice but the firmness of Cabernet quite evident.'

THE FACTS

Bottles produced
6,000
Composition
100% Cabernet Sauvignon
Yield
30hl/ha
Alcohol
14.2%
Release price
£30
Price today
None available, but estimated at £350

WEINERT, MALBEC ESTRELLA 1977

Luján de Cuyo, Mendoza, Argentina

A LEGEND BECAUSE...

This was a wine from only the second vintage produced at this estate, and spent an astonishing 19 years in casks before being bottled and released. It was one of the first pure Malbecs to be presented internationally as a fine wine, helping to establish it as Argentina's signature variety. The next Estrella Malbec would not be made until 1994 and, like its successors, was a selection of the very finest casks of wine. A few bottles of the 1977 Estrella remain in the Weinert cellars.

LOOKING BACK

Brazilian-born Bernardo Weinert bought a ruinous 19th-century winery in 1975, having previously made an extended study of soils and vines in the Mendoza area, and, after renovating the winery, he produced his first wines two years later. The winemaker then and for the next 20 years was Raúl de la Mota. From the outset, Estrella (meaning 'star') was the top wine from Weinert, showcasing the estate's finest single-varietal Malbec, Cabernet Sauvignon or Merlot, depending on the year.

THE VINTAGE

Little is recorded about the climatic conditions in 1977, but construction work at the winery delayed the harvest, so the Malbec was picked at riper levels than was usual at the time.

THE TERROIR

The Weinert vineyards are mainly in Luján de Cuyo and also in the higher sections of Maipú. There are 40ha here as well as a further 20ha in Patagonia. The elevation in Luján de Cuyo ranges from 850m to 1,100m, and the soils are rocky and sandy, although deep silt soils are preferred for Malbec. The vineyards drain well, although rainfall is low at 240mm and is amplified by flood irrigation. In 1977, however, most of the grapes were purchased, and those used for Estrella were more than 50 years old.

THE WINE

After a manual harvest the grapes are destemmed and fermented in concrete vats for up to nine days without prolonged maceration. For the first winter the wine stays on its fine lees. Weinert always ages its wines for a minimum of two years in underground cellars, but this 1977 is unusual in having spent 19 years in casks of 2,500 to 6,000 litres. For more than a year, Bernardo Weinert and current winemaker Hubert Weber taste various casks and make up the final blend before bottling.

THE REACTION

Decanter's Anthony Rose tasted one of the surviving bottles at the winery in 2011, noting 'Still very much alive, with the leathery maturity of a fine Bordeaux.' Julia Harding MW of *JancisRobinson.com* tried it with other tasters in 2008: 'A wine that was either loved or spurned. Still quite deeply coloured though it is browning a little. Complex developed nose – a little meaty and leathery. Tobacco and herbs and coffee on the palate. Meaty, leathery and still has fruit. Cool and fresh and elegant in this very old-fashioned style.'

'This wine spent an astonishing 19 years in casks before being bottled'

In the same year US critic Robert Parker tasted one of the remaining bottles from his own cellar: 'One of the historic wines of Argentina, and at age 31, it continues to strut its stuff. Possessing the complexity of a first- or second-growth Bordeaux, wonderful freshness, depth and ripeness, it offers spicy, earthy, complex fruit in a full-bodied style.'

In 2001 James Molesworth of *The Wine Spectator*, wrote: 'Like an old Rioja or Chateau Musar with guts, this shows brown sugar, tea and liquorice flavours, but still has fleshy, albeit pruney fruit. Though a touch dry on the finish this wine has stood the test of time.'

THE FACTS

Bottles produced
30,000
Composition
100% Malbec
Yield
2hl/ha
Alcohol
15%
Release price
US$25
Price today
£476

SOUTH AFRICA

The country's isolation during the apartheid years led to viticultural decline, as viruses proliferated and styles became parochial. Nonetheless some fine wines were produced by the most conscientious estates, although they are likely to be surpassed by the wines, in a wider range of styles, being produced today.

KANONKOP, PINOTAGE 1995

Stellenbosch, South Africa

A LEGEND BECAUSE...

Pinotage is a grape variety that divides critics and consumers alike, but Kanonkop's version, championed by long-term winemaker Beyers Truter, has always been hailed as a benchmark by those who believe Pinotage demands to be taken seriously. Kanonkop is a Stellenbosch estate now run by the fourth generation; it began bottling its wines in 1973. The Pinotage variety was created in 1925 by Dr Izak Perold by crossing Pinot Noir with Cinsault. It was soon being widely planted and became both a workhorse grape and South Africa's unique if controversial contribution to the world of varietal wines. It likes a warm climate and ripens early. It is not a difficult variety to grow, and although it doesn't raisin easily, it can attain high sugar levels which can give jammy flavours. Truter, both at Kanonkop and his own winery Beyerskloof, was long recognised as the master of Pinotage.

LOOKING BACK

By the 1980s Pinotage had fallen out of fashion, and existing vines were often used to produce Port-style wines. It was Beyers Truter who realised that excessive yields were the culprit, resulting in the production of many mediocre wines, marked by aromas of banana, nail varnish and acetate. Truter curbed yields and began ageing the wine in barrel from the early 1980s, a process that gives his Pinotage far more complexity and structure. Truter realised the often unpleasant acetate aromas were the consequence of fermenting at low temperatures – he would let the temperature rise to around 30°C so as to replace those aromas with those of ripe red fruits.

THE VINTAGE

Stellenbosch growers enjoyed an excellent growing season in 1995, warm and dry. These conditions resulted in a relatively small crop of bunches, often with small berries that gave great concentration to the wines, as well as formidable power and flavour. Kanonkop's owner Johann Krige considers 1995 to be one of the three top vintages of the past 20 years.

THE TERROIR

Kanonkop's Pinotage was planted on southwest-facing soils of decomposed granite, and the bush vines have been here since 1953. Thus by 1995 the vines were over 40 years old. They were dry-farmed bush vines rather than grown on trellises, which helped to restrain the variety's tendency to crop heavily (bush vines tend to be self-regulating).

THE WINE

The wine was given a relatively short maceration of around three days, and fermented in open-top vats at around 30°C. The array of shallow vats resembles the lagares found in the Douro Valley. The cap was punched down by hand. Once fermentation had terminated, the wine was decanted into Nevers barriques, of which half were new, and aged for 14 months.

THE REACTION

In 1997 the *Platter Wine Guide* remarked pithily: 'Among the most accessible so far, juicy, ripe flavours, oak vanilla adding charm.' In the same year Kim Marcus of *The Wine Spectator*

'Winemaker Beyers Truter was long recognised as the master of Pinotage'

noted: 'A rich, remarkable South African red, impressively structured, with plenty of jammy flavours in the mid-palate framed by chocolate, leather and smoke notes. Good acidity as well.'

Tasting the wine in June 2016, Michael Fridjhon observed: 'Still remarkably youthful, with fabulous fruit intensity – hints of plum and blackberry – contributing freshness to the more evolved, earthier notes of leather and spice; savoury tannins, nuanced and detailed on the finish.'

THE FACTS

Bottles produced
58,000
Composition
100% Pinotage
Yield
42hl/ha
Alcohol
13%
Release price
N/A
Price today
£49.20

KLEIN CONSTANTIA, VIN DE CONSTANCE 1986

Constantia, South Africa

A LEGEND BECAUSE...

Constantia was one of the most famous and expensive sweet wines in the 18th and 19th centuries. Jane Austen and Charles Baudelaire referred to the wine in their writings, and it was favoured by the likes of Frederick the Great, Napoleon Bonaparte, George IV of England and Otto von Bismarck. Most of those fortunate enough to taste 19th-century bottles, including Michael Broadbent, are of the opinion that Constantia was fortified. The outbreak of phylloxera in the late 19th century brought production to an end, and with it the precise details of how it was made. Nonetheless, in the 1980s Duggie Jooste of the Klein Constantia estate, together with winemaker Ross Gower, resolved to try to recreate the original wine. The idea was first proposed by viticulturist Professor Chris Orffer. His formula has proved a great success, with consistent quality over the years. The 1986 was the first year of production, but that wine was never released commercially, as the Joostes had no idea how well the wine would turn out. The special bottle, still in use, was designed in Italy.

LOOKING BACK

Klein Constantia is one of the original estates in the Constantia zone close to Cape Town. It forms part of the larger 900-hectare estate created in 1685 by Simon Van der Stel, who planted grapes here. Its long history explains why South African producers bristle when they are patronisingly described as 'New World' estates. Constantia seems to have made its first appearances in Europe in the 1720s. The Jooste family, who sold the property in 2011, was an admirable custodian of the estate, one of the finest in the region.

THE VINTAGE

1986 is remembered as a good vintage for red wines in the Cape. Very dry conditions in January and February led to early ripening and to perfect conditions for the Muscat de Frontignan to form perfect raisins.

THE TERROIR

The wine is made from Muscat de Frontignan (aka Muscat à Petits Grains) and picked very ripe with no botrytis. The eight hectares of vines were planted in 1983 on a slope with varied soils: sandstone higher up, clay and decomposed granite in the middle, and sand below. For the maiden 1986 vintage, most of the crop was thinned so as not to stress the young plants and a small amount was left to mature on the vines until it raisined.

THE WINE

Very little is known about how the 1986 vintage was made, but the tiny harvest would have been macerated on the skins before a hard pressing designed to extract not just sugar and flavour but tannins too, giving the finished wine more texture. The wine was fermented in two 500-litre barrels and aged for 18 months before being bottled. There is no fortification and fermentation stops naturally because of the high levels of sugar and alcohol. In current vintages the grapes are picked in various stages to bring in a range of sugar and acidity levels. Each batch is made using a variety of methods: some are fermented on the skins, while others are macerated for two weeks. Then the finished wine is aged in barrels for up to five years, providing a light oxidation that forms the stable yet complex character so typical of Vin de Constance.

'The wine was favoured by the likes of Frederick the Great and Napoleon Bonaparte'

THE REACTION

As the wine was never released, printed comments are scarce. South African wine writer Angela Lloyd tasted the wine in 2002 and wrote: 'Intense, lifted, fresh honey and lemon bouquet. Racy, minerally acid lends vivid clarity to the rich fruit, silky texture. Excellent balance. Incisively clean, long. Amazingly youthful.' A few years later, Tuscan wine producer Sebastiano Castiglioni of Querciabella acquired some cases at the Nederburg auction, so more bottles may become available for tasting. In 2014 Klein Constantia winemaker Matthew Day brought a bottle to London for tasting. I noted: 'Startling caramelised orange nose, smoky, a touch of rancio, vivid. Medium-bodied, moderate concentration, good acidity, a trace of oxidation, yet vibrant, with some tropical fruit. Peppery finish, fine length.'

THE FACTS

Bottles produced
950 500ml bottles
Composition
100% Muscat de Frontignan
Yield
3.3hl/ha
Alcohol
13.7%
Release price
Not sold, but the 1987 was ZAR22 ex-cellar (about £6.80)
Price today
N/A

LANZERAC, PINOTAGE 1959

Stellenbosch, South Africa

A LEGEND BECAUSE...

This was the first-ever monovarietal Pinotage bottled and released in South Africa. Nowadays, Pinotage is a staple variety in many parts of the country, even though it is not universally loved. This wine was produced by the huge cooperative Stellenbosch Farmers' Winery (SFW) and was not released until 1961. In the late 1950s, SFW had purchased the trademark of Lanzerac, an estate founded in 1692, and decided to use that label for its pioneering Pinotage. It went on to win the trophy at the Cape Young Wine Show in 1959.

LOOKING BACK

It was the inspiration of Professor Abraham Perold of Stellenbosch University in 1924 to cross Pinot Noir with the more widely planted Cinsault, resulting in a hardy variety that could give wines of deep colour and good structure. Perold was obliged to leave his house soon after, and seedlings planted close by were neglected. Indeed, just one survived, and all Pinotage wines thereafter are its descendants. It wasn't until 1941 that there was sufficient Pinotage in the ground to fill a barrel. This wine was made by CT de Waal of Stellenbosch University; Perold himself never tasted it, as he died that same year. A decade went by before Pinotage was first planted on an experimental basis in 1951. Soon the variety was performing well at local wine shows. The SFW took notice and decided to produce the wine under its Lanzerac label. It didn't own the property but had been entrusted with managing it. Today, Pinotage occupies more than 7% of South African wine-grape plantings.

THE VINTAGE

It has proved difficult to find any information on the vintage. The wine's longevity suggests it was of good quality.

THE TERROIR

This wine was a blend from two Stellenbosch vineyards: Bellevue Estate, owned by Pieter Morkel, with vines planted in 1953; and Kanonkop, planted by Paul Sauer. The latter would go on to produce the best known of all South African Pinotages, but at this time it was a blending component, as plantings were limited in the 1950s.

THE WINE

Pinotage is notorious for an acetone aroma and flavour that is hailed as the variety's footprint, or detested as an unwelcome intrusion of nail-varnish aromas into a sturdy red wine. A by-product of fermentation, its presence can be moderated by fermenting at cooler temperatures. It hasn't proved possible to unearth details about how this wine was made, but it's known that the 1961, the second release of Lanzerac Pinotage, was fermented in concrete and aged in 50-hectolitre vats. The bottled wine may have followed common practice at the time as a blend of different vintages, despite the label's vintage indication.

THE REACTION

Greg Sherwood MW tasted the wine in 2018: 'The wine carries a now-legendary status and does not disappoint in the glass... Fantastically fine, complex nose of sweet leafy savoury bramble berry fruits, sweet tobacco leaf, black chai tea, dried herbs, earthy wood spice and notes of macerated cherries. All the wonderful tertiary complexity of a very classy, expressive red wine that retains an impressive harmony and poise, textural elegance with pinpoint vibrant acidity, freshness and an all-round air of elder statesman confidence. You know you are in the presence of greatness when you taste this old beauty.'

Jamie Goode reported on the same tasting: 'Very fine and expressive with a hint of green and some notes of tobacco and tea, together with vibrant berry and cherry fruit. Harmonious and expressive with maturity but also freshness. This has aged so nicely with amazing purity considering its vintage. Subtle earthy notes, too. A really beautiful wine.'

In 2019, DWWA Regional Chair for South Africa Fiona McDonald was fortunate enough to taste one of the two remaining half-bottles from the Lanzerac cellars: 'The wine was evolved and tertiary with toasty coffee bean, a touch of leather and macerated red- and black-cherry fruit. It was drinking well, showing distinct signs of life in its relative freshness and succulence.'

THE FACTS

Bottles produced
82,400
Composition
95% Pinotage, 5% Cinsault

MEERLUST, RUBICON 1995

Stellenbosch, South Africa

A LEGEND BECAUSE...

This ancient property was one of the first in South Africa to offer a high-quality Bordeaux-style blend, and it remains a benchmark for Stellenbosch wines. Meerlust has been in the hands of the Myburgh family since 1756, and the incumbent now, as in 1995, is Hannes Myburgh, who represents the eighth generation of his family. Although the precise proportions of the Meerlust blend do vary from vintage to vintage, the wine is always dominated by Cabernet Sauvignon, which comprises about 70% of the blend. Stellenbosch may in recent years have produced Bordeaux blends with greater power or concentration, but few can match Rubicon for sheer finesse.

LOOKING BACK

Rubicon was first produced in 1980, after Nico Myburgh, the father of Hannes, visited Bordeaux and perceived that its climate was similar to that of Stellenbosch. Always intended as a top-of-the range wine, it is not made in every vintage. Thus no Rubicon was produced in 1985 or 1990. In such years the fruit is used for Meerlust's varietal wines from Merlot and Cabernet Sauvignon. The ebullient and perfectionist Giorgio Dalla Cia was the winemaker of this 1995 vintage, and had come to South Africa from his native Friuli in Italy to establish a distillery. He decided to stay on and joined Meerlust in 1978. He eventually retired in 2003, and was replaced the following year by Chris Williams. Williams had been Dalla Cia's assistant winemaker in 1995.

THE VINTAGE

The southern hemisphere winter of 1994 was cold and wet, but conditions improved when spring came early, with a perfect bud break. The growing season was warm, but so dry that water stress became a problem that was only alleviated when rain arrived in February. Ripening resumed rapidly and the harvest was able to take place in ideal conditions.

THE TERROIR

Meerlust lies 15km south of the town of Stellenbosch, and its 160 hectares of vineyards are cooler than most in the region, thanks to their proximity to False Bay, which is just 5km away. This brings in cooling breezes and mist during the summer months, which helps moderate the temperature and give a slower, more even ripening season. The soil is mainly decomposed granite mixed with clay, alongside parcels of gravelly loam. The gravel components provide excellent drainage, even in the clay soils. Merlot is planted on the richer, heavier soils, while Cabernet grows in the stonier sectors. The Meerlust estate is fortunate in that it is never affected by frost or hail. Up to half the crop is removed each year, ensuring excellent concentration and even ripening.

THE WINE

After the grapes have been picked by hand, the varieties are vinified separately. The Merlot tends to be fermented at relatively cool temperatures. But for the Cabernet Sauvignon Dalla Cia favoured an extended maceration in order to give the wine sufficient structure for long ageing. The selection for Rubicon is made after the malolactic fermentation is completed. Today the malolactic takes place in barrels, but in 1995 the wine remained in tanks. At this stage the blend is

'Stellenbosch may have produced Bordeaux blends with greater power or concentration, but few can match Rubicon for sheer finesse'

composed. Rubicon is aged in 80% new, 300-litre Nevers oak and 20% second-year barrels. It is then given two years' bottle age before being released.

THE REACTION

In 2000 *Decanter*'s Michael Broadbent described the vintage as 'One of the Cape's classics... Good fruit, lovely flavour and remarkably good value.' In the same year Pierre Rovani reviewed the wine for *The Wine Advocate*, finding a cornucopia of fruits: 'It exhibits fabulous aromas of dark fruits, spices, and some candied strawberries. It has a lovely satiny structure, excellent focus, elegance, and is crafted in a feminine style. This concentrated, spicy, cherry and blackberry syrup-flavoured offering has an exceptional finish filled with plums and tangy blackcurrants.'

THE FACTS

Bottles produced
60,000
Composition
68% Cabernet Sauvignon, 23% Merlot, 9% Cabernet Franc
Yield
35hl/ha
Alcohol
12.8%
Release price
85 Rand
Price today
£28

Nederburg, Cabernet Sauvignon 1974

Paarl, South Africa

A legend because…

South Africa is not short of historic estates, and with vineyards first planted in the late 17th century, its wine industry is not best pleased when it is considered a 'New World' region. Most of those original plantings were in Constantia, close to Cape Town, but other regions enjoy a long history too. Nederburg in Paarl was founded in 1791 and consolidated its reputation by hosting – and producing wines for – its celebrated annual auction. International sanctions during the apartheid era were a setback for wine quality overall, so the auctions helped to maintain standards.

Looking back

German-born Günter Brözel was winemaker here from 1956 to 1989, and was responsible for the excellent Cabernet Sauvignons. These were something of an exception in the context of South African wine in the 1970s, as so many vineyards were badly virused and struggled to ripen. Brözel was probably better known for Edelkeur, a botrytised Chenin Blanc, though its high residual sugar did not meet the requirements of the wine regulations at that time so it could not be sold. As a compromise, allowing Edelkeur to be offered to a limited clientele, the Nederburg Auction was founded in 1975. The annual event continues to this day.

The vintage

The 1974 vintage was of exceptional quality and the vines remained entirely healthy. It was widely regarded as the best vintage of the decade.

The terroir

Records are sparse, but it seems probable that the grapes for this wine were grown at Plaisir de Merle farm in Simondium. This lies on the east-facing lower slope of the Simonsberg Mountain. Its well-drained soil is mostly composed of weathered granite that retains sufficient water to help the vines survive even a very hot summer.

The wine

In the 1970s regulations for South African wine were lax, and many wines that were labelled as Cabernet Sauvignon also included a generous, sometimes even dominant proportion of Cinsault. The variety Cinsault was widely planted and high-yielding, helping estates to stretch their so-called Cabernets. However, winemaker Brözel often insisted that this wine was indeed 100% Cabernet. It was fermented to full dryness.

The reaction

Shortly after release in the late 1970s, *Platter's South African Wine Guide* noted: 'Richly flavoured dry red with great depth and excellent keeping qualities, an elegant wine, not too heavy on the palate.'

Robert Mondavi was enthusiastic in 1992: 'Rapture! Sweet spice, cake mix and whiffs of thatch. A beautiful, gentle, sweet-fruited entry. Still fresh and juicy with lovely structure and plum pudding, spice and fruitcake flavours. Long and lingering finish. Magnificent!'

In 2014 Michael Fridjhon wrote: 'Maroon, with great depth, only now bricking at the edge. Almost Porty in its ripeness and texture, yet surprisingly elegant on the finish.'

Roland Peens reviewed the 1974 on his blog *Wine Cellar* in 2015: 'Many wines from this era and vintage show a slightly Porty character... This 1974, however, is utterly composed, fresh and deeply complex. The nose reminded me of an aged Hermitage... So elegant and pure, with red berries, a hint of toast, nuts and exotic spice. The palate was astonishingly refined, deep and elegant.'

THE FACTS

Bottles produced
N/A
Composition
100% Cabernet Sauvignon
Yield
N/A
Alcohol
12.9%
Release price
N/A
Price today
£66

UNITED STATES

Napa Valley, with its long tradition of rich, seductive wines, dominates the selection here, but room was found for a great red from Santa Cruz and pioneering Pinot Noirs from Oregon and the Sonoma Coast. In future the Napa classics will be joined by cool-climate wines from many parts of California and Washington state.

BEAULIEU VINEYARD, BV, GEORGES DE LATOUR, PRIVATE RESERVE 1947

Rutherford, Napa Valley, California, USA

A LEGEND BECAUSE...

In the 1930s, Beaulieu Vineyard persuaded the Russian-born winemaker André Tchelistcheff to come over from France and make its wines after Prohibition ended. He succeeded Leon Bonnet as winemaker, and it was Bonnet who, encouraged by BV founder Georges de Latour, created the Georges de Latour Private Reserve in 1936. Latour was keen to create what today would be called an icon wine, one that fully represented the finest Cabernet Sauvignon vineyards in the Rutherford sub-region and followed the great winemaking traditions of Bordeaux. It was named after BV's Bordeaux-born founder, who established the property in 1900, planting 40 hectares in Rutherford, though his first vintage was 1909.

LOOKING BACK

Tchelistcheff was still firmly in place at BV in 1947 (only retiring in 1973) and was rapidly becoming a revered figure in Napa's winemaking circles, with many disciples working at other wineries in the valley. Fine wine was still a niche product in the 1940s, when fortified styles dominated the market and wine quality overall was not that high. The golden era for BV came to an end in 1969, when the property was sold to the giant Heublein drinks company, which rapidly increased volumes and downgraded quality. Recent decades have seen steady improvements in quality at the top end of the range.

THE VINTAGE

This was an exceptional year for Cabernet Sauvignon in Napa Valley; however, BV was unable to provide more detail on specific conditions at its vineyards.

THE TERROIR

Rutherford soils are essentially gravelly loam on gently sloping and well-drained alluvial fans. Tchelistcheff detected an earthy note in the wines grown here, and dubbed that character 'Rutherford dust'. Although many Rutherford Cabernets are of exceptional quality, it would be hard in a blind tasting to pick them out on the basis of their 'dustiness'.

THE WINE

The Private Reserve was aged from the outset in French barriques, but after the war it was difficult to import barrels from France, so until 1989 the Private Reserve was aged in American oak. This was also a stylistic choice. In an article by Frank Prial, Tchelistcheff declared: 'I changed to American oak because I wanted more flavour, a more aggressive wine. Today I dislike the American oak.'

THE REACTION

James Laube in 1991 wrote: 'A claret-style wine - dry, elegant and meaty, with spice and generous, plummy Cabernet flavours on the finish.' In the late-1990s he tasted it again: 'From an excellent vintage, it shows incredible richness, complexity and harmony for a wine past its 50th birthday. There is still much to admire in this amazing wine that seems suspended in time.'

Michael Broadbent, writing about his first tasting of the wine in 1972, noted that it was 'the first really top-class Napa Cabernet Sauvignon I had ever tasted'. In 1999 he found it 'medium-deep; fragrant, autumnal bouquet, very interesting and very attractive, soft entry, dry finish.' At the same tasting Steven Spurrier noted: 'Typical minty nose, ripe, almost sweet fruit and a touch of volatile acidity, balanced with some life ahead of it.'

Stephen Brook also tasted the wine on the same occasion in 1999. It showed little sign of age; the nose had 'dense, rich, cassis aromas', while on the palate it was 'medium-bodied and assertive', and was 'beginning to lose some fruit. Herbs and pepper underlay the fruit, but there's not much depth or complexity. It's still lively, long, and has good concentration, filling out with aeration.'

THE FACTS

Bottles produced
N/A
Composition
100% Cabernet Sauvignon
Yield
N/A
Alcohol
N/A
Release price
N/A
Price today
US$1,100

CHATEAU MONTELENA 1973

Calistoga, Napa Valley, California, USA

A LEGEND BECAUSE…

This was the wine that dethroned some of the most prestigious white Burgundies at the legendary Judgement of Paris tasting organised by Steven Spurrier in 1976. It came top out of the 10 French and Californian Chardonnays poured blind at the event. Moreover, no fewer than six of the nine French judges awarded Montelena their highest score. After the scores were totted up, it became clear it had won by a sizeable margin. Even more galling, it was a wine that had been made from young vines, confounding the French conviction that vines need to be mature to deliver top-class wine.

LOOKING BACK

Miljenko 'Mike' Grgich was a Croatian who in 1958 emigrated to California. There he worked with many of the existing wineries from the late 1960s, including Souverain, Christian Brothers, Beaulieu and Mondavi. In 1972 he was offered a job at Chateau Montelena, founded in 1882, but owned since 1969 by lawyer Jim Barrett and his partners. Grgich's wines met with an enthusiastic reception and he remained at Montelena until 1975, when he left after some acrimonious disputes to found his own winery.

THE VINTAGE

Winter was cool and damp, but the growing season in Napa and Sonoma, which was relatively cool, left the Chardonnay vines free from mildew and other diseases. August was very hot and the grapes ripened rapidly, yet preserved enough natural acidity so that Grgich did not have to add tartaric acid to the must.

THE TERROIR

Although Montelena owned extensive vineyards, they were being partly replanted to supply the winery with better quality fruit. So the Chardonnay in 1973 was sourced from independent growers. Montelena in 2014 stated that 39% of the grapes came from the Belle Terre Vineyard in Alexander Valley; 35% from Bacigalupi Vineyard in Russian River Valley; 23% from the Hanna Vineyard in Oak Knoll near Napa and just 3% from Calistoga. So the wine was a blend, without any clear terroir character. However, Grgich himself monitored the growing patterns in each site, and decided on the harvesting dates.

THE WINE

As they arrived at the winery, the grapes were crushed and destemmed before being pressed in a modern bladder press. The juice was clarified in steel tanks and racked after four days. Grgich inoculated the must with yeasts and fermentation began. He opted to ferment at low temperatures, so the extraction was prolonged to six weeks. He blocked the malolactic fermentation, and then stabilised and filtered the new wine. It was tranferred to second-fill Limousin barriques and left to age for eight months. In December 1974 Grgich made the final blend and filtered the final wine. It was released in September 1975.

THE REACTION

Unfortunately the written comments of the judges in 1976 have not been preserved – with one exception. Christian Vannequé, head sommelier at the Tour d'Argent in Paris, noted: 'A very agreeable wine, which will blossom pleasantly and has a good equilibrium. To be followed.' The owner of the celebrated

'No fewer than six of the nine French judges awarded it their top score'

restaurant would later rebuke Vannequé for having participated. Michael Broadbent tasted the wine in 1980, writing: 'It is certainly my idea of a fine California Chardonnay... broad, slightly sweet, fully developed ... positive but not excessive; dryish, more body than a Sauzet Puligny-Montrachet, but not heavy. Fine, rich, a touch of meatiness. Very good acidity. Perfect.'

THE FACTS

Bottles produced
26,400

Composition
100% Chardonnay

Yield
N/A

Alcohol
13.2%

Release price
US$6.50

Price today
There is no listed stockist for this wine, but a bottle was sold at a charity auction in 2010 for US$11,325

The Eyrie Vineyards, South Block Reserve Pinot Noir 1975

Willamette Valley, Oregon, USA

A legend because…

Even as a student at UC Davis, David Lett had a passion for Pinot Noir, which was not rated in California at the time. Carefully considering the ideal terroir for producing Pinot outside Burgundy, he pioneered a region that would swiftly become known for the quality of its Pinot Noir: Oregon's Willamette Valley. He planted vines in 1965 and his first vintage was 1970. Some months before he died in 2008, his son, Jason Lett, led a vertical tasting to celebrate his retirement. The 1970 was still very much alive, but of those early bottles 1975 was the best. It had also triumphed in a blind tasting of worldwide Pinots in Paris organised in 1979 by Gault-Millau, thus becoming a benchmark for the variety.

Looking back

David was a Willamette Valley pioneer; but he wasn't alone for long. Dick Erath and Dick Ponzi were among those drawn to Oregon. In the 1960s and 1970s the valley was a kind of bohemian centre, drawing in people attracted by an artisanal, even rustic way of life. David was particular in producing a consistent style of Pinot Noir that favoured perfume and delicacy rather than power. His delicate style was not universally admired, but proved enormously influential. The Eyrie style only evolved slightly after Jason took over the winemaking in 2005.

The vintage

1975 was an exceptional year. A warm, dry June was balanced by a rainy July, which restored balance to the vines. August was superb, with just a little rain late in the month, and then fine dry weather continued through September. The grapes for this Reserve were picked between 4 and 6 October.

The terroir

David's early Pinot plantings were in the Dundee Hills, on clay-loam soils that were rich in iron deposits. Farming was essentially organic, although it was not yet certified. Elevation ranged from 110m-125m. These original vines were ungrafted and, as French clones were unavailable in the 1960s, David opted for Davis clone 1A, although other clones were planted in subsequent years.

The wine

David liked to pick at slightly lower sugars than his neighbours, and fermented the wines in bins at low temperatures, using cultivated yeasts (replaced by wild yeasts from 2008) and retaining only a few whole clusters. This and the oak regime probably account for the pale colour of his Pinots. The regular Pinots were aged in barrels, none new, for 18-24 months, while Reserves spent an extra year in wood.

The reaction

The vertical tasting at the winery in 2008 allowed many writers to assess the wine. Mark Savage MW, Eyrie's British importer, wrote: 'A wine of subtlety, with beautiful balance, no harsh edges, great complexity and delicacy. Infinitely intriguing, a wine one wants to return to again and again!'

Stephen Brook, another participant, commented: 'Delicate nose showing lift and poise, aromas of potpourri and coffee. Rich and silky, this retains sweet fruit and is not that evolved. It still has vigour and flesh, integrated tannins, and a long cappuccino finish.'

Tyler Colman recalls: 'It was still tasting lovely and rich, with great aromas and serious character. When people in the room were asked to pick the favourite of the flight, this was the clear winner.'

THE FACTS

Bottles produced
1,172
Composition
100% Pinot Noir
Yield
28hl/ha
Alcohol
13.7%
Release price
US$9
Price today
On two occasions in 2017, two bottles fetched US$1,000 each at benefit auctions

JOSEPH PHELPS, INSIGNIA 1997

Napa Valley, California USA

A LEGEND BECAUSE...

Insignia was one of Napa's first proprietary Bordeaux-style blends, although the very first vintage, 1974, was pure Cabernet Sauvignon, as was the 1976. By 1977 it had taken on its present form. Although the precise blend has varied over the years, it has always been Cabernet-dominant. In an appealing contrast to many of Napa's cult wines, Insignia is made in substantial quantities. The 1997 represents the peak of production, and today Insignia ranges from 120,000 to 180,000 bottles.

LOOKING BACK

Construction tycoon Joseph Phelps began a new career as wine producer in 1973. As well as excellent Cabernets, his winery became known, under its German winemaker Walter Schug, for its Rieslings and botrytis wines and for some of California's first Syrah bottlings. The idea of a proprietary blend is now commonplace in Napa and Sonoma, but again Phelps was the pioneer of this style. Craig Williams took over as winemaker in 1983 and continued to fine-tune the Insignia blends, sourcing more and more of the fruit from Phelps's own Napa vineyards.

THE VINTAGE

This was both an early and big vintage. Cabernet Sauvignon resisted a rainy and humid mid-August, though some Merlot suffered. The huge crop led to some dilution in poorly managed vineyards. A dry September with moderate temperatures brought the Cabernet to perfect ripeness, with picking lasting four weeks until 8 October. Insignia was always hailed as one of the wines of 1997; some other Napa reds were clearly overripe and are now in decline.

THE TERROIR

From 2004 Insignia was produced only from Phelps's own estate vineyards in various parts of Napa Valley, but in 1997 about 40% of the grapes were purchased from other growers with whom the winery had long-term relationships. As a selection it was produced from many different lots, so that it doesn't make much sense to speak of a precise terroir behind the wine. The Cabernet Sauvignon came from vineyards in Rutherford and Stags Leap; the Merlot was sourced from Carneros, and the Petit Verdot from Napa Valley.

THE WINE

The grapes from different sources were sorted and fermented separately in stainless steel tanks, then aged separately until the spring of 1998. The various lots were then tasted and the final blend composed. This definitive version of the 1997 was aged in new barriques for a total of 26 months before being bottled.

THE REACTION

James Laube of *The Wine Spectator* noted in 2008: 'Youthful and concentrated, with hints of maturity. Wonderful vibrancy and intensity for a wine of this age.' Robert Parker was enthusiastic about the wine from the outset, and in 2013 wrote: 'A stunning bouquet of violets, charcoal, crème de cassis and toast. There is not a hard edge to be found, only velvety tannins, compelling depth and fruit intensity, and stunning purity. Should continue to age effortlessly for two

'Insignia was always hailed as one of the wines of 1997'

decades or more.' But in the same year Jancis Robinson MW was not so impressed: 'Not much nose. Minty, cough medicine. Lots of alcohol and dried spices on the finish. Still youthful and a little brutal at the moment. Quite a dry finish.' I've tasted this vintage four times, most recently in 2012: 'Very ripe and intense mint and blackcurrant nose, with eucalyptus tones. Very rich palate, but lifted and vigorous, with pungent acidity. Not tiring at all.'

THE FACTS

Bottles produced
240,000
Composition
83% Cabernet Sauvignon, 14% Merlot, 3% Petit Verdot
Yield
N/A
Alcohol
13.9%
Release price
US$120
Price today
£312

MARTINELLI, JACKASS HILL ZINFANDEL 1994

Russian River Valley, Sonoma County, California, USA

A LEGEND BECAUSE...

The Martinelli family have been grape growers in Sonoma since the late 1880s. It remains their primary business to this day, with most of the fruit contracted to other wineries. The family stopped producing their own wines after 1949, but the winery reopened in the late 1980s under winemaker Daniel Moore. Helen Turley came on board in 1992 as consultant winemaker; she only left in 2010. Turley was a name to conjure with, admired by Robert Parker and other influential wine writers. Sonoma Zinfandel was typically a big, ripe wine with more heft than finesse. European palates often found it Porty and fatiguing, but Americans – the main buyers of these wines – adored it, their predilection boosted by wine critics' rave reviews.

LOOKING BACK

Visitors flocked to the Martinelli facility on River Road in droves after the reviews of the 1990s. They must have been surprised to find it a large, rather scruffy former hop-barn. There was no Napa Valley bling here at that time, although today the tasting room has been expanded and tidied up. Indeed, this rustic atmosphere and the welcome from the family members were part of the appeal. This was also a period when bold, full-bodied, high-alcohol wines were in fashion. Helen Turley's brother Larry founded his own winery in Napa Valley, where he produced numerous single-vineyard Zinfandels in exactly this style.

THE VINTAGE

The spring this year was cool, with some stormy weather. The summer was warm and mild, giving slow and consistent maturation, and the grapes retained good acidity. The autumn was cool and the harvest free of challenges. Problems at flowering did result in a below-average crop of Zinfandel, although the low yields didn't impact quality.

THE TERROIR

Jackass Hill is an estate vineyard on a southeast-facing slope that was planted in the 1890s by Giuseppe and Luisa Martinelli. This served as the mother block for massal selections for other Zinfandel vineyards planted by their descendants. Jackass Hill is believed to be the steepest unterraced vineyard in Sonoma county, with a 60°-65° slope, which it would be illegal to plant today for safety reasons. The site is dry-farmed and composed solely of bush vines.

THE WINE

The grapes were picked by hand and fermented with natural yeasts, and then aged for 10 months in 50% new French oak. The wine was bottled without fining or filtration.

THE REACTION

In 1996, Robert Parker was impressed: 'The 1994 Jackass Hill Vineyard Zinfandel... rivals the extraordinary 1994 Hayne Vineyard Zinfandel produced by Turley Cellars... Martinelli's Zinfandel is amazingly rich and unctuous, with huge flavour concentration, and a blockbuster finish that must be tasted to be believed.'

That same year, *The Wine Spectator* was slightly less enthusiastic: 'Dark, ripe and intense. Delivers an elegant core of complex, rich, plush plum, cherry, currant and berry flavours, with a tarry, spicy aftertaste. Delicious now and worthy of short-term cellaring.'

In 2018, Lisa Perrotti-Brown MW reviewed the wine on the Parker website: 'Medium garnet with a touch of brick... scented of potpourri, Chinese five spice, citrus peel, liquorice and chargrill with a core of dried mulberries, preserved cherries and figs plus a touch of smoked meats. Full-bodied, super-concentrated and still sporting a firm frame of chewy tannins, it delivers incredible freshness and a very long, savoury finish.'

THE FACTS

Bottles produced
3,300
Composition
100% Zinfandel
Yield
N/A
Alcohol
14.9%
Release price
US$16
Price today
US$130

OPUS ONE 1991

Napa Valley, California, USA

A LEGEND BECAUSE...

In retrospect it still seems astonishing that a great Bordeaux personality such as Baron Philippe de Rothschild, owner of Château Mouton Rothschild, should embark on a joint venture in Napa Valley with visionary local producer Robert Mondavi. The baron's first approach was made in 1970, but it wasn't until 1978 that the deal was sealed. New vineyards in Oakville were planted for this venture, with Tim Mondavi – and from 1986, Mouton winemaker Patrick Léon – overseeing the winemaking. The first vintage was 1979, with 1991 widely recognised as an exceptional year.

LOOKING BACK

In this year the magnificent new winery for Opus One was inaugurated. The new facility was gravity-operated, which in 1991 was by no means as common as today. The winery, with its eye-catching circular design and magnificent underground barrel cellar, large enough to hold 1,000 barriques without stacking, signified an ambition to create the Californian equivalent of a Bordeaux first growth. That also meant establishing a very high price for the wine, a risky strategy given that Opus One is a brand releasing more than 20,000 cases each year. But it has worked and the wine is a staple of international wine lists.

THE VINTAGE

The growing season was cool and long. A trouble-free flowering ensured a generous crop too. The fine summer was followed by a balmy autumn that led to fully mature bunches. The Cabernets were deep in colour, with good acidity levels.

THE TERROIR

The Opus vineyards were planted at the Mondavi winery from 1981, but some of the early plantings succumbed to phylloxera and had to be replanted. Also in 1981, Mondavi sold 14ha of his celebrated To Kalon vineyard to the new joint venture. Much replanting took place after 1991, again due to phylloxera, and this was done to a far higher density than was usual in Napa. This was controversial, as some thought that the greater vigour of the Napa climate led to more generous canopies that provided too much shade, discouraging even ripening. Later plantings were more widely spaced as a consequence.

THE WINE

After harvesting by hand and careful sorting, the destemmed grapes fall by gravity into fermentation tanks below, without pumping. Maceration was unusually long, at 33 days. After fermentation the skins were pressed in specially designed basket presses. The wine was aged for 18 months in new barrique, and was egg-white-fined before bottling.

THE REACTION

Robert Parker wrote in 1995: 'A knock-out nose of smoke, cassis, vanilla, and a whiff of herbs and liquorice. Full-bodied, with surprisingly supple, concentrated, chocolatey, cassis and blackcurrant flavours that ooze across the palate.'

In 1997 Michael Broadbent noted: 'Deep, velvety... crisp, fruity, mouthwatering, very sweet, fairly full-bodied, tolerable tannin, good acidity.'

Jancis Robinson was intrigued in 2007: 'Not quite charming – but is this a question of time? Fresh and lively. But not especially long. When they pressed they saw there was lots of sugar left in the whole berry fermentation, so long fermentation really added to the complexity of the wine.'

In 2019 Stephen Brook was impressed: 'Smoky, cedary nose, distinctly Bordelais in style, blackberry fruit; aromatic, elegant and refined. It's rich and opulent, but not too extracted; lovely texture, still fresh. Stylistically more Pauillac than Oakville. Long, with piquant acidity on the finish.'

THE FACTS

Bottles produced
270,000

Composition
93.4% Cabernet Sauvignon, 6% Cabernet Franc, 0.5% Merlot, 0.1% Malbec

Yield
45hl/ha

Alcohol
13.5%

Release price
US$70

Price today
£352

Ridge, Monte Bello 1970

Santa Cruz Mountains, California, USA

A legend because...

The original Monte Bello vineyard was first planted high in the Santa Cruz Mountains in the 1880s, and the site was acquired in the 1950s by a group of scientists from Stanford University. They bought the property as a weekend retreat but realised the handful of remaining vines made exceptional wine. Production was extremely limited at first but as it gradually grew, the decision was made to hire a full-time winemaker. Paul Draper, who had been working in Chile at the time, was taken on in 1969. His first vintage, in 1970, proved to be one of the most outstanding wines from Monte Bello. Although it was the 1971 that dazzled tasters at Steven Spurrier's celebrated Judgment of Paris tasting in 1976, Draper himself always preferred the 1970. When he was named Decanter Man of the Year in 2000, it was the 1970 vintage that he chose to be served at the dinner held in his honour.

Looking back

In 1970 Ridge was still in its infancy, and total production was no more than 3,000 cases. The Stanford partners had intended to sell grapes rather than make their own wines, but the early vintages had such intensity of flavour that they changed their mind, deciding to bring the historic vineyard back into production. The first commercial vintage from Monte Bello was in 1962 and the 1964 is still very much alive.

The vintage

Despite spring frosts in some areas, 1970 was a very successful growing season, with some hot spells that led to raisining in some valley floor locations, but not at Monte Bello, where the wines emerged as balanced and long-lived.

The terroir

With vines at between 400m and 800m, the Monte Bello vineyard is, according to Draper, one of the highest and coolest Cabernet Sauvignon sites in California. The soil is decomposing Franciscan greenstone mixed with clay over a subsoil of 100-million-yearold limestone, which is very rare in California. The average age of the vines is more than 30 years and yields do not exceed 30hl/ha. Elevation keeps the site free of sea fogs, but the ocean is just 24km to the west so the vines still benefit from maritime influence. The climate is as cool as Bordeaux, but much drier in summer, and its imprint on the Cabernet from here is relatively high acidity and a taut structure that requires bottle age to show at its best. Early vintages of Monte Bello were pure Cabernet, although in subsequent years other Bordeaux varieties were added to the vineyard.

The wine

The grapes would have been destemmed, and fermented with natural yeasts. Draper finds a short maceration necessary to avoid overextraction of tough tannins, which typically means racking off the skins at between 1% and 4% residual sugar. The fermentation then continues to dryness. The blend is made up soon after the malolactic fermentation is completed and between 10% and 20% press wine is added. Monte Bello differs from other prestigious Californian Cabernets in being aged primarily in new, air-dried American oak, as Draper has always wanted to avoid making a wine that could be regarded as an imitation claret. However about 5% of the barrels are of French oak as an annual experiment since 1971. After about 18 months the wine is bottled with minimal filtration. Despite the specifics above, the

'An exceptional wine, still bursting with life'

Mike Steinberger

winemaking is never formulaic, and Draper adapts the vinification to the conditions of each vintage, aiming for wines that are accessible young but have the capacity to age for at least two or three decades. Today, when there is a greater variation in vine age than there was in 1970, the youngest vines are relegated to the second wine. But longevity alone is not sufficient for a lot to qualify for Monte Bello, and the blend is decided on the base of blind tasting.

THE REACTION

American critic James Laube has been emphatic about the 1970: 'The Monte Bello of the decade: a supple, complex, harmonious wine with layers of currant, anise, cedary oak and earthy mineral flavours.' Tyler Colman ('Dr Vino') noted in 2010: 'The legendary 1970 ... is in a lovely place, mature yet still very much alive.' In the same year Mike Steinberger was equally enthusiastic: 'A sensational bouquet redolent of leather, blackcurrant and tobacco. A rich, warm wine with fantastic depth of flavour, buttery tannins, a superb menthol kick... and a long graceful finish. An exceptional wine, still bursting with life.'

THE FACTS

Bottles produced	Alcohol
5,544	**13.5%**
Composition	Release price
100% Cabernet Sauvignon	**US$10**
	Price today
Yield	**US$500**
25hl/ha	

SCREAMING EAGLE, CABERNET SAUVIGNON 1997

Napa Valley, California, USA

A LEGEND BECAUSE...

In 1986, a successful Napa Valley estate agent, Jean Phillips, acquired a 23ha property on the eastern side of the valley in Oakville. There was a tiny parcel of Cabernet Sauvignon, and André Tchelistcheff was among those who recommended replanting the white-grape vines with Bordeaux varieties. The first commercial release of the dramatically named wine was 1992, with Heidi Peterson Barrett as the winemaker. Just under 1ha was used for this wine, as Phillips sold off most of the grapes. Robert Parker gave this 1992 wine a perfect score, and the rest is history.

LOOKING BACK

Screaming Eagle was the best known of a number of micro-estates that took Napa Valley, and wealthy wine collectors, by storm in the 1990s. Screaming Eagle and its ilk were produced in minute quantities, ensuring scarcity and justifying a very high price, encouraging queues to join the waiting list for new releases. These bottlings had much in common with Bordeaux garagiste releases, with the crucial difference that the Napa terroir was generally far superior to garagiste vineyards. In 2006, Phillips sold the brand to Charles Banks and Stan Kroenke. They replanted the vineyard and hired Michel Rolland as a consultant. In 2009, Kroenke became the sole owner.

THE VINTAGE

Despite a cool summer in Napa in 1997, ripening was rapid and the harvest early. Mid-August rains provoked rot in poorly managed vineyards, but not in the best properties such as Screaming Eagle. There was more rain in September, but it did little damage and brought no dilution to Cabernet grapes. It was to prove a controversial vintage, initially claimed as a great Cabernet year in Napa, but 10 years on, tasters found many wines were not holding up, probably because of excessive ripeness and high pH levels.

THE TERROIR

Planted on a west-facing slope, drainage and exposure are excellent, and the soils contain reddish rocks of volcanic origin. Afternoon breezes from the San Pablo Bay moderate the daytime heat and help achieve an ideal balance in the grapes.

THE WINE

After harvest, the grapes are placed into small open-top vats for fermentation, with extraction achieved by punchdowns rather than pumpovers. The wine is aged for 18-20 months in up to 75% new oak, and bottled without filtration. Selection is severe, and no more than 30% of the wine vinified is bottled as Screaming Eagle.

THE REACTION

In 2000, Robert Parker reviewed the newly released wine: 'It doesn't get any better than [the] 1997... the essence of cassis liqueur with blackberries, minerals, liquorice and toast, this full-bodied, multi-dimensional classic is fabulous, with extraordinary purity, symmetry, and a finish that lasts for nearly a minute. It has the equilibrium to evolve for nearly two decades...'

A year later, James Laube wrote in *The Wine Spectator*: 'A potent wine of finesse and grace, this weaves together a rich and complex array of cedary currant, toasty oak, hazelnut and black-cherry flavours that finish in a long, intricate aftertaste.'

Stephen Tanzer was less impressed: 'Leaner than the 1996 at a similar stage... Conveys a strong impression of terroir, but I don't yet find the texture or depth of the best vintages of Screaming Eagle.'

In 2015, Jeff Leve of *The Wine Cellar Insider* noted: 'With an attention-seeking nose of incense, cherry blossoms, liquorice and fresh, black cherry liqueur, you're already hooked. On the palate, the wine is elegant, refined, lush, supple and polished. There is a freshness to the perfectly ripe fruit and a silky, sweet, cherry finish.'

THE FACTS

Bottles produced
6,000
Composition
100% Cabernet Sauvignon
Yield
N/A
Alcohol
14.5%
Release price
US$125
Price today
£6,980

WILLIAMS SELYEM, SUMMA VINEYARD PINOT NOIR 1988

Sonoma, California, USA

A LEGEND BECAUSE...

Williams Selyem was not the first serious producer of Californian Pinot Noir, but by the late 1980s it was probably the most highly acclaimed. Although based in Russian River Valley, it bought fruit from several different vineyards. During the 1980s growers began seeking out cool sites near the Sonoma Coast and Summa Vineyard was one of these. The debut Summa bottling from Williams Selyem was 1988 and before long it became both the most expensive Pinot Noir from California and one of the most scarce. By the 1991 vintage, the release price was $100; nonetheless it sold out within three days. Demand for Williams Selyem wines exceeded supply, with a two-year wait to join the mailing list.

LOOKING BACK

Williams Selyem was an unusual partnership. Burt Williams was a newspaper typesetter by trade, Ed Selyem a wine retailer. Beginning as hobby winemakers in 1979, their first proper vintage was 1981. In 1983 they moved into an old garage on River Road, building a new winery nearby in 1989. This was a boom time for Russian River Valley Pinot, however in 1998 the duo sold the brand. The purchaser was New York politician John Dyson, who had the good sense to retain Williams as his winemaker for a few years. Dyson expanded the winery but maintained the founding principles under a new winemaker, Bob Cabral, succeeded in 2014 by Jeff Mangahas.

THE VINTAGE

A difficult flowering reduced Pinot yields by up to 20%. Summer saw wild swings of temperature, but conditions during harvest were good. Berries were small and the Pinots showed fine concentration. Overall the vintage was considered above average, though very dry conditions halved normal yields in many sites.

THE TERROIR

Summa's elevation and proximity to the ocean means that although the days are cool, the nights are relatively warm, allowing the grapes to ripen. However, the location just 10km from the Pacific meant that mildew and rot were constant threats. The Pinot planted here in the early 1980s was an unidentified clone but had desirably small clusters. (Williams always suspected it was the Swan clone.) These original blocks were dry-farmed.

THE WINE

Winemaking was always artisanal, following Burgundian principles. The bunches were hand-sorted, then given a five-day cold soak before fermentation with the winery's own yeast selection. There was no pumping. Up to 30% whole clusters were usually retained, with punchdowns by foot or by hand. After pressing, wines were aged in heavily toasted Burgundian barrels, with the proportion of new oak ranging from 35% to 100%.

THE REACTION

Given the tiny production of this wine, reviews are scarce. James Laube of *The Wine Spectator* tasted the wine in 1995, writing: 'Lean, with a smoky orange rind and tea leaf edge to the barely ripe fruit flavours.'

In 2016 Jordan Mackay noted: 'Still vital and pulsing after more than 25 years. On the palate, the acidity has just enough zip left to hold it all together, while tannins have faded... surrounding a vibrant, luminous sense of strawberry.'

In 2017 William Kelley said, 'Cruising along beautifully [with] an exotic blend of blood orange, Asian spice and dried rose petals – the signature from this site. On the palate the wine is glossy, with fully resolved tannins, but just impeccable balance and no signs of decline. Superb!'

THE FACTS

Bottles produced
1,296
Composition
100% Pinot Noir
Yield
8hl/ha
Alcohol
12.2%
Release price
US$25
Price today
N/A

PICTURE CREDITS

The publishers would like to thank the following sources for their kind permission to reproduce the pictures in this book.

[p3] Wine glass (*edge2edge-media*); [p7] Wine bottle and glass (*Getty Images/SW Productions*); [p9] Cellars of Dom Pérignon in Epernay (*Hemis/Alamy Stock Photo*); [pp10-11] Margaret River grapevines under protective bird netting, Western Australia (*tap10*); [pp12-13] Château Pichon Baron vineyard in Médoc (*travelstock 44/Alamy Stock Photo*); [pp38-39] Gevrey-Chambertin vineyard, Côte de Nuits (*Hemis/Alamy Stock Photo*); [pp56-57] Bollinger vineyard at Aÿ (*REUTERS/Alamy Stock Photo*); [pp72-73] The terraced vineyards of Hermitage Hill, Tournon-sur-Rhône, Ardèche (*Jason Knott/Alamy Stock Photo*); [pp86-87] Clos Sainte-Hune vineyard, Alsace (*Milena Pigdanowicz-Fidera*); [pp100-01] The vineyards of Bremm and the loop of the Moselle, Rhineland-Palatinate (*Jorg Greuel*); [pp106-07] Vineyard in Tuscany before harvest (*ah_fotobox*); [pp126-27] Hotel Marqués de Rical, Elciego (*mauritius images GmbH/Alamy Stock Photo*); [pp146-47] Hungarian Tukaji wine region in spring sunset (*Andfoto/Alamy Stock Photo*); [pp156-57] Douro Valley vineyards in autumn (*Mikehoward 2/Alamy Stock Photo*); [pp172-73] Vineyard in South Australia (*RooM the Agency/Alamy Stock Photo*); [pp194-95] Santa Rita vineyard, Maipo Valley (*robertharding/Alamy Stock Photo*); [pp208-09] Tokara Wine Estate and vineyards near Stellenbosch, Western Cape (*frans lemmens/Alamy Stock Photo*); [pp220-21] Vines at The Eyrie Vineyards, Williamette Valley, Oregon (*Cannon Photography LLC/Alamy Stock Photo*).

All wine bottle images courtesy of Decanter/Future Publishing.

Every effort has been made to acknowledge correctly and contact the source and/or copyright holder of each picture and Sona Books apologises for any unintentional errors or omissions, which will be corrected in future editions of the book.